NO MORE EXCUSES

NoMore Excuses

BE THE MAN
GOD MADE YOU TO BE

TONY EVANS

Renaissance Productions

CROSSWAY BOOKS • WHEATON, ILLINOIS
A DIVISION OF GOOD NEWS PUBLISHERS

ISBN 0-89107-896-7

CONTENTS

Dedication / With Gratitude   vii

Foreword by Bill McCartney   ix

Introduction   xi

1 No More Hiding Behind the Past   13

2 No More Feeling Worthless   33

3 No More Allowing for Immorality   51

4 No More Going Through the Motions   69

5 No More Dabbling in Defiance   85

6 No More Compromising Your Integrity   101

7 No More Sifting Through the Rubble   117

8 No More Giving in to Tempation   133

9 No More Second-rate Marriages   149

10 No More Passive Fathering   167

11 No More Sissified Males   183

12 No More Playing the Lone Ranger   199

13 No More Ownership   215

14 No More Clock-punching   233

15 No More Business as Usual   249

16 No More Half-stepping   267

17 No More Standing on the Sidelines   285

18 No More "Loser's Limp"   301

Epilogue   317

Dedication

With Gratitude

Once again I want to say thanks to my friend Philip Rawley for the way he organizes my ideas and words into a sharp, clear literary style. My appreciation also goes to Lane Dennis and Leonard Goss of Crossway Books for their guidance and patience with this book. The editorial skills of Len Goss helped bring *No More Excuses* to its finished state.

FOREWORD

BY BILL MCCARTNEY

Whe n I was coaching football, I used to sit down with my players one at a time the night before a game and ask each young man what I could expect from him on the field the next day.

I didn't do it to make them nervous, of course. It was a way of letting them know that I had confidence in them, that I knew what they were capable of, and that I would be looking for their best effort supported by the best coaching our staff was capable of giving.

That's something of what I believe God is doing with men all across America. He's sitting us down, so to speak, and asking, "What can I expect of you in light of what I've given you?" God is calling men to faithfulness to Him and to their families, to godly leadership in the home and in the workplace.

This is the heart of the movement known as Promise Keepers. And one of the men who has given this movement its vitality and its spiritual direction is Dr. Tony Evans. Tony has been speaking to men straight from his heart for a long time, and in this book he takes his challenge to godly manhood to a higher level.

No More Excuses is not a book you read for a breezy morning devotional thought to get you through the day. It's honest and masculine, it's biblical and straightforward. It speaks to us as men in every area of our lives. It probes and convicts and disciples and empowers and encourages men—everything a good coach wants to do with his players.

There have been a lot of forces pushing men down over the last thirty years, and it would be easy for a man to say, "I'm a victim of forces beyond my control." But Tony doesn't buy that, because the Bible doesn't speak to men as victims. It speaks to them as the ones ultimately responsible for the spiritual health of home, neighborhood, church, and nation.

So don't expect *No More Excuses* to reinforce the reasons a man might offer for being less than God wants him to be. Don't expect Tony to pull his punches—but do expect to be encouraged, loved as a brother, and given a crystal-clear picture of what God wants from men.

In this book, Tony Evans speaks to us as a comrade-in-arms, as a fellow disciple seeking to keep his promises and be a man of God. He's not looking to hammer men down, but to hammer and shape us into men of God who will change this world.

You'll find biblical truth communicated in these pages in a clear way so that you can understand and apply it. I have discovered that Tony possesses that rare talent to challenge us to press through the darkness and enter the light.

So if you're tired of the excuses; if you want to break through your problems, get into the clear, and start running to win; if you are willing to open your heart to the ministry of the Holy Spirit; then I commend *No More Excuses* to you as a book you can't afford to overlook.

Bill McCartney
Founder, Promise Keepers

INTRODUCTION

Today we have a generation of men who suffer from "loser's limp." Anyone who has competed in sports knows what I mean by "loser's limp." It's what happens when an outfielder misjudges a fly ball and misses the catch, or when a wide receiver drops an easy pass. They fall to the ground and get up limping.

The purpose of the limp is to camouflage their failure. The impression they want to give their teammates and the fans is that the reason they didn't make the catch was because of a cramp or a muscle pull or some other sudden malady of the leg rather than their misjudgment.

So the limp becomes the athlete's excuse, his attempt to be exonerated of blame for his misplay. But while the consequences of a misplay in a ball game are relatively small, the unfortunate fact is that many men have developed a "loser's limp" when it comes to life. Instead of owning up to their failures and responsibilities, they excuse them, giving the impression that forces beyond their control are responsible for their circumstances.

It's true that circumstances beyond our control can sometimes make it difficult for us to be all that God wants us to be. But we need to start looking at these things as challenges and opportunities for success rather than as excuses for failure or not doing anything. It's high time that we stop blaming past circumstances or present pressures and start living as real men.

Now I'm not saying that real men just leap over every obstacle like Superman. No, we all stumble and fall. But being real men means we don't allow our past to control our present by coming up with a "limp" to hide our mistakes. Instead, we accept responsibility for our actions, identify what needs to be corrected, and set about being the men God wants us to be.

That's what this book is all about. It's about Christian men repudiating the "loser's limp" and becoming real men of God. It's about men winning back their families, their churches, and their culture by rising above their circumstances through the grace and power of God.

This book is about men finding purpose, meaning, and direction for their lives despite past setbacks or present pressures. It's about becoming men of character, commitment, power, and influence for Jesus Christ. That's the kind of man I want to be. Are you with me, brother?

It's my contention that when men know God and apply His truths to their lives, they truly will need no more excuses!

ONE

NO MORE HIDING BEHIND THE PAST

"I'M THE WAY I AM TODAY BECAUSE OF WHAT HAPPENED TO ME IN MY PAST."

Some time ago, I was in my backyard and noticed a piece of wood lying beside the air conditioner. It had been there for a long time, so I finally decided to move it. You can probably guess what happened when I picked it up. The insects that had been making their home under that piece of wood began to scurry for new cover.

Now, when I was just walking by, that piece of wood looked normal. But it had actually become a home for varmints, a dwelling place for colonies of insects who stayed hidden beneath the veneer of the wood until someone disturbed their nest.

That incident seems to me a good metaphor for what I want to do in this book, and especially in this opening chapter. That is, I want to show you that we need to "pick up" our lives as men and see what's hiding under them. When we are willing to deal with whatever comes out, we will see God do a fantastic work in us and then through us.

Now don't get me wrong. I'm not suggesting there are any "varmints" in your past. And I'm not a psychiatrist, so we're not going to probe your psyche for deep, dark secrets. But we all have a past, as they say. And since no man among us is perfect, we tend to cover our hurts and fears with Sunday smiles, nice suits, firm handshakes—and sometimes lies.

Someone says, "How are you doing this morning, brother?"

"Wonderful! Praise the Lord!"

"How's the family?"

"Couldn't be better!"

But if we picked up that piece of wood in that man's "backyard," stuff might scatter everywhere. We men have become very adept at covering up our pain. And one of the things that causes us great pain is broken relationships. One reason they are so painful and so crippling is that no one has ever showed us how to fix a fractured relationship. That is for women only, right?

Not in God's kingdom, it isn't. In this chapter, I want to share with you some principles from God's Word that will enable you, by His grace, to step out from under the shadow of your past and stop letting it control your present and your future. I want to help you lay aside what happened yesterday as an excuse for what's happening today.

I'm not denying that something happened in the past. It may even have been something devastating, such as rejection by your father or mother when you were a child, or a divorce that was so painful and/or bitter that you have never been able to get past its effects. Or you may have brothers, sisters, or good friends you don't talk to anymore and wouldn't speak to if they called.

Painful pasts come in all shapes and sizes and degrees of intensity. In some cases, the person who has been the focus of our pain isn't even around anymore. It's too late to say you're sorry, or to hear those healing words from the other person's lips. What can you do in cases like that?

Well, the Bible has a lot to teach us on this subject, because whatever your situation may be, it is no surprise to God. He is very aware of your past, and He knows that when things go wrong in your relationships, it can have a staggering effect. I want to show you how to start overcoming and stop blaming your past by taking you on a biblical journey through the life of Joseph.

Here was a young man with a painful past—and none of it was

his fault. The story of what Joseph did about it is very special, because more than one-fourth of the book of Genesis (chapters 37–50) is devoted to this remarkable man. Let's meet him now.

JOSEPH: A SHAKY FAMILY TREE

I told you Joseph had a past. It started before he was even born, because his daddy was Jacob. Now Jacob would not win the "Father of the Year" award from the local Kiwanis or Rotary Club. As a young man, Jacob was a deceiver. We know from Genesis chapter 27 that he deceived his brother Esau right out of the family birthright, linking up with his mother Rebekah to trick Isaac and gain the blessing.

When the deal was exposed, Jacob had to run for his life because Esau tried to kill him. Jacob fled to the land of a relative named Laban and fell in love with Laban's daughter Rachel. Now there is a biblical principle that says, "you may be sure that your sin will find you out." (Numbers 32:23) Jacob was a trickster, but in Laban he met a better trickster.

Laban told Jacob, "If you will work for me seven years, I will give you my beautiful, vivacious daughter Rachel to be your wife." Genesis 29:18 says that Jacob loved Rachel so much he accepted Laban's terms—only to be tricked into marrying her sister Leah instead. He had to serve another seven years to get Rachel, who would become Joseph's mother.

But because Rachel was barren (before God opened her womb) and Leah stopped having children after four sons, each of them gave their maidens to Jacob as additional wives (Genesis 30:1-9). So here is this patchwork family of a husband and four wives, three of whom the man didn't really plan to marry. Are you getting the picture of the kind of family into which Joseph was born? In today's terms, it was dysfunctional.

Jacob's life of deception continued when he "deceived Laban" by fleeing without telling him (Genesis 31:20). His trickery carried over to Rachel, who stole her father's household idols and then deceived her father about having them (31:19, 33-35).

Is it any wonder that by the time Jacob had eleven sons, counting Joseph (Benjamin was born later), his older boys turned out to be as treacherous as their daddy? In fact, they were worse because their treachery involved killing all the men in the city of Shechem in revenge for the rape of their sister (34:25).

Reuben, the firstborn son, then slept with one of his father's wives (Genesis 35:22), and his brother Judah was seduced by his daughter-in-law (38:18). This is not what you would call a well-adjusted family. This is not the kind of family you would want to grow up in, but this was Joseph's family. Here was a young man who had every excuse he needed not to turn out right.

Yet when the Bible presents Joseph to us, it presents a man of greatness, godliness, and dignity. I point this out to let you know that just because your daddy was bad and your mama was messed up and your brothers and sisters turned out rotten, you don't have to wind up the same way.

In other words, a bad environment need not control your present decision-making. Now don't misunderstand. Your past can influence you, but it doesn't have to control you. Joseph could have given up before he ever really got started, but he refused to let the sins of others control him. He refused to hide behind his past.

REJECTED BY MEN, PROTECTED BY GOD

Joseph's story begins in Genesis chapter 37 with the incident that marked him for the rest of his life. He was out with his older brothers in the pasture, and "he brought their father a bad report about them." (verse 2). Nothing is said about this report, so we can assume it was accurate. But here was the real problem:

> Now Israel loved Joseph more than any of his other sons, because he had been born to him in his old age; and he made a richly ornamented robe for him. When his brothers saw that their father loved him more than any of them, they hated him and could not speak a kind word to him.
>
> —*verses 3-4*

So here was serious sibling rivalry. The ten older boys couldn't stand Joseph. A lot of this had to do with bad judgment on Jacob's part. He was openly partial to Joseph, the first son born to Rachel, who was his favorite wife and true love.

So as far as Jacob was concerned, Joseph was his number-one son. He showered Joseph with affection and gave him a multicolored coat. When the brothers saw that coat, they blew.

You say, "Why would they go off over a trench coat?"

Oh, but that was a very special coat. That was the kind of coat you would give to royalty. Not only was it expensive, but the other brothers knew what it meant. It meant that Pop had chosen Joseph, not Reuben, to be the heir to the family birthright.

The older boys weren't about to let a baby brother, born of a woman who wasn't mother to any of them, horn in on their territory. It didn't help when Joseph told them his dream that they would all bow down to him someday (37:5-11)! So they concocted a plan to kill him, but Reuben talked them into throwing Joseph into a pit instead (37:20-24).

So they tossed Joseph down into an empty cistern and sat down to eat. What they did to him didn't even curb their appetites! Then they sold him into slavery to some passing traders (37:25), and the rest of the chapter relates how they tricked old Jacob into thinking his favorite boy was dead. I would call that rejection by your family.

Perhaps you were rejected by your family or some other important person in your life. Maybe you found out that people who claimed to love you really didn't love you. Maybe someone you trusted deeply turned on you, and you got hung out to dry.

What are you going to do now? Stay where you are? Decide never to trust anyone again? All of this and more happened to Joseph. Let's follow him down to Egypt where he began his life as a slave:

> Now Joseph had been taken down to Egypt. Potiphar, an Egyptian who was one of Pharaoh's officials, the captain of the guard, bought him from the Ishmaelites. . . . [But] the LORD was with Joseph.
> —*Genesis 39:1-2a*

Don't miss that last phrase. You say, "Joseph sure had a lousy family background." Yes, but "the LORD was with Joseph."

You say, "Yeah, but his brothers couldn't stand him." True, but "the LORD was with Joseph."

"But he had such a bad break." No, you didn't hear me. "The LORD was with Joseph."

WHOM WILL YOU TURN TO?

Do you get my drift? The first step to overcoming the past is realizing that no matter what others do to you, if the Lord is with you, you can still get somewhere. So your assignment is to stay with the Lord. Joseph was rejected by his family, but he was accepted by the Lord. Even though he was mistreated, he didn't turn against the Lord. His faith held him firm.

Regardless of what happened yesterday, if you will stick with the Lord today, your yesterday doesn't have to control your tomorrow. If you are still thinking about the people who caused your problem, you are focusing on the wrong thing. You need to focus on Someone who is there to help you.

The Lord was with Joseph, so this rejected child was now under God's watchful eye in slavery:

> The LORD was with Joseph and he prospered, and he lived in the house of his Egyptian master . . . his master saw that the LORD was with him and that the LORD gave him success in everything he did.
>
> —*verses 2-3*

Joseph had a job to do. He worked for Potiphar now. In fact, Pot turned his whole house over to Joseph (Genesis 39:4-6). The Lord met Joseph where he was and made him successful in a strange land.

If you will walk with the Lord, He can do the same for you. All Joseph did was allow God to use him. The problem with the past is that it can become a dictator that rules you today. The only way to overcome that is to change dictators—to allow the Lord to dictate your life today.

There are things from the past that you may not be able to fix. You may never be able to get your parents to accept you, your brothers and sisters to talk to you, or your boss to atone for previous injustices. But with the Lord in your present, He can always make something happen.

Now let me tell you one reason Joseph may have turned out better than Jacob's older boys. There's a part of Jacob's story I didn't mention. He was a mess for a long time, but when he got old he had a confrontation with God. According to Genesis 32:24-32, Jacob wrestled with someone whom the prophet Hosea later called an angel (Hosea 12:4).

Jacob asked for a blessing, so this heavenly being, who may have been Christ in a pre-incarnate appearance, blessed him with a new name, Israel. Jacob also got crippled in the deal, so this was a life-changing experience in more ways than one. Jacob said, "I saw God face to face, and yet my life was spared." (Genesis 32:30) Later he renewed his covenant with God at Bethel (Genesis 35:1-5).

So in his later years, Jacob made a decision for God that Joseph was able to benefit from because he was still young. It may have been too late for Jacob's ten older sons, but he made the decision anyway and it made a difference in his family.

I want to encourage you with that reminder if you're a husband and father who can look back and see bad decisions that messed up your family. You may not, by your own effort, be able to fix what is broken. You can't raise your children over again. But if you will start walking with God now, He can make up some of those lost days and years and opportunities. He can fix what you can't even touch anymore because it's behind you.

By the time Joseph was a young boy, Jacob was committed to God. He could not fix the past, but he could walk with God in the present and see God bless his present in spite of his past. And that's just what he did.

COMMITTED TO GODLINESS

Besides knowing Joseph's background and his rejection, you need to know that Joseph was committed to living a godly life.

That becomes very apparent beginning in Genesis 39:7: "After a while his master's wife took notice of Joseph and said, 'Come to bed with me!'" Now this is a bold sister here. She wanted Joseph because he was "well-built and handsome." (39:6) He looked good, and so Potiphar's wife said, "Uh, huh!"

Mrs. Potiphar made a move on Joseph, but he refused and he said to her:

> "With me in charge, my master does not concern himself with anything in the house; everything he owns he has entrusted to my care. No one is greater in this house than I am. My master has withheld nothing from me except you, because you are his wife. How then could I do such a wicked thing and sin against God?"
>
> —*verses 8-9*

Do you see the mind-set of Joseph? He says, "Look, I'm in a situation that I can't possibly explain other than that God is doing it. How can I be in the midst of what God is doing and do what you are asking me to do?"

So Joseph refused her advances, but she persisted in trying to seduce him. Finally she made a grab for him, and he fled without his shirt. Mrs. Potiphar got mad, cried rape, and framed Joseph for a crime that never happened. Potiphar took one look at the "evidence," heard her phony testimony, and slapped Joe in jail (Genesis 39:10-20).

Now at this point in the story you may want to say, "Come on. The man is living right. He refuses the illegitimate demands of his boss's wife because he wants to obey God, and he cares about his boss. And for that he gets fired and lands in jail. I mean, Joseph has done absolutely nothing wrong!"

I think by now some men in Joseph's shoes would be pacing back and forth in that jail cell talking about, "Lord, have mercy. I try to do right and I get fired. Shucks! I should have at least had some fun. I could have held on to my job and had some fun too. Now I don't have either one." But that wasn't Joseph's mind-set because he had already learned something important: the Lord was with him (verse 21).

GOING SOMEWHERE WITH GOD

No matter what has gone on in the past, if you are willing to stay with God on this thing, then even going to jail is where you ought to go if it is within God's will for you. For Joseph, there was no better place to be than in the king's jail, because he was right where God wanted him to be.

Sometimes God must lead you downhill to take you uphill. He must take you to the bottom in order to get you to the top. The problem comes when we're at the bottom, because we tend to assume that it's the end of the trip. But when the Lord is with you, something is going to happen.

That's why I love verse 21 of Genesis 39: "the LORD was with him; he showed him kindness and granted him favor in the eyes of the prison warden." The head turnkey put Joseph in charge of everything in the place. My man was busy again. Joseph didn't have time to dwell on the past and let it eat at him, even if he had wanted to. The Lord was with him and had something more important for him to do.

When you commit your life totally to God, your past no longer has to be the controlling factor in your life. It means that what happened to you five years or ten years ago—or even last month—no longer dictates your steps. Is what happened to you still real? Of course it is. I'm not talking about having a frontal lobotomy so you don't remember anything. I'm talking about breaking the past's control.

This is the sense in which Paul says, "Forgetting what is behind and straining toward what is ahead, I press on toward the goal to win the prize for which God has called me heavenward in Christ Jesus." (Philippians 3:13-14) Yet he was keenly aware of his past as a persecutor of the church (1 Corinthians 15:9).

I think as men we really need to come to grips with this, because we tend to let past failures keep us from trying again. But once we are committed to the Lord, we have His power available to help us move forward instead of looking back.

That's what Joseph did. We're now up to Genesis 40, and Joe is still a jailbird. Chapter 40 is the story of his interpretation of the dreams experienced by Pharaoh's baker and cupbearer, who were in the King of Egypt's doghouse. I don't have the space here to go through each verse in detail. If you're not familiar with the story, or if you've forgotten how it goes, you can read Genesis 40 in just a few minutes.

I want to focus on verses 12-15. The news was good for the cupbearer. He was going to be released from prison and restored to Pharaoh's service. So Joseph made a small request—to be remembered to Pharaoh (verse 14). In verse 15, Joseph protested his innocence without any apparent bitterness, which is very enlightening when you're talking about getting free of the past.

But the cupbearer forgot about Joseph (40:23), and Joseph stayed in the dungeon for two more years (Genesis 41:1). Now Joseph could really be feeling sorry for himself, saying, "You know, life would be good if it weren't for people. Every time I try to help someone, something wrong happens."

Nothing is recorded about those two years, however. What's interesting is that when Pharaoh had his dream and needed someone to interpret it, Joseph was ready to go. So I don't believe he could have spent those two years seething with bitterness and resentment, or he would not have been ready for God to use him so dramatically.

Now again, since my purpose is not to retell the whole story of Joseph's life, let me summarize what happened in verses 1-45 of Genesis 41. Things really started popping for my man Joe when Pharaoh woke up from his dream in a cold sweat. The cupbearer got his memory back, and Joseph was summoned.

The message of Pharaoh's dream was that Egypt would have seven good years followed by seven years of famine. Joseph's advice was that Pharaoh had better appoint a "famine commissioner," and do it pretty quick so that Egypt could survive the "seven ugly cows" years (vv. 4, 30). Pharaoh said, "Great idea, Joseph. I appoint you. You're now number-two man in Egypt. In fact, if anyone asks my permission to do something, I'm sending him to you."

I have only one theological observation to make about the story of Joseph at this point: wow! Here we've got a young slave going nowhere and rotting in jail, and now he's going somewhere—if you call being the number-two ruler in the most powerful nation on earth going somewhere. No one can do that but God.

The lesson here is simply this: God knows where He's taking you. And He knows the lessons you need to know in order to be equipped when you get there. God knew what you were going to go through as a five-, ten-, or fifteen-year-old. He knew how people were going to mess over you at twenty-five.

But He allowed those things in his purpose because of where He's going to take you when you're forty or fifty. And when you get there, there will be no question as to who gets the glory. Joseph could never sit beside Pharaoh as second in command and say, "Look who I am and what I did." He knew God was doing the work, so he was able to look at his circumstances in terms of his relationship with God and not just in terms of the nasty things people did to him.

Joseph was thirty when the promotion came (Genesis 41:46). He was seventeen when he was sold into slavery (37:2). He had thirteen years of a messed-up life, thirteen years of confusion, of not knowing whether he was going to be up or down, in or out, dead or alive.

Yet through it all Joseph maintained his faithfulness and his commitment, so God was able to use the negatives in his life to achieve His good plan. God was able to take Joseph somewhere—and He has a definite "somewhere" He wants to take you too.

BREAKING THE POWER OF THE PAST

Please take note also that Joseph didn't let his bad family background interfere with his present responsibility.

Let me say again what we've been trying to say throughout this chapter: we can't use someone else's irresponsibility in the past as an excuse for our irresponsibility in the present. If you are blaming what your parents or your wife or the government did for what you are not doing now, you need a wake-up call, my brother. You need to live up to your responsibilities.

I know your father or mother or "the system" may have stripped away your self-esteem. But Jesus Christ can give it back to you. I sometimes get into a lot of trouble when I talk to African-American groups because I reject the idea of using the reality of slavery as a reason for irresponsible behavior today.

Please read me very carefully here. Slavery was bad. Slavery was horrible. It was inhuman, ungodly, and unbiblical. It did a number on my people who were oppressed. But to tell me that what happened to our forefathers then is keeping African-American men from being what God wants us to be now is just giving us an out, an excuse, for our irresponsibility. No more excuses.

Let me tell you something. When the Dallas Cowboys get into their huddle during a football game, they don't say, "We'd better not try to move the ball, or those men on the other side of the line are going to nail us." The whole point of the game is to run your plays and find the ones your opponent can't stop so you can move the ball and score without getting nailed every time.

What I am saying is that you can learn from your past, but you cannot allow your past to control your present decisions. When you do that, your life becomes a self-fulfilling prophecy. "Well, I knew I was going to get nailed because of what has happened to me. But I tried, and sure enough, I got nailed."

Too many of us are looking for an excuse to hang our fears and shortcomings on. If I weren't in the ministry, I would be a psychiatrist because I would be free to charge people $200 an hour to tell them why they need to come back next week. They would come back too, because a lot of people want to keep blaming.

You say, "My father wouldn't work." Well, you'd better get a job. You say, "My father beat my mother." Then you'd better learn some self-control. The problems in your past should become object lessons to show you where you need to be different, not excuses for you to repeat them.

Let's go back to Joseph, because his story gets even more interesting from here on out. His brothers had done a number on him. He didn't just forget it. Anyone who tells you, "Just forget it, don't think about it" is not living in the real world. If it happened, you can't just pretend like it didn't happen. In Joseph's case other people did some bad things to him, but God also did something.

MAKING THE MOST OF THE PRESENT

The first thing God did was elevate Joseph to the rank of prime minister in Egypt. So that took care of his living conditions. But he was still bereft of his family, so God gave him a new family, new relationships to replace the bad ones. Joseph married Asenath (Genesis 41:45), which, by the way, was an interracial marriage; and God gave the couple two sons to whom Joseph gave very interesting names:

> Before the years of famine came, two sons were born to Joseph
> by Asenath, daughter of Potiphera, priest of On. Joseph named
> his firstborn Manasseh and said, "It is because God has made
> me forget all my trouble and all my father's household." The
> second son he named Ephraim and said, "It is because God has
> made me fruitful in the land of my suffering."
> —*Genesis 41:50-52*

By naming his sons this way, Joseph was saying that here was one more way he resolved to look ahead and let the pain of his past stay behind. That's what he meant by forgetting. Obviously, as we will see, he didn't forget the facts of his past. Those facts just didn't hurt anymore.

Appropriate relationships will help you not to dwell on the negative things in the past that hurt you, but on the positive things that God is doing in your life. You can't beat something with nothing.

If old relationships are destroying you, maybe it's because you have not yet replaced them with appropriate relationships. Now I'm not talking about replacing your wife with a new one, so don't tell anyone I said that. I'm talking about hanging out with people who remind you how bad off you are and how you have every reason to be mad and not set things right. The reason some men are depressed is because they hang out with depression; that is, with other guys who are as messed-up as they are, and who aren't planning to go anywhere either. That just reinforces the pain.

Sure, you still have scars from the past. We all do. But it's like a surgical incision. That cut may have hurt tremendously when you first woke up from your operation, but ten years later the pain should be long forgotten. If that scar still hurts ten years later, something is wrong.

Why? Because God wants you to have a "Manasseh" experience. He wants to help you forget. He also wants to give you an "Ephraim" experience. He wants to make you fruitful in the very place where you were afflicted before.

God took a slave jailbird, a nobody in the world's eyes, and made him the second biggest somebody in Egypt. A lot of men are fretting about the nobodies in their lives while God is waiting to make them somebody.

As Christian men, you and I need to develop thankful hearts toward God. We need to say, "Even though someone messed over me, I'm still here to talk about it. Even though someone tried to stop me, I'm still progressing. Lord, I'm going to stop focusing on how they messed up my yesterday, and I'm going to look at how You are putting me together today."

Many of us can't love our families because we are remembering the other family we grew up in. So we are causing misery rather than enjoying our relationships. If you had a bad father, you need a new father. If you had a bad mother, you need a new mother. If you had bad siblings, how about some new ones?

You say, "But you only have one father and mother." Not according to Jesus. Jesus told his disciples, "And everyone who has left houses or brothers or sisters or father or mother or children or fields for my sake will receive a hundred times as much and will inherit eternal life." (Matthew 19:29) God says He will be "a father to the fatherless." (Psalm 68:5)

But you say, "Where am I going to find this new family?" That's what the church is all about. In the church you can say, "Lady, you never had a son? You've got one now." "Mister, you never had a boy? You have one now." "I need a brother. Will you be my brother? I need a sister. Will you be my sister?"

The family of God is the replacement family for the messed-up family relationships we used to have. That's what Joseph's family was for him. But he had one more step to take.

LETTING GOD BE GOD

This is the hard one. Joseph let God take care of the people who messed him over rather than trying to take care of it himself. A Scripture you need to know is Romans 12:17-19:

> Do not repay anyone evil for evil. Be careful to do what is right in the eyes of everybody. If it is possible, as far as it depends on you, live at peace with everyone. Do not take revenge, my friends, but leave room for God's wrath, for it is written: "It is mine to avenge; I will repay," says the Lord.

If you are thinking about revenge on those who have hurt you, you're stuck. Why? Because once you look back, you can't move forward. Besides, God commands you to leave the thing in His hands. And He can do a better job of settling things than you could ever do anyway. Look at what He did in Joseph's case.

Genesis 41:56-57 describes the fulfillment of Pharaoh's dream about the coming famine. And because the famine reached into Canaan, Jacob's family was affected by it. So he sent his ten older sons to Egypt to buy food (42:1-3).

So when they arrived in Egypt, guess who they had to deal with?

My boy Joe, who recognized them right off. "But he pretended to be a stranger and spoke harshly to them. 'Where do you come from?' he asked. 'From the land of Canaan,' they replied, 'to buy food.'" (42:7)

We have arrived at the part of this story that could have been written by a Hollywood screenwriter. The intrigue, drama, and emotion of Genesis 42–45 are incredible. God has dropped all ten of the offending brothers in Joseph's lap. It's time for these boys to face what they did. It's reckoning time.

You'll want to read these chapters for yourself, because even if you remember the gist of the story, there are so many poignant moments and side plots going on that you need to know the whole story to get the full flavor.

The key thread of the story is that Joseph kept Simeon and sent the others back home, warning them not to return without their little brother Benjamin. Jacob reluctantly agreed to let Benjamin go to Egypt with his brothers, where, after further testing of the brothers' attitudes, Joseph revealed his identity to them. After this they were tearfully reunited. Then they sent for Jacob to live in Egypt where food was plentiful. So the family was restored, and their lives were saved.

That's the main story, but there is so much going on here that we need to learn from. I think one reason Joseph put his brothers through such a scary time was to test the depth of their repentance and see if there was ground for a renewed relationship with them. He wanted to make sure they were moving forward like he was or if they were going to hang around in the past.

If you and your wife are split up, for example, before you try to resolve your problem you need to make sure that both of you are moving forward. If one or the other is still dragging the past into the present, it will drag the marriage backwards. Both of you need to be moving forward.

Look at Genesis 42:36, which is the saddest part of the story. When Jacob heard that the boys had to take Benjamin back with them, he cried, "You have deprived me of my children. Joseph is no more and Simeon is no more, and now you want to take Benjamin. Everything is against me!"

Have you ever felt like that? Have you ever felt like everything has broken down, everything has gone wrong? Let me tell you something. It all depends on whose glasses you are looking through.

To Jacob, everything seemed to be against him because he was looking at the present through the lens of the past, and so his vision was blurred. He didn't know that Joseph was alive and that Simeon was eating at Joseph's table in Egypt. Jacob didn't know that Joseph was getting ready to bring the whole family to Egypt so they could eat again.

When all things seem to be against you, it may be because your vision is obscured by the past. When you look at your situation from a heavenly perspective, all these things may be for you. They just haven't been put together yet.

Things are about to get put together for Jacob and his sons. At first, Jacob refused to let Benjamin go to Egypt with the remaining ten brothers. But by the time we come to Genesis chapter 43, the food shortage is again so severe that Jacob told the boys to get themselves back to Egypt to buy more grain.

That's when Judah reminded Jacob of Joseph's warning about Benjamin: "The man warned us solemnly, 'You will not see my face again unless your brother is with you.'" (43:3) So Jacob reluctantly agreed to let baby brother go with the older boys.

It was during this visit, in which Simeon was reunited with his brothers (43:23), that Joseph's emotions really began to kick in. He had the brothers come over to his house for a little luncheon, and when he saw Benjamin again (he had seen him briefly back in verse 16), Joseph couldn't control his emotions. He went off for a good cry, then came out for the meal (verses 29-31).

Here Joseph apparently decided to plant a little bit of consternation in the minds of the brothers, because he had them seated in rank according to their age without anything being said. He went from number one right on down to number eleven without missing a beat. No wonder verse 33 concludes by saying, "they looked at each other in astonishment." How did this Egyptian know their birth order? What's the deal here?

SEEKING GOD'S GREATER PURPOSE

What Joseph was doing was getting ready to bring it on home. He had all the factual information he needed. He knew Jacob was well, and he had seen his beloved brother Benjamin—remember, they were both sons of Rachel—with his own eyes.

Now it was time to test his older brothers again. Joseph had a good idea how they felt about him, but he wanted to see if they had any love for Benjamin. So he had incriminating evidence planted in Benjamin's sack and hauled the brothers back to his house after sending them away. Judah pled for Benjamin's life, which meant they passed the test (Genesis 44:1-34).

All of that sets the stage for the high point of this drama, the moment when Joseph revealed his identity:

> Then Joseph could no longer control himself before all his attendants, and he cried out, "Have everyone leave my presence!" So there was no one with Joseph when he made himself known to his brothers. And he wept so loudly that the Egyptians heard him, and Pharaoh's household heard about it. Joseph said to his brothers, "I am Joseph! Is my father still living?" But his brothers were not able to answer him, because they were terrified at his presence. Then Joseph said to his brothers, "Come close to me."
>
> —*Genesis 45:1-4a*

Joseph wanted his brothers to get close and see that it was really him. He may have even revealed his circumcision to them as proof that he was a Hebrew, because no Egyptian would have borne that mark of the Hebrews. This would explain his sending everyone else out of the room and telling his brothers to come close.

But they were afraid to get close because they thought the next words out of his mouth would be, "Yeah, I'm Joseph, and you're dead, you good-for-nothing jive turkeys! I've waited twenty years for this, and now I'm going to kill you!"

But that's not what Joseph said. In a great declaration of forgiveness and a tremendous statement of God's sovereignty, Joseph told his brothers three times that God sent him there to save their lives (45:5, 7-8).

Later he said, "You intended to harm me, but God intended it for good." (50:20) That's the Old Testament version of Romans 8:28: "And we know that in all things God works for the good of those who love him." Joseph's vision wasn't blurred because he saw the past in the light of God's purpose.

Don't miss what's happening here. You don't read where the brothers wailed and lamented and begged Joseph's forgiveness, because it wasn't necessary. His forgiveness took care of the terrible wrong they had done to him.

FORGETTING WHAT LIES BEHIND

If someone who has wronged you is not going to come around for another twenty years, you'd better get on with your life. You don't want to look up one day and realize you've made no progress for the past twenty or however many years because that thing and those people from the past have been controlling your mind. Let God catch them up with you while you keep moving.

Obviously, if they want to repent and get things straight, you must reach back to them. But I'm saying don't be stifled by folk who want to hang out in the past and keep you there. Even if you don't understand why certain things happened, God will always work out his purposes if you'll give Him a chance.

But you say, "My life is a lemon." Oh, but God can make lemonade. He can take a messed-up scenario and totally transform it if His sovereignty is allowed to work in your life. That's what God is after. He wants to mend your broken past so you can be fully useful again.

A few years ago an old lamp in our house fell and broke. It was in pretty bad shape, but we liked that old lamp, so I got out the Super Glue and went to work. I fit the pieces back together, let the glue dry, and put that lamp back on the stand. It's still there. In fact, if you saw this lamp you would never know it was once broken. I know it, but that's irrelevant now because the glue worked and the lamp is giving light.

You may have a broken past, cracked by an uncaring father, a domineering mother, jealous siblings, perverted relatives, or a careless mate. But I want you to know that if you will bring that cracked vessel to Jesus Christ and let the Holy Spirit do the "glue thing," He can put your life together where only you will know it was ever cracked. And you may even forget it was once cracked because your light is still shining. That's what God can do. Because of Him now you can bring light to others.

My challenge to you, as one man to another and as a brother in Christ, is not to allow your past to control your walk with God in the present as you keep moving toward the future He has for you. It can happen if you will submit your past, and your present, to the Lordship of Jesus Christ. Then you won't need the past as an excuse anymore.

TWO

NO MORE
FEELING WORTHLESS

"I CAN'T GET IT TOGETHER BECAUSE I WAS
REJECTED BY THE PEOPLE WHO SHOULD
HAVE LOVED AND ACCEPTED ME."

It's one thing to fall down. I fall down, you fall down, all the King's men fall down. The question is, are you going to stay down, or are you going to get back up?

We men pride ourselves on being able to take a hit and keep going. We admire the fighter who gets up off the canvas, the basketball player who follows his missed shot, gets the rebound, and puts it back up. We can't even imagine Emmitt Smith lying on the turf, saying, "The other team knocked me down, so I'm not going to get up. I'm just going to lay here."

You may say, "Tony, I didn't just fall down. I was pushed." That's probably how you feel if you were rejected by the people closest to you. Rejection hurts at any level, at any stage of life. It's hard to overcome.

But what I want you to see is that God has made a way for you to come out from under the stigma of rejection so that it no longer needs to trip you up and cause you to fall. I want to help you lay aside the excuse of rejection.

We are going to look at a biblical giant who was rejected by his people, ran away, and lived under the cloud of that rejection for the next forty years. His name was Moses.

If you have experienced rejection, you may be suffering from what psychologists might call a lack of self-esteem, the feeling that you're not worth much and can't do much. Well, that was Moses' problem.

MOSES: A BEGINNING YOU WON'T BELIEVE!

Moses was a man who had a spectacular beginning. You might even call it a supernatural beginning:

> Now a man of the house of Levi married a Levite woman, and she became pregnant and gave birth to a son. When she saw that he was a fine child, she hid him for three months.
> —*Exodus 2:1-2*

Moses was called a beautiful child not just because his mother thought he was cute. The Scripture says, "He was fair in the sight of God." (Acts 7:20, NIV margin) In other words, God had plans for this young man.

The only problem was that Moses was born during a time of great turmoil for the Hebrew slaves in Egypt. They were multiplying too fast, so Pharaoh ordered all Hebrew baby boys to be thrown into the Nile River (Exodus 1:22). Moses was born under a death order, but his mother feared God more than Pharaoh and hid him as long as she could.

But when that became too dangerous, Moses' mother sealed a wicker basket with tar and pitch, put baby Moses in it, and hid the basket on the banks of the Nile. Then she stationed his sister Miriam nearby to see what would happen:

> Then Pharaoh's daughter went down to the Nile to bathe. . . . She saw the basket among the reeds. . . . She opened it and saw the baby. He was crying, and she felt sorry for him. "This is one

of the Hebrew babies," she said. Then his sister asked Pharaoh's daughter, "Shall I go and get one of the Hebrew women to nurse the baby for you?" "Yes, go," she answered. And the girl went and got the baby's mother.

—verses 5-8

What a miraculous turn of events. It just so happened that the wicker basket was in the spot where Pharaoh's daughter chose to bathe. It just so happened that Moses' sister was on the scene to ask and receive permission to find a nurse for the baby. Moses' mother got to raise him anyway, and in the king's palace no less. This is called the sovereignty of God.

BEING RAISED ROYAL

So Moses was raised with the silver spoon of royalty in his mouth. "When the child grew older, she took him to Pharaoh's daughter and he became her son. She named him Moses, saying, 'I drew him out of the water.'" (Exodus 2:10)

Now please understand that this kid had no ordinary upbringing. We are talking about a prince here. Moses was raised with the best and the brightest of Egyptian society, and that was saying a lot in those days. He was Pharaoh's son. He had more money than he could ever spend. He had more power than he could ever wield. He had prestige and recognition. He had the world at his fingertips.

Now since Moses wrote the book of Exodus, he probably didn't want to brag about all that. So Exodus chapter 2 skips the details of his upbringing and goes right to the problem. But to help us understand the full significance of what was about to happen, we need to jump all the way to Acts chapter 7, where Stephen supplies us with some information not found in Exodus.

Stephen was defending himself before the Sanhedrin (the court of justice in Jerusalem), and in the course of his defense he preached a great sermon outlining the wonderful privileges Israel had enjoyed. When he came to the era of Moses, Stephen said this:

"At that time Moses was born, and he was no ordinary child. For three months he was cared for in his father's house. When he was placed outside, Pharaoh's daughter took him and brought him up as her own son. Moses was educated in all the wisdom of the Egyptians and was powerful in speech and action."

—verses 20-22

Now this was during the height of Egypt's reign as a world power. The pyramids were already standing when Moses was born. So we are talking about one of the most brilliant kingdoms in world history in terms of engineering and mathematics. Moses knew all of that stuff.

My point is, this man was no loser. Moses could talk, and he could back it up. In modern terminology, he could put his money where his mouth was. He was a powerful man, educated and handsome. Now notice how Stephen continued in Acts 7:23: "When Moses was forty years old [stuff goes wrong when you hit forty], he decided to visit his fellow Israelites."

A Monumental Miscalculation

With that bit of background, let's go back to Exodus 2 and pick up the story:

One day, after Moses had grown up, he went out to where his own people were and watched them at their hard labor. He saw an Egyptian beating a Hebrew, one of his own people. Glancing this way and that and seeing no one, he killed the Egyptian and hid him in the sand.

—verses 11-12

Moses decided one day to see what was up with the Hebrew slaves. But when he saw one of the brothers being mistreated, he decided to take action right then and there.

What led Moses to make this decision? It doesn't seem like a wise choice for a rich and well-educated son of Pharaoh to make, does it? If we only had this second chapter of Exodus to go by, we might think that Moses just lost his temper and killed that Egyptian. But Acts 7 helps us again:

> "He saw one of them being mistreated by an Egyptian, so he went to his defense and avenged him by killing the Egyptian. Moses thought that his own people would realize that God was using him to rescue them, but they did not."
>
> —*verses 24-25*

Moses' miscalculation wasn't that he committed murder. That wasn't a miscalculation. That was a sin. His miscalculation was supposing that if he showed his oppressed fellow Hebrews that he was on their side by killing an Egyptian, they would throw a parade in his honor and welcome him as their great liberator. Watch out when you start supposing. Moses supposed wrong.

Moses believed he had a purpose for his life, which was to deliver the Hebrews from Egyptian oppression. And he was right. He just wasn't ready. He badly miscalculated God's timing and God's means for setting His people free. But there was nothing wrong with his decision to identify with God's people. In fact, the writer of Hebrews says it was a faith decision.

> By faith Moses, when he had grown up, refused to be known as the son of Pharaoh's daughter. He chose to be mistreated along with the people of God rather than to enjoy the pleasures of sin for a short time. He regarded disgrace for the sake of Christ as of greater value than the treasures of Egypt, because he was looking ahead to his reward.
>
> —*Hebrews 11:24-26*

At some point before he turned forty, Moses made a decision. "I am a Hebrew," he told himself. "I am going to identify with my people and use my position to deliver them." Hebrews says he based that decision on his commitment to God and his people.

Now how did Moses know all of this? He got it from his nurse, who was his mother. Thank God for mothers. He had a mother who told him, "Boy, this is who you really are, and don't you forget it. Don't get tricked by all this money. Don't be fooled by all this power. God saved you because He has a purpose for you. He didn't send you to school just so you can make a lot of money in Egypt. He sent you to school so you could use all your knowledge and expertise to deliver your people."

Moses heard that, and at forty years of age he finally bought it. The problem was that he "supposed" everyone else knew what he and his mama knew—that he was to be Israel's deliverer. So when he saw a chance to be a hero, he took it. As he was kicking sand on the Egyptian's grave, he was probably thinking, "That takes care of one of those Egyptians. A couple of million to go."

But the extent of Moses' miscalculation became obvious the next day when he went back to the scene of his crime (Exodus 2:13-14). He found two Hebrew brothers beating on each other and tried to stop the offender. But the guy turned on him. "Who do you think you are? This is none of your business. Who died and made you boss? Are you going to kill me like you killed the Egyptian?" In other words, "You aren't anybody's deliverer."

When Moses heard that, he became afraid. The word was out. He thought he had looked both ways before killing that Egyptian. But his crime had gone public, and he didn't even know it. His picture was on the wall at the Cairo post office. What he thought he had done in secret had been witnessed by someone, and the word was out.

According to Exodus 2:15, Moses had good reason to be afraid: "When Pharaoh heard of this, he tried to kill Moses, but Moses fled from Pharaoh and went to live in Midian, where he sat down by a well." This is what you call big-time rejection.

A ROYAL REJECT

Here was a man whose life had crumbled. Moses was rejected by his own folk, the Hebrews. He was rejected and hunted like a dog by Pharaoh, his step-daddy. His world had fallen apart. No one seemed to want this guy. And it was all because he tried to do a good thing, to set his people free.

Now it's bad enough if your world crumbles because you are doing a bad thing. But it's even worse when you try to do a good thing and people reject you. Moses tried to do right, but he miscalculated. And the result of his miscalculation was rejection. He was rejected by people on both sides of the track, and he had nowhere to go but into the desert.

Some men experience this kind of dual rejection because of their race. African-American men who are successful in business or other spheres may be rejected by white people simply because they are black. But they may also be rejected by other African-Americans because they are not black enough. This puts them in a racial "twilight zone."

If a white man associates with too many blacks, he may be written off by other whites. But if he pulls away from his black friends, he's caught in another trap. If you grew up in my generation or earlier, you know exactly what I'm talking about.

For other men, the problem isn't so much racial as it is family. They may be caught between two parents who are fighting with each other and trying to pull the kids in opposite directions. So no matter whether the son does or does not take sides, he gets rejected by somebody.

But a far more common scenario for American men is the son who can never live up to his father's expectations. No matter how hard he tries or what he accomplishes, it's never good enough for Dad. Somewhere out there is a middle-aged man still striving for his father's approval, even though his dad has been dead for twenty years. Men like this are paying a high price for their fathers' rejection.

Moses was well-intentioned. He had the right desire, but what he didn't understand was that you can't do the right thing the wrong way. As I said earlier, he wasn't ready to be a deliverer. When it comes to God, timing is everything. You may want to do something real bad, and it may be something you know God wants you to do real bad. But is it His time?

There is only one way I know to determine whether it is God's time, and that is, are you using God's method? Moses did the right thing the wrong way. God never intended Moses to liberate the Hebrews by killing one Egyptian at a time.

But Moses didn't wait around for God's strategy. He desperately needed God's perspective, but he didn't ask, "Is this how I'm supposed to do this?" He figured his training and his high position were the only things he needed to get the job done.

Does that sound like any man you know? "What, ask directions? I know what I'm doing. I don't need any help." So Moses acted impulsively and paid an awful price. Now he was a fugitive and a reject, hiding in the desert.

It's natural to want to run away when you've been rejected, whether the mess was your fault or not. Most men handle rejection by running from it. We aren't usually well prepared emotionally to deal with it, so we skip out. That's why many young men join the military. Things are bad at home, or a man can't find acceptance in the community, so he decides to join the army and see the world, get a fresh start.

If you or someone else has made a mess and now you're running, I have some good news for you. The beauty of God's grace is that even when you run, He knows where you are going. In fact, He will be there to greet you when you arrive. And if you'll allow Him to, He will help you put that rejection behind you and make a fresh start.

FROM HEIR TO HERDER FOR HIRE

So here was Moses in the land of Midian (Exodus 2:15). It didn't take him long to find a new profession or a new family, because right off he got introduced to the family of Reuel or Jethro—a man of Hamitic or African descent, by the way.

Jethro gave his daughter Zipporah, an African woman, to Moses in marriage (2:16-22), and Moses settled down to start his new "profession" as a shepherd—quite a humbling step down from being heir to the throne in Egypt. But while Moses was putting in forty years following sheep around, things were starting to rumble back in Egypt:

During that long period, the king of Egypt died. The Israelites groaned in their slavery and cried out, and their cry for help because of their slavery went up to God. God heard their groaning and he remembered his covenant with Abraham, with Isaac and with Jacob. So God looked on the Israelites and was concerned about them.

—Exodus 2:23-25

What a difference between Exodus 2:11 and 2:25! In the first instance, Moses "saw" the oppression of Israel by Egypt. But now, forty years later, "God looked on the Israelites . . ."

There are two different sets of eyes here. When you react to what you see, if you're not also reacting to what God sees, you are getting ready to make a big mistake because you don't know all the calculations. You don't have all the figures and formulas. You aren't aware of all the pertinent data.

Moses had a good idea, but it wasn't God's timing. He had a *great* idea, in fact, but he didn't wait for God's data. So Moses acted in the flesh. He did it his way. He got mad and lashed out. You know how it is when we men get mad. We don't care about God, the devil, Mama, or Daddy. We take matters into our own hands.

Moses did that, and his life as the deliverer of Israel got put on a forty-year hold. He was eating the dust of the sheep he was herding. He had been next in line to Pharaoh, and now he was baby-sitting sheep.

Have you ever been humbled like that? It's a blow to your male pride, but sometimes it's necessary. Sometimes, to get you where he wants you to be, God has to take you low before He can take you high. He's got to bring you down so that when you come up, you come up right.

God may use rejection to bring us low and open our eyes so that we see the way He sees, but don't miss the point. He doesn't intend for that rejection to become a prison cell, an excuse for not doing anything now. He wants to use your rejection as a stepping-stone, not a stumbling-block. That's what we're about to see with Moses.

GOD'S TURF, GOD'S TIMING, GOD'S TERMS

Up to now, Moses has had too much Egyptian in him. He had more than enough Egyptian knowledge, but he didn't have enough God knowledge. He had great Egyptian power, but he didn't have great God power. He was forty years old, but he wasn't mature yet. He had all the natural tools, but still he wasn't ready.

If God had allowed Moses to get away with killing that Egyptian forty years earlier, Moses would never have *known* he wasn't ready to lead anybody anywhere. Now, forty years later, he's about to find out he is ready:

> There the angel of the LORD appeared to him in flames of fire from within a bush. Moses saw that though the bush was on fire it did not burn up. So Moses thought, "I will go over and see this strange sight—why the bush does not burn up." When the LORD saw that he had gone over to look, God called to him from within the bush, "Moses! Moses!" And Moses said, "Here I am."
> *—Exodus 3:2-4*

Notice that Moses had enough interest and enough curiosity to turn aside and look. The text says that God didn't call until Moses turned aside. Before, Moses didn't consult with God. He said, "I'm going to kill me an Egyptian!" Now he says, "Let me turn aside."

You think twice when you didn't turn aside the last time. The last time, Moses just acted without considering what God might have to say. This time, he was ready to listen, and his reward was a new view of God.

As Moses stood before the bush, God commanded him, "Do not come any closer. Take off your sandals, for the place where you are standing is holy ground." (verse 5)

Wait a minute. Aren't we talking about scrub wilderness, dirt, and rocks? Not anymore, because the blazing Shekinah glory of God has arrived. Why did God tell Moses to take off his sandals? What difference did a half inch or so of shoe leather make?

Well, when are you standing in the presence of God, even half an inch of height is too high. You go as low as you can possibly go; that's humility.

God was saying, "Moses, you are not this big-shot Egyptian now. Are you ready to obey Me? Are you ready to listen to Me? Are you ready to allow Me to be God? Can I run this deliverance of the Hebrews show? Have you been humbled enough with the sheep to learn? Have you got the message that I do things My way?"

Many of us who have experienced rejection have been trying to fix our lives our way for a long time. Like guys in a pickup basketball game, we keep taking our best shot. And we keep missing. But we get the ball once more and say, "I'm going to make it this time."

So we shoot again, and miss again. We say, "It was close!" But you don't get points for being close. That's horseshoes. The way you deal with rejection and get beyond it is *not* to give it your best shot. What you need is a whole new revelation of God and a new vision of what He wants to do in and through you.

That's the process God began with Moses when he turned aside to see the burning bush. God said, "Moses, I want you to understand that I'm in charge on this ground. This is holy ground. This is My territory."

God identified himself to Moses and then announced his plan:

> "I am the God of your father, the God of Abraham, the God of Isaac and the God of Jacob." At this, Moses hid his face, because he was afraid to look at God. The LORD said, "I have indeed seen the misery of my people in Egypt. I have heard them crying out because of their slave drivers, and I am concerned about their suffering."
>
> —*Exodus 3:6-7*

Do you see how God went straight from His identity to His plan? There was no discussion or debate. Moses was in no position to argue with God. He was staring straight into the burning presence of a holy

God, and he was overcome. The fact that he had been rejected forty years earlier was suddenly irrelevant.

If you've been rejected, you need a new view of God. You need to see a "burning bush" kind of God. When I talk about rejection, I don't mean a little incident somewhere in the past. I mean the kind of rejection that tears your life up, the kind of circumstances that have altered the course of your life and left you with real and dramatic scars.

To deal with that kind of rejection, you need to see a God who takes responsibility for people, including you. Those Hebrews Moses tried to liberate were *God's* people. He's the One who made the covenant with them. He was their God. God was saying, "Moses, these are not your people. They're *My* people. I will deliver them in My time and My way, not yours. I will deliver them when *they* cry, not when you cry."

There is a great lesson here because a lot of us are trying to fix our lives up by fixing other people whom God is not ready to fix yet. A lot of us are trying to fix our wives or our children or our coworkers or our bosses, when God wants to fix us first.

It took forty years for God to fix Moses. But the job finally got done, so God said to Moses, "Now I'm ready to do something. I'm ready to come down in power to deliver My people and bring them to their own land. I've heard them cry, and I've seen the oppression, and I've had enough."

Moses got a new view of God. First, he saw God's presence. Second, he saw God's program. And third, he saw God's person. "So now, go. I am sending you to Pharaoh." (3:10) What was God saying? "Now that you've seen Me, you are ready to go back home. Now that you've seen Me, you can do what you tried to do forty years ago on your own. The timing is right."

I'm afraid too many Christian men are still wandering around in Midian because too many wrong things have happened to us and we have not seen the right God yet. It's not that we aren't sincere. It's not that we haven't made spiritual commitments.

Moses made a serious commitment. He chose "to be mistreated

along with the people of God." (Hebrews 11:25) He had the right idea, but he wasn't ready for the high calling yet. Some flaws in his spiritual personality emerged. But now he had come to grips with God on a whole new level. No matter how people have messed you over, it will be all right if you will turn aside to see the burning bush.

KNOWING OUR PRESENT-TENSE GOD

Now I don't want you to think all of this is easy or just automatic. As we saw in the last chapter, God never asks us to pretend as if the past never happened. Moses had a new view of God's presence and God's plan, and that was great. But he wasn't so sure about God's person.

The lingering effects of what had happened to Moses when he tried to act as deliverer now began to surface. His first question was, "Who am I, that I should go to Pharaoh and bring the Israelites out of Egypt?" (Exodus 3:11)

This can't be my boy Mo talking, can it? This can't be the man who was mighty in words and deeds, educated, self-confident, walking around saying, "I'm not going to let any Egyptian mess with my Hebrew brother. He's my homeboy. He's from the 'hood. If you jump on him, you've got to jump on both of us."

Now he is saying fearfully, "Who am I?" Rejection will kill your cocky self-confidence. What we need is a settled God-confidence. Moses was rattled by his rejection at the hands of the Hebrews. He had been a lowly sheepherder for forty years. He had lost the confidence that God could use him. He was operating from a feeling of inferiority.

So God answered in Exodus 3:12, saying, "I will be with you." God knew Moses had been humbled and pressed down. But the question was no longer who Moses was, but who God is.

But Moses had another objection. "Suppose I go to the Israelites and say to them, 'The God of your fathers has sent me to you,' and they ask me, 'What is his name?' Then what shall I tell them?" (3:13)

Remember what we read in Acts? Moses had a definite way with words. This guy never had a problem coming up with an answer. But now he is saying, "I don't know what to say. I can't just say a voice from a bush told me to come down here. What will I say when the people question me?"

I love Exodus 3:14. "God said to Moses, 'I AM WHO I AM. This is what you are to say to the Israelites: "I AM has sent me to you."'" *I* is a personal pronoun; *AM* is the present tense. The eternal God who always lives in the present tense is the One who sent Moses. That's the name of God Moses needed to know, and so do we.

God always lives in the present. He does not have a past or a future. You and I have a past, and we also have a future. But everything is present tense to God. Therefore, if He tells you about your tomorrow, He's not waiting to see if it's coming true. It has already come true because for God, everything is present.

So God was telling Moses, "You can go to Egypt and set My people free because everything I'm telling you is in My today." Then, in the remaining verses of the third chapter of Exodus, God proceeded to tell Moses exactly what would happen when he went to Pharaoh. It was as good as done in God's sight.

But Moses said, "I was rejected."

God said, "But I AM."

Moses said, "I tried this once, and it didn't work."

God said, "But I AM. If they ask you who sent you, tell them I AM sent you."

Moses wasn't quite finished yet, however. He was still acting like a rejected, defeated failure. "What if they do not believe me or listen to me . . . ?" (Exodus 4:1)

This time God answered with a question: "What is that in your hand?" (4:2) Moses was holding his staff, his shepherd's crook. God told him to throw it on the ground, and when he did, it became a snake. Moses jumped back in fear, but then God told him to pick it up by its tail.

Moses: "Say what?"

God: "Pick it up by its tail."

So Moses reached out and grabbed the snake, and it became a staff in his hand again (4:4). God then gave Moses a second sign in verses 6-7, the changing of his hand from normal to leprous and then back to normal again.

Moses was just about out of objections, but he had one more saved for emergencies. "O Lord, I have never been eloquent, neither in the past nor since you have spoken to your servant. I am slow of speech and tongue." (4:10)

That's what rejection will do to you. It will make you lose sight of who you really are and what you really have. Have you ever seen kids who have been beaten down by parents or schoolteachers? They are told, "You are nothing, and you are never going to be anything."

So they walk around saying, "I'm nothing." It becomes a self-fulfilling prophecy. The rejection sinks in, and they don't see their capacity and their potential. Moses had been beaten down so low he said, "I can't talk. How can I go before Pharaoh?" But he was raised in Pharaoh's house. He had just gotten a little rusty. God took care of that objection with the promise of verse 12: "Now go; I will help you speak and will teach you what to say."

FACING THE FALLOUT

What can we learn from Moses about dealing with yesterday's rejection instead of using it as an excuse for today? Let me share four principles with you.

First, *our greatest need is not self-confidence, but God-confidence*. I have already referred briefly to this. Men are taught to be self-confident. We are taught to say, "I can do it!"

Now there's nothing necessarily wrong with a healthy sense of confidence in the gifts and abilities God has given you. But what most of us need is more confidence in the God who gives the gifts and abilities.

Second, *God uses even the bad experiences to prepare us for future service*. The things that God allows to go wrong in your yesterdays are things He wants to use to make you better in your tomorrows. Often the tragedy is not just that we go through these kinds of experiences. The tragedy is that we often go through them without learning from them or realizing that God can make something good out of them.

Third, *God wants to do something with what you already have before He gives you something new*. Some people say, "God, what are you going to do for me tomorrow?" God says, as He said to Moses, "What is in your hand today? Let me do something with what I've already given you, and then I can show you great and mighty things."

Fourth, *obeying God leads to a new self-image*. No matter how much you were rejected by your father, mother, or anyone else, if you will follow God in obedience, He can make up all of the loss and then some. We have a great example in Moses.

Turn ahead to Exodus 11:3. This is after Moses has gone to Egypt and has presented God's plan to Pharaoh. Just before Moses announced the tenth and final plague on Egypt, this verse says, "Moses himself was highly regarded in Egypt by Pharaoh's officials and by the people."

This is what you call a reversal of fortunes. Moses got back all the esteem he lost, but this time he got it from God. Then in Exodus chapter 14, the Israelites have left Egypt and are caught between a rock and a hard place. Pharaoh is coming with his army to attack them. Their backs are to the Red Sea. There was no escape. So in verses 11-12 the people turned against Moses, accusing him of bringing them into the wilderness to die like dogs.

Here is the rejection syndrome again. The people are turning on him again. But listen to Moses this time:

> "Do not be afraid. Stand firm and you will see the deliverance the LORD will bring you today. The Egyptians you see today you will never see again."
>
> —*Exodus 14:13*

Moses has become a true deliverer now. He's doing it in God's time and God's way. And so God tells him, "Raise your staff and stretch out your hand over the sea to divide the water so that the Israelites can go through the sea on dry ground." (verse 16)

You probably know what happened. The Red Sea opened up,

Israel passed through, and then it closed. Pharaoh and his army drowned. Notice how the story culminates in Exodus 14:31: "And when the Israelites saw the great power the LORD displayed against the Egyptians, the people feared the LORD and put their trust in him and in Moses his servant."

I have to give you just one more example. In Exodus chapter 17 we find the famous account in which Joshua was to fight against the Amalekites while Moses went up on the mountain to hold up his arms (with a little help from his friends Aaron and Hur). In verse 9, Moses called his staff "the staff of God."

Back in Exodus 3:2, it was Moses' staff. Now it was "the staff of God." Same stick, but different power. Whatever is in your hand today, throw it down, let God touch it, and pick it back up. Then you will be able to do something great with it for God's glory—no matter who told you anything different!

· THREE ·

NO MORE
ALLOWING FOR
IMMORALITY

"I'M ONLY HUMAN. I'M JUST DOING WHAT COMES
NATURALLY. AFTER ALL, GOD KNOWS A MAN
HAS NEEDS. HE MADE ME THIS WAY."

One of the most devastating sins I know of is that of sexual immorality. Of all the things that can crush a man spiritually, emotionally, and physically, none can do it faster or more completely than a plunge into sexual sin.

Some of the strongest and finest men in this generation have bitten the dust because of failure to bring this area of their lives under God's control. And even those who have never fallen physically regularly fall mentally.

The reason sexual sin is so destructive is because sex is such a potent gift. Our sexuality is an integral part of our makeup as human beings. God created us as man and woman. Like all of God's good gifts, sex can bring great joy and fulfillment to life when used correctly. But when used incorrectly, it brings great devastation.

We might liken sex to a fire. A fire in the fireplace is warm and delightful. But if that fire gets out of the fireplace, it can burn the house down. The fire of sex has been given for the fireplace of marriage. Once it leaves there, someone is going to get burned.

Unfortunately, there are a lot of burn victims out there, even in the Christian community. Some very successful men have lost their careers over their sexual behavior. Husbands have sacrificed their marriages for sex. Fathers have deserted their families for sex. Single men have traded their sexual integrity and purity for sex. And gay men are at constant risk of their very lives for it.

Yet with all of this, the great irony is that for most men, sexual sin is one of the easiest sins to excuse and rationalize. The man who devours pornography tells himself they're only pictures. The man who lives on lust excuses it by saying his fantasies are harmless. The single man who engages in sex tries to excuse his sin by shifting the responsibility to the woman. The adulterer says, "Well, at least I'm not homosexual." And the homosexual says, "I can't help it. God made me this way."

The sad thing about excusing sexual sin, or any sin for that matter, is that it actually makes things worse. It doesn't relieve the offender's sense of guilt. In fact, it increases guilt, because neither God nor the people hurt by the sin are buying the offender's excuse—and he knows it deep down.

In addition, excusing sin lessens the chance of getting to the root of the problem and dealing with it, leaving the pornography user, the adulterer, or the homosexual mired in his sin. Many men trapped in sexual sin say they feel helpless to stop. They think there is no hope for them—and there really isn't, as long as they insist on excusing their actions.

Now every man has experienced sexual temptation on some level. All of us have felt the flames of this fire. Some of us have been set aflame, and others have been scorched. If you have never been touched by it, you may want to check your pulse!

So I am proceeding on the assumption that I am not talking a foreign language to most men. But my purpose is not to add to any load of guilt you may be carrying. The Holy Spirit is the Convicter.

I have three purposes in this chapter. First, I want to help you lay aside the excuses that make it easy for a man to commit and justify sexual sin. Second, I want to help you deal with this sin if the need is there. Third, I want to fortify your spiritual defenses against the sexual temptation that is common to all of us (1 Corinthians 10:13).

It should not surprise us to learn that the Bible does not hesitate to talk about sex. The Bible does not blush to tell us the truth about sex, both as God created it to be and as humankind has twisted and misused it.

THE CONCEPTION OF SEXUAL SIN

Since one of the most powerful methods of teaching is by real-life example, we are going to look at a biblical story of a man who committed adultery. We are going to watch his life crumble as a result of his sin and his attempts to excuse and cover it up, and then we are going to see the grace of God put this man back together.

King David is our man here, and 2 Samuel 11:1 tells us right off that he was in the wrong place at the wrong time: "In the spring, at the time when kings go off to war, David sent Joab out with the king's men and the whole Israelite army. . . . But David remained in Jerusalem."

Normally a king would lead his army into battle. But David had already solidified his kingdom. There were just a few skirmishes to take care of, so he decided to stay home. Now David was about fifty years old here, a time when many men peer into the mirror and see some gray hair and some wrinkles. Then the question comes, "Do I still have it?"

So we have a middle-aged man hanging around the house with nothing to do. It's springtime, the season for love. And he's a king, so he can have anything he wants. Bad combination.

Then it happened. David got up from his late-afternoon nap and decided to walk around on the roof of the palace, which was situated high above the city. From there, he could see down into other homes. As David scanned the city, "he saw a woman bathing." (1 Samuel 11:2) And not just any woman. We are talking about a "bad mamma-jamma." She was "very beautiful."

David looked out over that rooftop and saw one of God's choicest specimens, with all the right measurements. He watched as the

water ran down her hair and over her skin. The early evening's moon-
light only added to her beauty. David looked and looked until he could
not stop looking. Then he inquired about her and found out her name
was Bathsheba.

Now you must understand that King David was coming off
about twenty years of spiritual success. He was walking with God. He
had his failures, but he had lived many years in spiritual strength. We
are talking about the David who killed Goliath, the poet who wrote
most of the Psalms.

It was David who said, "I will extol the LORD at all times; his
praise will always be on my lips" (Psalm 34:1); "As the deer pants for
streams of water, so my soul pants for you, O God" (Psalm 42:1);
"Your word is a lamp to my feet and a light for my path" (Psalm
119:105); "I lift up my eyes to the hills—where does my help come
from?" (Psalm 121:1)

But on that evening David wasn't "mountain looking." This
woman captivated him. We need to remember that David was not trying to be carnal or looking to fall that night. But he was a man, and he
saw a woman. The Bible says, "If you think you are standing firm, be
careful that you don't fall!" (1 Corinthians 10:12)

Many of us would say, "I would have never gone so far as to try
and find out the woman's name." Take heed, because you can do anything when Satan gets ahold of you. David not only found out
Bathsheba's name, he learned something else about her. She was "the
wife of Uriah the Hittite." (2 Samuel 11:3)

Uriah was one of David's most loyal soldiers. The woman was
married to a man who was faithful to David. But that didn't stop David
from carrying out the sin he was formulating in his mind. Sexual sin
blinds a man to the consequences.

The Bible says David saw Bathsheba. But what he didn't see was
that this one night would change the rest of his life. What he didn't
see was that this one night would cause four of his children to die, as
we will learn later. What he didn't see was that this one night would

split his kingdom in half. What he didn't see was that he would become a first-degree murderer.

So as a man thumbs through his pornographic magazines or watches X-rated videos, as he looks at what he ought not to be looking at, he gets spiritually blinded. He doesn't see the whole picture, the real story. And that's a tragedy.

The Complications of Sexual Sin

A tragedy was unfolding in this case for sure. David sent for Bathsheba, and "she came to him, and he slept with her." Tomorrow didn't matter. The only thing that mattered was right now. The only thing that mattered was his passion. In the midst of his idleness, David made the mistake of his life. But he didn't count on Bathsheba getting pregnant.

Just one night and it's over, it's finished, we think. David said, "I had my party. The party's over." No, Bathsheba was pregnant. Sin can get complicated.

Bathsheba's pregnancy was the start of the tomorrow that David didn't think about the night before. Now he's got to do something. He's got to cover this up. He can't let anyone know. A king can not only have whomever he wants, he can also do whatever he wants to get rid of his problems. David thought about it and formulated three plans to cover up this mess (2 Samuel 11:6-17). We could call this the "Davidic Watergate."

Plan A was to send a message to Joab, his army chief of staff, and have him send Uriah home to Jerusalem. "Tell Uriah that I want him to come back home and rest up. He's been fighting hard, and I want him to spend a nice weekend with his wife, take a little 'R & R.'" Of course, David hoped Uriah and Bathsheba would make love, and Uriah would then think the baby was his.

But David didn't bank on Uriah's loyalty. David tried to send Uriah home, but he curled up on David's front porch (vv. 8-9). David asked him what he was doing, and Uriah answered:

"The ark and Israel and Judah are staying in tents, and my master Joab and my lord's men are camped in the open fields. How could I go to my house to eat and drink and lie with my wife? As surely as you live, I will not do such a thing!"

—verse 11

Again, what a beautiful picture of faithfulness and integrity on Uriah's part. Now David had two problems he hadn't banked on: Bathsheba's pregnancy and her committed husband. Plan A crashed.

So David set Plan B in motion: get Uriah drunk and send him home, where he would finally sleep with his wife and David could get this nasty mess fixed (verse 13). But even drunk, Uriah wouldn't cooperate. He wouldn't go to his house. Then David pulled out Plan C, which was first-degree murder:

In the morning David wrote a letter to Joab and sent it with Uriah. In it he wrote, "Put Uriah in the front line where the fighting is fiercest. Then withdraw from him so he will be struck down and die."

—2 Samuel 11:14-15

When you read about the carrying out of the plot and the report to David in verses 16-25, what strikes you most, if you are like me, is the calculation and the coldness of the whole thing. David made Uriah deliver his own death warrant to Joab. Trying to cover up sin always leads to more sin. Sin not dealt with early becomes more sin to deal with later.

And when David was told, "Some of the king's servants are dead, and your servant Uriah the Hittite is also dead" (verse 24), his response was, "No big deal. Don't sweat it." David had become so cold and hard over his sin that he said, "Well, you win some, you lose some. That's the way it is. Life's unfair. Uriah lost out. Don't be upset about it."

If you're a Christian and you have been in moral sin for any time, you know how bad you felt at first. You felt kind of bad a little bit later, and then a little bad after that. But before long you were saying, "Everybody is doing it." Then finally, "I'm only human."

David was probably at this stage by the time Bathsheba's mourning period for Uriah was over and David married her. A baby boy came, and all was nice and legal. The cover-up seemed to be complete. Bathsheba was now his wife. The child was legitimate. And the only other person who knew was Joab, who wasn't about to say anything because he was an accomplice to murder. David had sinned, but he had covered his tracks . . . except for one.

Look at the end of 2 Samuel 11:27: "But the thing that David had done displeased the LORD." Things would be fine if the Lord didn't see it. Stuff would be perfect if the Lord didn't see it. If the Lord hadn't seen it, David would have gotten away with murder. Uriah died in battle. Let's play Taps. Let's fold the flag. But the Lord saw it.

Married man, if you are running around on your wife, the Lord sees it. If you are sleeping around, single man, the Lord sees it. You may not get caught today, but the Lord has a lot of tomorrows.

I have permission from a member of our church in Dallas to tell the following story. This person got involved in immorality and then got out of the relationship, and no one knew but the two people involved. About a year went by, and all was well.

But then the other person went to the doctor, who saw some problems that could be related to venereal disease. The doctor told this person, "We need to test you, but we also need to know everyone you've been sexually involved with over the last two years." That included this member of our church.

So a year later the whole thing was suddenly exposed because the doctor's office called this church member regarding concerns over possible venereal infection. When the Lord decides to deal with you, it doesn't matter how few people know.

THE CONSEQUENCES OF SEXUAL SIN

One reason I share that incident is because David's sin went unexposed for roughly the same length of time, about a year. But after a year, God sent the prophet Nathan to call on David (2 Samuel 12:1-4). Now Nathan knew better than to stroll into a king's throne room and start throwing accusations at him. So Nathan told David a touching story.

He said, "David, we've got a problem. There were two men in one of your cities. One man was rich and had a lot of flocks and herds, but the other man was poor. He had nothing but one little ewe lamb. It was like a daughter to him.

"Now someone came to visit the rich man, but he didn't want to kill one of his own animals to feed his guest. Instead, he took the poor man's ewe lamb and killed it to feed his guest." Nathan didn't say it, but the implication of his story was, "What do you think we ought to do about this, Dave?"

The Bible says David burned with anger (verse 5). To think that someone who had a lot of lambs would take a poor man's only lamb that he loved like one of his own children made David very hot. He slammed his fist on the arm of his throne and said, "Find me that man, and I'll put him to death! Then pay that poor man back four times as much as he lost from the rich man's stock."

The Law said if a thief stole a sheep, he had to pay the owner back with four sheep (Exodus 22:1). But David said, "That's not enough. Kill him!"

A lot of us do that. We look at the immorality of other people and say, "Throw the book at them!" As I said above, some adulterers do this with homosexuals. They say, "I know I'm doing this, but at least I'm not gay. Nothing funny here, honey. I'm not like them. They ought to die. I deserve to live, but not them."

Once David had incriminated himself, Nathan lowered the boom. "You are the man!" (verse 7) I think Nathan's story tells us something about the marriage of Uriah and Bathsheba. For instance, I think Uriah was older because Bathsheba was described as his "little ewe lamb," meaning she was a lot younger.

The story also shows that Uriah's life revolved around Bathsheba. Like the poor man's lamb, she was the darling of his life.

Bathsheba brought the Hittite a lot of joy and fulfillment, even though he was a little older.

But by his sin David said, "I know that old man isn't doing anything for this little darling." So he looked over and said, "Papa is here."

Notice the indictment that Nathan delivered against David. This wasn't Nathan's indictment. It was the Lord's.

> "This is what the LORD, the God of Israel, says: 'I anointed you king over Israel, and I delivered you from the hand of Saul. I gave your master's house to you, and your master's wives into your arms. I gave you the house of Israel and Judah. And if all this had been too little, I would have given you even more.'"
>
> —*2 Samuel 12:7-8*

Then in verse 9, David's crime was described in perfect detail, and his judgment was announced in verses 10-14. The punishment fit the crime, because "From everyone who has been given much, much will be demanded." (Luke 12:48) Yet this passage also reflects God's great grace, since as an adulterer and murderer David deserved death under the Law. God spared David's life, but he would reap what he had sown (Galatians 6:7).

Do you see what God is saying here? He is telling David, "Your problem is Me. Your problem is not Bathsheba or this baby. Your problem is not even Uriah. Your problem is Me! Look at what I've done for you. How could you sin against Me after all that I have given you?"

David's sin unleashed a whole series of consequences. He himself said the offender should pay back the debt fourfold, and in fact four of his own children eventually died. You can trace it through the rest of David's story.

First, the baby he conceived with Bathsheba died (2 Samuel 12:18). Second, David's son Amnon raped his half-sister, Tamar. Absalom, another of David's sons and Tamar's full brother, had Amnon killed in revenge (2 Samuel 13:28-29).

Then Absalom went up and violated all of David's wives, in fulfillment of the judgment pronounced against David in 2 Samuel 12:11. Absalom then became the third of David's sons to die when he got his hair caught in a tree and was slain by Joab (2 Samuel 18:9-14). And finally, years later, Adonijah was killed by Solomon (1 Kings 2:19-25).

And, of course, after the reign of Solomon the kingdom of Israel was split in two by his successors. So David's sin wasn't just a one-night stand. It was a lifetime wipeout.

Not only that; according to Psalm 32:3-4 David said that during the whole time he tried to hide his sin, his life was so spiritually empty that his strength was sapped. He felt guilt and shame. He had no relief day or night because he wouldn't come clean with God.

THE CHARACTER OF SEXUAL SIN

The ultimate issue in sexual sin is that immorality is an affront to a holy God. When David sinned, he broke God's holy commandments.

- He dishonored his family.
  "Honor your father and your mother." (Exodus 20:12)

- He killed Uriah.
  "You shall not murder." (Exodus 20:13)

- He committed adultery.
  "You shall not commit adultery." (Exodus 20:14)

- He stole Uriah's wife.
  "You shall not steal." (Exodus 20:15)

- He had to live a life of lies.
  "You shall not give false testimony." (Exodus 20:16)

- He lusted after that which belonged to his neighbor.
  "You shall not covet your neighbor's wife." (Exodus 20:17)

By my count, that's six of the Ten Commandments. David broke in this one act every Commandment dealing with how you are supposed to treat others. Even leaving off murder, you still wipe out five of the Commandments when you commit sexual sin. That's the whole second table of the Law. David did all of this, and yet God told him, "I gave you the house of Israel and Judah. And if all this had been too little, I would have given you even more." (2 Samuel 12:8)

So David's cover-up was uncovered. Hebrews 4:13 tells us that "nothing in all creation is hidden from God's sight." Ironically, David's sin wasn't covered up. It was recorded for millions of people to read over the last three thousand years.

David's sin caused God's name to be blasphemed (2 Samuel 12:14). God said, "You've made My name look bad. You have embarrassed My reputation. You have been an affront to Me."

It's like a parent who tells a child, "Don't play with the lamp." The kid plays with the lamp, knocks it over, and the lamp breaks into little pieces. Brother or sister comes along, steps on the glass, and gets cut.

Someone else got hurt because of that child's disobedience, but the problem was that the child didn't listen to the parent. God is the parent, and while your wife or children or other people may get hurt by your sexual sin, your *real* problem is with Daddy.

You may say, "Tony, I'm afraid that describes me. I've got a real problem right now. What should I do?" Or you may have a friend who is trapped in sexual sin and doesn't see any way out. Or it may be that sexual sin is not an addiction for you, but you know you've blown it at times and you want to know forgiveness. Whatever the case, I have good news for you. This is not the end of the story.

THE CONFESSION OF SEXUAL SIN

When David was confronted by Nathan the prophet, he showed why he was called a man after God's heart. David's immediate response was, "I have sinned against the LORD." (2 Samuel 12:13) His prayer of confession and repentance is recorded for us in Psalm 51.

This is a prayer every Christian man needs to make at one time or another. If you have fallen into fornication, adultery, homosexuality, pornography, lust, or any other form of moral compromise, this is the kind of prayer God is looking for from you:

"Have mercy on me, O God, according to your unfailing love; according to your great compassion blot out my transgressions. Wash away all my iniquity and cleanse me from my sin. For I know my transgressions, and my sin is always before me. Against you, you only, have I sinned and done what is evil in your sight, so that you are proved right when you speak and justified when you judge."

—*Psalm 51:1-4*

David repented. The only way back from moral compromise is to change your direction and confess your sin before God. Now many people don't know what God means when He says to confess. They whip out this little prayer and say, "Lord, I'm sorry for the sins I've done today. Forgive me. In Jesus' name, Amen."

That is not confession. The word *confess* means to agree with. In confession, you agree with God when He says that what you did was sin. Confession is not just some vague, "I'm sorry."

True repentance is coming to grips with your rebellion against a holy God. It means acknowledging your sin, being sorry for it, and doing away with it. You see yourself as sinful and in need of cleansing.

That's painful, but what a faithful and forgiving God we have. David uses a beautiful Hebrew word in Psalm 51:1, *hesed*, translated "lovingkindness" (NASB). The root of this word pictures a stork, a bird that is known for building its huge nests high in the treetops and for being tenaciously committed to its young. This commitment is why in popular American mythology the stork is said to deliver babies.

David is saying that God's love for him is "stork-like." David knew that God loved him with the same tenacity and commitment with which a stork loves its little ones. Another way of translating this word is "loyal love," which gives the same idea of devotion and commitment.

That's the kind of love God displays for the one who has sinned, but the sinner must display a true repentance that does not make excuses. The truly repentant person does not say, "Lord, I know I messed up, but it was the woman's fault."

Notice that Bathsheba's name never comes up in David's prayer.

He owns the sin himself. True repentance says, "This is my problem and my sin, because I didn't have to yield to it." David knows that God is "justified" and "blameless" in his judgments (NASB).

It is a great tragedy when we refuse to own up to moral failure. One guy tried to justify his immoral behavior to me by saying, "I'm a man." That's not the point. The point is that you are a *Christian* man. You are a redeemed man, and therefore, when you sin and you stand judged by God, you simply say, "You've got me. I'm guilty."

Now, God decides what He's going to expose and what He's not going to expose. He decides who He is going to expose and who He's not going to expose. He decides when He's going to expose it and when He's not going to expose it. He is gracious, but whatever He decides, we have to be ready to say, "Lord, You are righteous when You judge. You have the right to be God in my life."

David continues the prayer of Psalm 51 by asking for cleansing and restoration:

> Cleanse me with hyssop, and I will be clean; wash me, and I will be whiter than snow. Let me hear joy and gladness; let the bones you have crushed rejoice. Hide your face from my sins and blot out all my iniquity. Create in me a pure heart, O God, and renew a steadfast spirit within me. Do not cast me from your presence or take your Holy Spirit from me.
>
> —*verses 7-11*

Look at David's plea for a return of the joy and wholeness and power he once had with God. If you are living with unconfessed moral sin, that's why you have no joy, no peace, no power. That's why you don't have a sense of God's presence. That's why your prayers are not being answered.

David asked for a bath. Hyssop was a branch dipped into blood, which was sprinkled on the altar for the forgiveness of sin. Some of us need a spiritual bath. Many men are filthy. We wallow in the muck and mire of pornographic literature. We go by magazine stands and look around to make sure no one is watching before we flip the pages of magazines we wouldn't want our sons to look at. We choose our movies based on the amount of sex scenes.

We become spiritually dirty when we do things like this, and we need to be made clean before God. David was all out of excuses and rationalizations and twelve-step self-improvement plans at this point. All he could do was pray, "Wash me. Cleanse me."

What did David mean when he prayed that God would not take the Holy Spirit from him? When Saul sinned and forfeited his kingdom, the Bible says that the Spirit of the Lord departed from him (1 Samuel 16:14). As king, he lost the anointing of God.

I think that's what David is talking about here. He's saying, "Don't take away the Holy Spirit's anointing on my life. Don't take away my ministry." He's not just talking about the Person of the Spirit departing from him.

Now if you've messed up morally and you are ready to turn to God in real confession and repentance, David has good news for you. God can use you to teach other transgressors his ways (Psalm 51:13). You might be able to tell a potential homosexual why he doesn't have to go that way, because you have been there and it's a dead-end road. You might be able to tell other adulterers that this is not the way to go because you have paid the price. The result will be that "sinners will turn back to you."

What does God want? "The sacrifices of God are a broken spirit; a broken and contrite heart, O God, you will not despise." (verse 17). Say, "Lord, I am brokenhearted over my sin." But another tragedy of moral compromise is that it takes us men so long to get brokenhearted. We don't hurt over it. It doesn't turn our stomachs and make us want to throw up. But God wants to see a broken heart. He can fix broken hearts.

Did God answer David's prayer? He did. Psalm 32, which we looked at earlier, summarizes David's answer:

> Blessed is he whose transgressions are forgiven, whose sins are covered. Blessed is the man whose sin the LORD does not count against him and in whose spirit is no deceit.
>
> —*verses 1-2*

I acknowledged my sin to you and did not cover up my iniquity.
I said, "I will confess my transgressions to the LORD"—and you
forgave the guilt of my sin.

—verse 5

God forgave David and has used him throughout history to teach others. My prayer is that God will use His Word to help Christian men today avoid the degrading, destructive trap of sexual sin.

FIVE TRUTHS ABOUT SEXUAL SIN

To that end, let me give you five important principles you need to keep before you as you deal with this volatile area of sexuality and sexual temptation.

1. *Anyone can commit immorality.* I'm not immune to it; neither are you. It has nothing to do with how much you love your wife. It has nothing to do with how committed you are to your family. It doesn't even have anything to do with how much you love the Lord, because at a particular moment we are all vulnerable. Instead of saying, "That will never happen to me," say, "By God's grace, never."

2. *Past success is no guarantee of future success.* The fact that you haven't fallen in all these years has little to do with what might happen tomorrow. Don't underestimate the power of passion. Augustine said, "There is nothing more powerful in bringing down the spirit of a man than the caress of a woman." Passion is powerful. When you play with it, you will always want more.

Don't live off yesterday's spiritual victories. Keep your walk with God fresh every day.

3. *Sin is a choice.* It was David's decision to continue looking at Bathsheba, to send for her, to commit sin with her. He could have stopped the process at any time, but he chose to act on his desires.

4. *Immorality always brings consequences.* Forgiveness is available, but it does not undo all the consequences of sexual sin. The tearing apart of your family, the loss of respect, the threat of disease, and the danger of escalation to even more serious sin are also con-

sequences you need to consider before you enter into sexual immorality.

5. *God will forgive you*. If He forgave David, He will forgive you. You can't change what happened last night, but you have a lot to say about what will happen tonight. If you want to get right with God in this area, you have to do like they do in Alcoholics Anonymous. They go to the meeting and say, "My name is John. I am an alcoholic." You need to go before a holy God and say, "My name is (fill in the blank). I am a sinner, and I have blown it."

In John 8:1-11 we read about a woman who was brought to Jesus by the scribes and Pharisees. She had been caught in "the act of adultery." It wasn't hearsay. They brought the woman to Jesus to trip him up because the Law said she should be stoned. "Now what do you say?" they asked Jesus.

The Bible says Jesus just knelt down on the ground and started writing in the dirt. They kept asking Him, so He stood up and said, "If any one of you is without sin, let Him be the first to throw a stone at her." (verse 7) Then He knelt a second time and again started writing on the ground.

Then the men began to drop their stones and disappear one by one, until they were all gone. Obviously, none of them could claim to be without sin and back it up.

Was their disappearing act based partly on what Jesus was writing? It could have been. The Bible doesn't say what he wrote, but let me use some holy imagination. Whatever He wrote must have related to them, because it shook them up enough to make them leave. Whatever He wrote had to do with adultery, because that was the issue in question.

Now when I put all that together, I think what Jesus was writing was the names of some other women in town like the one standing before Him. What He was saying was, "Anyone here who is not connected to one of these ladies, throw the first stone."

In other words, don't condemn someone else for a sin you're guilty of yourself. You might be quick to condemn another man's adultery, but don't throw stones if you are into pornography.

Now I don't know if that's what Jesus was actually doing, and even if it was, He wasn't justifying the woman's adultery. The warning here is the one I quoted earlier in the chapter: "if you think you are standing firm, be careful that you don't fall!"

The word I want to leave you with is Jesus' word to this woman in John 8:10-11: "Where are they? Has no one condemned you?" And she said, "No one, sir." And Jesus said, "Then neither do I condemn you. . . . Go now and leave your life of sin."

· FOUR ·

No More Going Through The Motions

"THERE'S REALLY NO PURPOSE TO LIFE. I'M
JUST ALONG FOR THE RIDE. I'LL PUT IN
MY EIGHT HOURS, BUT THAT'S IT."

If I were to ask you who you are as a man, could you tell me with-out giving me your name, your occupation, your job title at work, or any of the other obvious means we use to identify ourselves? If I were to simply say, "Tell me who you are," what would you say?

Now it's not that your name and your occupation don't matter. These are very important and valid identifiers, but there are plenty of men who know their names and their occupations who don't really know who they are at the core of their being. Therefore, they have no real sense of purpose in life.

When you have no *purpose* for what you're doing, all you have left is the routine of what you're doing. Many men trudge to work every day and trudge home every night with little or no sense of why they do what they do.

Since thinking about the purpose of life can raise some uncom-fortable questions, a lot of men start to hide behind the daily routine. It becomes their escape, their excuse not to search for anything more. The routine may not be all that enjoyable, but at least it's safe. It's predictable.

ROUTINE-ITIS: THE MODERN MAN'S EPIDEMIC

This is why the twentieth-century American man is such an empty creature. Legions of modern men suffer from what I call the "same old same old" disease. You ask them how it's going, and they answer, "Oh, you know, same old same old."

What they mean is, every day they get out of that same old bed and go to that same old bathroom to stare in the mirror at that same old face. They go to that same old closet and thumb through those same old clothes to put on that same old body. They go to that same old kitchen, sit at that same old breakfast table, and eat that same old breakfast cooked by that same old wife (I'm treading dangerous ground here).

Then they go to that same old garage, get in that same old car, and drive down that same old road to that same old office. There they work with those same old people, doing that same old thing, receiving that same old pay. At five o'clock they end that same old work and get back in that same old car to drive that same old road back to that same old house.

At home they hear the same old noise from the same old kids while sitting in that same old easy chair reading that same old newspaper. They finish their day by sitting in front of that same old television watching those same old shows. Then they retire to that same old bed with that same old wife, so they can get up and start it all over again.

You may think that's a little overstated, but I guarantee you there are a lot of men living exactly that kind of life. And many of them are sincere Christians who have fallen into the rut of a meaningless existence because life has lost its sense of purpose and significance.

Men who find themselves in this rut are often driven to ask, "Is this all there is?" Now if the answer comes back that yes, this seems to be all there is, a man will usually react in one of two ways.

He may react by trying to climb out of the rut. This man says, "I've got to find myself. I've got to know who I am and why I'm here." He may not have the slightest idea who he is supposed to be or where to begin looking, but he starts searching for himself anyway—an interesting chore, to say the least.

But the man I'm more concerned about here is the man who reacts to his rut by looking around and deciding there's no way out and it's pointless to try. This is the man who heaves a deep sigh and plods on ahead, cutting even deeper grooves in his rut.

Then when he hits his middle years he becomes vulnerable in a lot of ways because he can look back and see more years behind him than he has ahead of him. This is when a lot of men begin raising questions about life and death and eternity.

We may not always admit it, because men have a way of covering themselves and preserving their pride. But there are not too many of us who don't raise the question at some point, "Why do I have to continue dealing with this?" I have talked to more than a few men who wanted to throw in the towel because they didn't see any reason to continue.

Many men today are like the father who sat his son down to talk to him about life. "Now, son, what I want you to do is go to school and get a good education."

The son replied, "Why, Dad?"

"Because if you go to school and get a good education, then you'll get a good job. And if you get a good job, you can live where you want, wear what you want, and buy what you want. You can be your own man."

The son said, "Dad, let me see if I understand you. You want me to go to school and get a good education so I can get a good job and make good money so I can live where I want, wear what I want to wear, and buy what I want. Is that right?"

"That's it."

"But why am I supposed to do all that?"

"Well, son, it's like this. I want you to do all of this so that when you have kids, you can send them to school so they can get a good education and a good job so they can live where they want, wear what they want, and buy what they want."

"Let me make sure I got this right, Dad. You want me to do all this stuff so I can help my children do all the same stuff I did when they grow up? Is that right, Dad?"

"You got it, kid."

"But what am I doing all of this for?"

The father said, "Son, you don't understand. I want you to do all of this so that you'll be able to retire in comfort. I want you to be able to travel and enjoy your golden years."

The son said, "Dad, you still haven't answered my question. If I achieve everything you want me to achieve, build up a good nest egg, retire in comfort, and enjoy my golden years, then what? You still haven't told me why."

By now Dad is getting a little frustrated, so he says, "Boy, just go to school, get a good education, and get a good job so you can live where you want, wear what you want, and buy what you want. Help your kids do the same, then retire in comfort and enjoy your golden years. That way, when you die you'll have something to leave behind."

If you think about it, there are a lot of people who live like that. They get the good education and the good job, they provide for their children so their children can provide for their own children, then they grow old, retire, die—and leave it all behind. As the song says, "If that's all there is, then let's keep dancing."

THE WORLD'S WISEST, WEALTHIEST MAN ASKS, "WHAT'S THE PURPOSE?"

I was on a cruise a couple of years ago, and as I stood on that boat looking out over that vast Pacific Ocean, I was reminded of my insignificance. All around me was water, the largest body of water in the world. Here I was, a little speck on a boat that seemed huge to me, but a boat that seemed like a little speck in the middle of that huge ocean.

Then I happened to turn around and look at the stern of the boat, and I noticed something that frustrated me more. As the ship went through the water, it caused a lot of turbulence. It made a dent, it did something in the water, but a couple of seconds afterwards, the water closed up and everything was back to normal.

As I thought about that, I thought about me. I thought to myself, "That's me. I'll go through here in seventy years, Lord willing, and cause a little stir. But after I'm gone, it will all go back to normal."

Do you know what frustrates me even more? The advertising boys on Madison Avenue have picked up on modern man's lack of significance. Virtually every commercial you see for men is designed to exploit our feeling of insignificance, to take advantage of our desire to be somebody.

To attract the women, you've got to splash on this. To be recognized as successful, you've got to drive that. Then, knowing how bored men get after a while, they make it new and improved to attack our sense of insignificance all over again.

The whole area of purpose and identity and significance in life is no small question for men today. If you are in the rut I described earlier, and you've gotten used to routine without real meaning, my purpose is not to chastise you or put you down for being there. I want to offer you a ladder and help hold it steady while you climb out.

If you are not in that rut and want to avoid falling into it down the road, I want to help you steer a clear course. And if you have a friend or family member, a brother in Christ, who is in the rut of a meaningless existence, I want to help you offer him a ladder too.

One reason I know this issue of purpose is important is that God has devoted a whole book of His Word to addressing it. The book of Ecclesiastes addresses our need for a sense of purpose in life. It was written by a man in search of life's purpose, so it speaks especially to us as men.

Now if you're going to get advice from somebody on a subject this important, you don't want to hear from a loser. You want to hear from a winner. You want advice from somebody who has made it. If you are trying to grow hair, you don't go to a hair growth expert who is bald. You want somebody with some hair. If you are trying to lose weight, you don't go to a three-hundred-pound nutritionist. That just doesn't compute.

So to get the real deal about life's purpose, we need to find somebody who can speak from experience. We need to hear from somebody we can respect, particularly as men. We need somebody who has it together, who has what we are looking for, who is going after what we are going after. That's why Solomon is the perfect person.

Here was a man who not only had it all, but could buy and sell everyone else who had it all. At the peak of his reign as the king of Israel, Solomon personally had more money than most other entire nations. He would have made Ross Perot look like a ghetto child.

Besides being filthy rich, the man had a thousand ladies—seven hundred wives and three hundred concubines. He probably could have added to that number with a snap of his fingers at any time too. No woman he desired was beyond his reach. So Solomon could soak himself in any pleasure any man could imagine.

And talk about a career. Solomon was king of a great kingdom. He was the top guy. If you make it to king, you can't go any higher. Everybody else worked for Solomon. So in addition to unimaginable wealth and pleasure, this guy also had the kind of power most men only dream about. Besides all of this, Solomon was also given wisdom beyond what anyone before or since has possessed.

Yet Solomon was also the man who wrote a book to tell us how empty and futile he found life to be. Given his credentials to speak on the subject, we had better sit up and listen to what Solomon had to say.

I used to teach preaching at my alma mater, Dallas Theological Seminary. One of the things you learn to do in preaching, or in any public speaking, is to prepare your introduction last, after you have prepared the body and conclusion of the sermon.

Of course, to students who have never preached before, that sounds backwards. But I explained to them that you can't do the introduction until you know what you are introducing. And you want to make sure your introduction not only grabs the hearers' attention, but points them in the direction the sermon is going to take them.

Well, I don't know if Solomon wrote Ecclesiastes 1:1-3 last or not, but it definitely meets all the criteria of a good introduction. We know something is up because in the very first verse Solomon calls himself "the Teacher." That means he has something to tell us, a message to deliver. He adds "son of David, king in Jerusalem" almost as an afterthought.

Solomon now has our attention, because we know he's somebody who has a lot of credibility and something to tell us. And his opening is a real attention-grabber:

> "Meaningless! Meaningless!" says the Teacher. "Utterly meaningless! Everything is meaningless." What does man gain from all his labor at which he toils under the sun?
>
> —*verses 2-3*

Solomon opens the book by telling us he has nothing good to tell us. In fact, he says he has nothing to talk about. That's what the word "*vanity*" (used in translations such as the *King James Version* and *New American Standard*; "meaningless" in *New International Version*) means. It means "empty, void, without meaning, purpose, or significance." Solomon is saying, "The topic of my sermon today is the nothingness of everything."

We say, "Wait a minute, Solomon. What are you talking about? You're the man. You're the guy with all the wealth and power and wisdom and all those ladies. You're the king. You've got the dream job. What's this vanity stuff?"

Hang on, because it gets worse. "Generations come and generations go, but the earth remains forever." (verse 4) Read on in 1:5-11 and you realize this sounds like the "same old same old" we talked about earlier. This is the water closing over the wake of the cruise ship without leaving a trace. This is the man at the top asking the same question we ordinary men ask: "Is this all there is?"

It reminds me of little kids at Christmas. They are so excited the night before. You send them to bed early. My kids would wake me up at some unearthly hour like 3 or 4 in the morning asking if they could start opening the presents yet. I had to keep shooing them back to bed.

By the time we got up and had some devotions the kids were full of life. I can remember the excitement of being around the tree with paper flying everywhere as the kids in all their exuberance and enthusiasm would open their presents. There was a lot of excitement.

But a week later the toys had been discarded. They didn't feel like riding the bike anymore. They didn't feel like playing with the doll anymore. In the vanity of youth what was so exciting last week has lost its meaning today.

Men, some of us are like that. We get our new toy, maybe that new car we wanted. We drive it, and we're so excited. It has that new car smell. We look good, we feel powerful, we have a sense of significance as we drive it. But as the months go by, it becomes just a car, and the new smell fades. The significance disappears. We have to find another toy.

This is reminiscent of Solomon as he writes the book of Ecclesiastes. He was a man who started off close to God. But by the time we meet him here, he has lost his way. He found it again, but not until after taking a long detour. God uses Solomon's detour to teach us about the question of purpose in life.

SEARCHING FOR SELF

So when a man says, "I gotta be me," he needs to ask himself this question: "Who is the *me* I gotta be?" That's an all-important question. Solomon didn't know the answer, so he went searching for himself, looking for meaning and purpose. In Ecclesiastes chapter 2, he describes his search.

THE SEARCH FOR PLEASURE

The first place Solomon went looking for purpose and meaning was in pleasure. He thought that if he could "party hearty," if he could have a good time, he would find the sense of purpose he sought:

> I thought in my heart, "Come now, I will test you with pleasure to find out what is good." But that also proved to be meaningless. "Laughter," I said, "is foolish. And what does pleasure

accomplish?" I tried cheering myself with wine, and embracing folly—my mind still guiding me with wisdom. . . . I undertook great projects: I built houses for myself and planted vineyards. I made gardens and parks. . . . I amassed silver and gold for myself, and the treasure of kings and provinces. I acquired men and women singers, and a harem as well—the delights of the heart of man.

—2:1-3a, 4-5a, 8

What are the key words here? *Me*, *myself*, and *I*. Solomon began living for these three people, and he said he didn't deny himself any pleasure his heart could imagine (2:10). Anything he wanted, he went out and got it.

Many men are living for that goal, working hard for the day when they are making enough money that they won't have to walk by the store and say, "You can't have that today." Then they won't have to limit themselves. They can live for the good times.

This is the world's call to men today. What does the bumper sticker say? "He who dies with the most toys wins." Many men are following this call, trying to accumulate purpose by accumulating toys and maximizing pleasure.

I was witnessing to a young man and talking to him about life, so I said, "Tell me about yourself." He said, "Man, all I care about is the parties and the honeys." Then he explained his approach to life. "On Monday, I find out where the parties are going to be for that Friday, Saturday, and Sunday. On Tuesday, I go through my little black book and find out who I am going to take to the parties. On Wednesday, I put my clothes in the cleaners so they will be ready for the weekend. On Thursday, I shine my shoes so they glisten in the sun and I'll be lookin' good for the parties. Then come the parties on Friday, Saturday, and Sunday. When Monday comes, I start doing the same thing all over again."

Well, Solomon could probably identify with that. So let's ask him where all this leads. I mean, this guy didn't go to parties. He *was* the party. He brought the party to himself. Did pleasure solve his problem of purpose? Did it gain him a sense of significance and a reason for living? Here is Solomon's answer:

> Yet when I surveyed all that my hands had done and what I had toiled to achieve, everything was meaningless, a chasing after the wind; nothing was gained under the sun.
>
> —2:11

Have you ever tried "chasing after the wind"? Talk about futility. Try to grab a fistful of wind, and you'll have the essence of what Solomon is saying. Try to grab for it, and there's nothing there. The moment you grab it, you've lost it.

That's what pleasure was like for Solomon. He threw the party, but the party ended. He had the good times, but the good times expired. He was left as empty as before he started. If you are banking on pleasure to give you a reason for living, you are going to be sorely disappointed.

THE SEARCH FOR WISDOM

Having been frustrated by pleasure, Solomon decided to call on his great wisdom:

> Then I turned my thoughts to consider wisdom, and also madness and folly. . . . I saw that wisdom is better than folly, just as light is better than darkness. The wise man has eyes in his head, while the fool walks in the darkness; but I came to realize that the same fate overtakes them both. Then I thought in my heart, "The fate of the fool will overtake me also. What then do I gain by being wise?" I said in my heart, "This too is meaningless."
>
> —2:12a, 13-15

You would think the wise man would have a great advantage over the fool. Wisdom beats folly any day. But not so, says Solomon. One day he looked out the palace window and saw the local kindergarten dropout. This guy had absolutely nothing going for himself, but it dawned on Solomon that one day both he and the dropout were going to die.

Then it hit him. In the grave, wisdom and foolishness won't matter. In the grave, all the education and all the earned degrees will have no value at all. The wise man and the fool will be equally dead. In fact, the fool may live to be eighty while the wise man dies at sixty. Solomon considered all of this and said, "There's got to be more to life than this."

In your quiet moments, when you are lying in bed at night, do you ever think about your life and the prospect of death and say, "There's got to be more to life than this"? Trying to use human wisdom to come up with a satisfying purpose for life will leave you just where it left Solomon: "This too is meaningless."

Solomon was looking ahead to the end of it all, and he realized something our modern society tries to ignore and deny. He realized that whether you go out in a pine box or a satin-lined casket, you go out dead.

Funerals were pretty crude in the old days. They used wooden boxes and horse-drawn carriages to take the deceased to the grave. Then they put ropes underneath the box and wriggled it down into the hole.

But when you die today, it's not like that. Today when you die, you die in style. If you've never been able to gain any significance in life, they make sure you get some in death.

Instead of a wooden box, you get a bronze casket. You've always wanted to lay your head on a satin pillow. Now you have the opportunity. They'll put a handsome suit on you, and a professional beautician will make you look good. Every hair will be in place. The makeup artist takes care of your fingernails and fixes any discoloration or disfigurement on your face.

You've always wanted to ride in a limousine. Now, you've got it. In fact, there's a whole fleet of limousines out in front waiting for you. You always wanted to lead the parade. On that day you will. You'll stop traffic. Folk are going to turn their lights on and pull over in your honor. You'll be able to go through red lights with two motorcycles stopping traffic for you.

Then, when you arrive at the grave, they won't use ropes to let you down. You'll have a nickel-plated machine to ease you down so as not to disturb you.

Now please don't misunderstand. I'm not making light of burial practices. I'm not saying that honoring someone at death is wrong. What I want to show you is the futility of trying to find your sense of purpose in the stuff that will pass away. As long as you do that, you'll always have an excuse to stay in the rut.

THE SEARCH FOR WORK

Solomon had one more place to look for something to give him a sense of purpose—his work. Now you would think that being Your Highness would be a pretty satisfying line of work. Just like some men today think that if they just get that great job, they'll finally have a reason to look forward to getting up in the morning. What about the job, Solomon?

> I hated all the things I had toiled for under the sun, because I must leave them to the one who comes after me. And who knows whether he will be a wise man or a fool? Yet he will have control over all the work into which I have poured my effort and skill under the sun. This too is meaningless. So my heart began to despair over all my toilsome labor under the sun.
>
> —2:18-20

It distressed Solomon to think that when he died, he would have to leave his kingdom to someone who didn't work for it the way he did. In fact, his successor might be a fool who would unwisely mess up what Solomon had built. Somebody might get everything Solomon had worked so hard for, simply because the king was dead.

That would be pretty frustrating, wouldn't it? Who wants to see all of his hard work undone by someone else? But that's the risk we all take with our careers. Someone has said that most family fortunes in America are dissipated within one generation of the person who amassed the fortune.

And even before that time comes, there are a lot of men lying awake at night worrying about how to hang on to what they have. Solomon says of the working man in this situation, "Even at night his mind does not rest." (2:23)

You say, "How did Solomon know?" He was a man just like you and me. He may not have been an average working man, but he spent his share of sleepless nights. How many men haven't spent at least a few sleepless nights worrying about their work? Well, if your whole identity and purpose in life is tied up in your job, you're going to spend a lot of waking nights fretting over it. Any physician or psychologist will tell you that's not good.

THE ONLY WAY TO MAKE A LIFE WITH MEANING

That brings us to Ecclesiastes chapter 3, the familiar chapter that tells us, "There is a time for everything." What Solomon is saying poetically in verses 2-8 is that we live in a closed universe. An open universe means you control your own destiny. You have the final say.

But in a closed universe, you don't have the final say. If our universe is closed, the question is, who closed it? Who locked us in? Solomon says God did, and He did it on purpose (verse 10). God has shut us up to the routines of life, but He has done something else. "He has also set eternity in the hearts of men," Solomon writes in verse 11.

In other words, God has put within each one of us a sense of the eternal, a yearning for the things that are beyond space and time, things like ultimate purpose and meaning. So while God has set us among the routines of life, He wants us to look beyond the things of earth for something greater.

But notice in verse 11 that God has set eternity in our hearts in such a way that men "cannot fathom what God has done from beginning to end."

Solomon is saying that while God has given us a yearning and a questioning for the eternal, He hasn't left the answers to life lying around in this world for us to find. To put it another way, you cannot find your ultimate purpose in life by looking at life.

God has made it so that the only way a man can find the answer to the eternal question in his heart is by looking into eternity. And when he looks into eternity, a man will find the eternal God waiting for him.

What this means is that the minute you start looking at life to find the meaning of life, you miss the very life you're looking for. As long as you go to wealth or power or pleasure or work or people—or anything else—to find the meaning of life, you have just lost what you're looking for.

That's why Solomon says:

> I know that there is nothing better for men than to be happy and
> do good while they live. That everyone may eat and drink, and
> find satisfaction in all his toil—this is the gift of God.
>
> —3:12-13

It's only as we view life as the gift of God that we begin to find its purpose. It's only as we live in time from the perspective of eternity that we find life's meaning.

In other words, if you want to find your purpose, don't go looking for your purpose. Look for the Purpose-giver. If you want to find the secret to life, look to the Author of Life. That's why the greatest way to find out who you are is not to look in the mirror, but to look to God, the One who gave you your identity. Because when you find your Creator, you find you.

Jesus said, "I have come that they may have life, and have it to the full." (John 10:10) Life is not found in the living, but in the Living One. Jesus agreed with Solomon. Life is a gift from God. So you find what you're looking for when you stop looking for it and let the Giver of Life grant it to you.

You may have to think about that for a minute. But when you do, you'll realize what a freeing thing this is. Instead of looking for your purpose within yourself, locate God and you will find yourself.

If you're like me, your life has a lot of pieces to it. There's the wife's piece, the kids' piece, the work piece, the financial piece, and so on. And as soon as you get one piece in place, another piece comes loose.

But things like that happen with a purpose. God is trying to tell us, "Look, quit trying to fix everything yourself. Quit trying to put it all together on your own. You men won't find the answer until you find it in Me."

But what do so many of us men do with our lives? We do like I did one year with the bicycle I bought my son for Christmas. It came with one of those thick assembly manuals written by someone for whom English is a second language. Now it was going to take a long time to read that manual, and I hate taking the time to read those things anyway. So like any intelligent, self-respecting American man, I figured, "Hey, I've got a doctoral degree. I can certainly put a bike together without any help."

Eight hours later I had nothing but the handlebar on. My wife came to the door with a novel suggestion. "Honey, why don't you just read the directions?"

In my frustration and futility, with my pride crushed, I finally did just that. I let the creator of the bike tell me how to put it together. Forty-five minutes later, it was done.

I saved another eight hours of frustration, irritation, and agitation because I surrendered to the fact that the bicycle-maker knew more than I did about assembling it. Once I humbled myself and let the bicycle-maker define me in terms of putting the bike together, my son had a bike and my frustration was gone.

The Life-maker knows more about fixing life than you or I ever will know. We need to humble ourselves and say, "Lord, I don't know how to find my purpose in life. It has too many pieces. Show me the purpose You have for me."

Life is God's gift to you. And the fastest way to find your purpose in life is through thanksgiving. What do you say when someone brings you a gift? You say, "Thank you," and then you enjoy the gift. You don't try to take it apart and figure it out.

So what is the purpose of life? The purpose of life is the discovery and the enjoyment of God. There is no greater purpose or passion in all of existence. That's why the Apostle Paul said he had one goal, and that was: "I want to know Christ and the power of his resurrection." (Philippians 3:10)

Now don't get me wrong. There's nothing wrong with wanting a better job or more pay. There's nothing wrong with being the best you can be at whatever you do. But if you make any of that your guiding purpose in life, after seventy years you'll look back and not know who you are or why you were here.

Do you want a way out of the rut of meaninglessness? Do you want an escape instead of an excuse? Then let me extend to you this ladder: "Now all has been heard; here is the conclusion of the matter: Fear God and keep his commandments, for this is the whole duty of man." (Ecclesiastes 12:13)

If you know God, you will know your purpose. Not because you went purpose hunting, but because you went God hunting. And when you find God, you will find you. Say, "God, I want to know You more than anything. I'll let You reveal me to me." When you do that, you will know why you are here and where you are going.

· FIVE ·

NO MORE DABBLING IN DEFIANCE

"I DON'T LIKE ANYONE TELLING ME WHAT
TO DO. I NEVER HAVE. PEOPLE WILL
JUST HAVE TO ADJUST."

If there's one thing American men learn early, it's to be self-reliant. From Daniel Boone to Donald Trump, our culture lionizes men who do it on their own. The Lone Ranger was a boyhood hero of my generation. There he was, firing silver bullets and standing tall for justice in the Old West.

You get the idea. What I'm talking about is one of masculine America's most cherished myths, the myth of the "self-made man." I have a feeling that millions of American men dream of being in a position where they call their own shots, march to the beat of their own drum, and take orders from no one.

That scenario may be attractive to many men, but it's a myth nonetheless. The fact is that none of us is self-made, unless you count sin. Now don't get me wrong. I'm not putting down men of courage and vision who have done great things. If God has given you a great vision, go for it.

The problem I want to zero in on is that rebellious spirit we men are so prone to adopt, the attitude we had when we were very young—that Mama wasn't going to tell *us* what to do. Neither was

Daddy. Now that we're grown, no one is going to tell us what to do—including God.

Even as Christian men, many of us still have a streak of defiance in us. We're like the stubborn little boy whose mama told him to sit in the corner. He told her, "I may be sitting down on the outside, but I'm standing up on the inside." Too often we excuse our rebellion by saying things like, "This is the way God made me," or "I can't change the way I am. Everyone else will just have to get used to it."

Well, let me show you where that spirit can lead and how to get past another excuse that keeps a lot of men stuck in spiritual neutral. This is important because if you are rebellious toward the Lord, nothing else in your Christian life is going to work.

You want God to do something in your family, but He says, "Let's talk about you first." You try to get to second base in your spiritual life, and the Holy Spirit says, "But you missed first base." God will keep bringing you back to this issue of rebellion.

JONAH'S CHOICE: GOD'S WAY—OR THE HIGHWAY

How do I know that? Because that's exactly what God did with a reluctant, rebellious prophet named Jonah. This story has a lot to teach us as we learn how to stop dabbling in defiance. The opening verses of Jonah set the scene for us.

> The word of the LORD came to Jonah son of Amittai: "Go to the great city of Nineveh and preach against it, because its wickedness has come up before me." But Jonah ran away from the LORD and headed for Tarshish. He went down to Joppa, where he found a ship bound for that port. After paying the fare, he went aboard and sailed for Tarshish to flee from the LORD.
>
> —*1:1-3*

Jonah was a prophet in Israel during a time when Israel itself was in rebellion against God. Two of his contemporaries were Hosea and Amos, who declared God's anger at Israel's sin and his call to repentance. So we might say Jonah reflected the spirit of his times. But his calling was unique. God sent Jonah not to his own people, but to Nineveh, Israel's hated enemy. Jonah said no and took off in the opposite direction.

Why did Jonah refuse to go to Nineveh? Were those people *that* bad? In a word, yes. Nineveh was the capital of Assyria, a Gentile power God was going to use to judge his own people for their disobedience. The Assyrians were notorious for their destruction and cruelty. To get a picture of Assyria you won't soon forget, read the little book of Nahum, just two books after Jonah.

Nahum prophesied the doom of Nineveh more than a hundred years after God sent Jonah to call the city to repentance. Nahum pictures the Assyrians swooping down on their victims so ferociously that they stumbled over the dead bodies (3:3).

The Assyrians were a bloodthirsty people. They were known to decapitate their enemies and write graffiti on the walls with their blood. They were experts at inflicting pain on those they conquered. They were feared and hated.

This helps us to understand why Jonah was so put off when he heard God's call to Nineveh. Jonah figures he has two problems. If he goes to Nineveh and preaches and the Assyrians get right with God, he has just helped to preserve Israel's dreaded enemy. After all, Jonah is an Israelite first and foremost. He doesn't want God using these Gentiles to judge his people.

But if Jonah goes to Nineveh and preaches and they *don't* repent, he can just see his body parts falling off. No one has to paint him a picture of what these people could do if they took an intense disliking to him. Jonah figures he loses either way.

So he concludes, "Rather than put myself in this predicament, I am not going to go at all." And thus rebellion rises in the heart of Jonah, that defiant spirit that says, "I am not going to do what God said to do. God will just have to adjust on this one."

We have all seen defiant children. A close friend was once telling me how defiant his three-year-old son had become. His son did a horrible thing that wouldn't be appropriate for me to talk about. His father spanked him and said, "Son, don't ever do that again. Do you want me to spank you again for doing that?"

The boy looked at him and said, "Yeah!"

I told my friend, "You'd better get that boy saved fast because he's either going to be in jail or dead."

I've seen this defiant spirit in counseling with a husband who sits across from my desk with his wife and says, "I am not going to do what it would take to put this marriage back together. I don't care what God says about it. I am not going to do it!"

So Jonah headed in the opposite direction from Nineveh. Now, he was no dummy. He knew that he couldn't get away from God in the sense of going someplace where God couldn't find him. He was trying to flee from the Lord in that he was refusing to submit to God's will for him. He found a ship going to Tarshish, paid his fare, and got on board.

Now let me draw you a little mental map here. Nineveh was about 550 miles east of Israel. Tarshish was about 2,500 miles west of Israel. Do you get the picture? My boy Jonah was doing some serious running. With apologies to the University of Nevada-Las Vegas, Jonah was the original "Runnin' Rebel."

Now think about this. Rather than go 550 miles in God's will, Jonah was ready to travel 2,500 miles out of God's will. It's always a longer trip when you defy God. But that's the decision many of us men have made with our lives. We say, "I'll do things my way." But "my way" is a long, hard road, and God wants to spare us the extra mileage.

But there's something else here. Not only is it a long trip out when you defy God, but if you ever change your mind and decide you want to come back, you've now got 2,500 miles between you and where you started—to say nothing of getting to where God wanted you in the first place. In other words, you've got to make a longer trip back.

Jonah ran from the presence of God because he didn't like the plan of God. It didn't make sense to him. But human logic has never been the measure of God's will. Many times God's will seems illogical. You and I can understand Jonah emotionally. We can see why he felt the way he did.

It's hard for us men to put ourselves in a position where we are either vulnerable ourselves or else helping people who may turn around and do us in. No self-respecting Israelite man wanted to mix it up with Ninevites. But when we say, "Let me do it my way, God," we are really saying, "You obviously don't know what You are doing."

Jonah figured God made a mistake, so he pulled out his coins. "I'll pay for this one myself." There's a lesson in Jonah's paying his own fare. When you run from the will of God, you get to pick up the tab. Whenever you defy God, you pay the freight. The beautiful thing about going to Nineveh was that God would have paid Jonah's fare. But Tarshish? Put that on Jonah's tab.

Many of us are paying a high price for our "Tarshish trip," when if we had done it God's way, He would have picked up the tab. The good news about obeying God is that He always supplies that which He demands. The bad news about rebelling against Him is that in your rebellion, you pick up the tab.

I'm convinced that far too many men are picking up heavy emotional, psychological, spiritual, and even physical tabs for their refusal to submit to God. The result is heavy scars on bodies and souls.

God wasn't about to let His defiant prophet get away with rebellion, so He "sent a great wind on the sea, and such a violent storm arose that the ship threatened to break up." (verse 4) The only problem with running from God is that when you get to where you are going, He has already been there waiting for you.

God looked at Jonah and said, "Jone, are you running from Me? Let's examine this. You are sailing on the sea that I made, through the air that I control. So let's make some adjustments here." We talk about Mother Nature. We'd better be talking about Father God. Nature is in God's hand, so He sent a special "Jonah storm."

Unfortunately, when Jonah messed up and God had to come after him, the people near Jonah got messed up too. Rebellion always hurts those around you. The storm scared the sailors so bad, they started throwing the cargo into the sea to lighten the ship (verse 5).

Now this was a cargo ship. These sailors were delivering cargo to Tarshish. That's how they made their money to feed their families. But if the cargo doesn't get to Tarshish, they don't get paid. But because this preacher is out of the will of God, the cargo goes overboard; there will be no pay for the sailors on *this* voyage.

I'll say it again. When you are out of God's will, you not only mess up you. You mess up those in the neighborhood. Those in Jonah's "neighborhood" were in bad shape, so the ship's captain approached him and said, "How can you sleep? Get up and call on your god! Maybe he will take notice of us, and we will not perish." (verse 6)

You can get so content in rebellion that you don't even know God is after you. So here a sinner had to ask a saint, "How come you are sleeping? You ought to be praying." This shows how bad God's people can get. We can go so far away from God that we sleep when He is trying to deal with us.

These sailors were pagans, but they knew some supernatural power was very upset with someone on that ship. So they cast lots to find out who the bad guy was. According to verse 7, "the lot fell on Jonah." Bingo.

What God did was control the throw of these stones. Now don't go to Las Vegas talking about how God can control the dice. That's not what we are talking about here. These were sinners doing the throwing, not the saint. But God controlled the throw.

There followed a brief interview in which it was determined not only that Jonah was the problem, but that if something wasn't done fast, they were all going to go down with him (verses 8-11). Hebrews 12:6 says that "Whom the Lord loveth, he skinneth alive" (Evans translation). And whom the Lord loveth, he spanketh. Jonas was about to get spanked bigtime.

The Lord didn't stop him from getting on the boat in Joppa to go to Tarshish. But the Lord met him in the middle of nowhere. In the words of that great boxing philosopher Muhammad Ali, "He can run, but he can't hide."

Some of us have been running from God, and now we are asleep in the storm, thinking this is the way things are supposed to be. We think we are supposed to be sick like this; we are supposed to be depressed like this; the family is supposed to be in turmoil like this. We say, "Well, that's life. I'll just tough it out until things get better." We men always figure we can outlast any problem, right?

But maybe things aren't meant to get better. Maybe God has thrown a turbulence into your life to get you back to where he wants you. Where Jonah thought God wanted him was dead. Once he knew God was after him, he figured it was all over. He actually told the sailors to throw him into the sea (verse 12).

Did you know that Christians can be suicidal? Christians can want to end it all. Rebellion can take you so low you don't want to live anymore.

Well, the sailors weren't murderers, so they rowed harder trying to get to land. But they were rowing against God, which meant they weren't going anywhere. There was nothing to do but toss Jonah overboard. When they did that, the storm stopped—and a revival broke out! "At this the men greatly feared the LORD, and they offered a sacrifice to the LORD and made vows to him." (verse 16)

So here's a disobedient saint on a boat with sinners. We know they were not believers in the true God because earlier they were praying to their own gods (verse 5). But even though Jonah was outside the will of God, God still used him to lead these men to faith.

So Jonah was preaching even when he wasn't obeying! That reminds us that God is sovereign in accomplishing His will, whether we're cooperating or not. Now for sure, Jonah didn't get to enjoy the fact of the sailors' conversion. He didn't even know about it. He was too busy doing his little stroke thing in the water because they had tossed him overboard.

So Jonah was seemingly content in his rebellion until God woke him up and got his attention with adverse circumstances. We know that throwing him overboard was the right thing because the sea got real calm (verse 15).

Has it occurred to you that the adverse circumstances in your life may be related to a decision you made where God said go and you said no? It may have been months ago or even years ago, but whatever the case, a storm has broken loose on you. The harder you row your boat, the farther away from shore you get. The more you fight to get your finances together, the more in debt you go. The harder you work to get your marriage or some other relationship back on track, the worse it gets. I don't know your situation, of course, but the problem could be that you are fighting the "wind" of God's Spirit.

I like the final verse of the first chapter of Jonah: "But the LORD provided a great fish to swallow Jonah." (verse 17) You might call this a "whale-o-gram." Now it doesn't say that God created a great fish, but that He "provided" one. God didn't make a special fish just for Jonah.

People get hung up on this story, but there are known cases of people being swallowed by a large fish, like a great white shark, and surviving. The fish swallowing Jonah is not the big deal here. The big deal is that the fish did what Jonah didn't do. The fish obeyed God. So now we have the wind, the sea, and the fish obeying God. But we still have problems with the preacher.

A WHALE OF A RIDE

Jonah chapter 2 begins with an interesting statement: "From inside the fish Jonah prayed to the LORD his God." Jonah wasn't praying when he ran to Joppa. He wasn't praying when he got on the boat and paid the fare. He wasn't even praying when the storm came and the sinners chastised him for his disobedience. He didn't pray until he got swallowed.

Some of us are not going to get right with God until we are swallowed, until God puts us in a place so tight that going to Him in prayer is the only thing left to do. Jonah could have repented anywhere along the line, but it took this cataclysmic circumstance to turn him back to God. Then he was ready to pray:

"In my distress I called to the LORD, and he answered me. From the depths of the grave I called for help, and you listened to my cry. You hurled me into the deep, into the very heart of the seas, and the currents swirled about me; all your waves and breakers swept over me. I said, 'I have been banished from your sight; yet I will look again toward your holy temple.' The engulfing waters threatened me, the deep surrounded me; seaweed was wrapped around my head. To the roots of the mountains I sank down; the earth beneath barred me in forever. But you brought my life up from the pit, O LORD my God."

—2:2-6

I hate to hear Christians talking about being unlucky. *Luck* is one word you should never use as a Christian. There are no chance happenings for Christians. There is no fate. Jonah recognized that it was God who threw him overboard. Those sailors were just doing what God wanted done.

This prayer of Jonah's is remarkable. All the things he should have admitted earlier, he admits now. He sees that God is sovereign and has his life under control. It all makes sense now. Jonah says, "I'm out of fellowship with You. That's why I'm down here in this dark place, tangled up in seaweed and choking on sea water."

But in Jonah 2:7 we find some good news. Jonah was in the pit of darkness and despair. He felt like his life was ebbing away. But then he said, "I remembered You, Lord."

Are you in the pit right now? The pit is not a fun place to be, but if it gets you back into the will of God, thank Him for the pit. The pit is a bad place to be, but if it takes going into the pit to get you back on the mountaintop, thank God for the pit. As Corrie ten Boom said, "There is no pit so deep that our God is not deeper still."

Now, many of us will make promises to God when we're in the pit. Suppose you had the horrifying experience of seeing a huge fish come toward you in the water with his mouth open and gulp you down. You're stuffed in this fish's stomach, and God says, "Can we talk now?" Don't you think you would be pretty agreeable to whatever He wanted you to do?

That's what happens, for example, when we think we have cancer and we pray, "Lord, if you'll just give me a negative report this time I will . . ." We make promises to the Lord in the pit, but sometimes we forget them once we're back on dry land. Jonah said:

> "My prayer rose to you, to your holy temple. Those who cling to worthless idols forfeit the grace that could be theirs. But I, with a song of thanksgiving, will sacrifice to you. What I have vowed I will make good. Salvation comes from the LORD."
>
> *—2:7b-9*

Jonah said, "Lord, what I told You I'm going to do, I'm going to do." He had made a vow as a prophet to preach the Word of God, but he was failing to do this. I think I know how he felt. I'm scared not to preach, because I know that's what I've been called to do.

Notice that God didn't act until Jonah remembered. God didn't act until Jonah confessed. God didn't act until Jonah got right. Many times we want God to do something before we have done anything. But Jonah acted and God responded, commanding the fish to vomit Jonah onto the dry land (verse 10). We might call him the "flying prophet." The fish came to the shore and hurled Jonah out. At least the fish got rid of his problem.

My Christian brother, let me tell you something. You can go straight to Nineveh when God first calls you, or you can let Him take you there. Now it's going to be a wet, scary ride if God has to take you, but sometimes that's what has to happen because we don't like anyone telling us what to do.

Sometimes, because of our rebellion, we don't get it right until the third marriage. Sometimes we don't get it right until the age of fifty, when we could have gotten it right at twenty. Sometimes we wait longer than necessary to overcome that addiction. Sometimes we have to hit rock bottom before we start looking up.

One of the names that men have given God is "the Hound of Heaven." He just keeps on tracking you. Jonah was still unwrapping the seaweed from around his head when God came to him:

> Then the word of the LORD came to Jonah a second time: "Go to the great city of Nineveh and proclaim to it the message I give you."
>
> —3:1-2

This is the heavy one. Note that God didn't change. He told Jonah the same thing He told him the first time. Now if God's not going to change, it seems like we ought to do what He says the first time.

You are either a father yourself or you had a father. Think of how often your dad tried to teach you, "Son, you may as well do it right the first time, because you're not going anywhere until you do it right." Think of the times you have said this to your children. You want them to learn this because you know that's what will be expected of them in the real world.

GETTING A SECOND CHANCE TO GET IT RIGHT

Should God expect any less from us? Jonah was now stinky and ugly, but he still had to preach. His rebellion didn't cause God to change or adjust his plan at all. God's second word to Jonah was the same as His first word. Jonah's wishes, preferences, and prejudices didn't enter the picture.

But the beauty of the third chapter of Jonah is that Jonah got a second chance. The wonder is that instead of dying in the stomach of that fish, Jonah got a return trip back to God's will.

Now it definitely was not a convenient return trip. But then, you can't run to Tarshish to avoid having to obey God and then expect to have an easy trip back. This is a principle we often forget. This is the part of the process we don't want.

Men are especially bad here. We mess up, then we expect to do one little thing or make one little adjustment and have everything running smoothly again. I wonder how many times a wife has said to a husband, "You men are all alike. You expect everything to be wonderful again just because you said you're sorry."

Our wives have a point. You can't defy God and take off in the other direction the way Jonah did without having a few bumps on the return trip. The longer you stay on that boat to Tarshish, the farther and bumpier the ride back is going to be.

God told Jonah to go to Nineveh, but He had another stop for Jonah to make first. The text says the fish vomited Jonah onto dry land (2:10), not at the front gate of Nineveh. He still had to go to Nineveh.

What I think happened here is that God took Jonah back to Joppa, his port of departure, so he could start off right from the point where he started off wrong. God often brings us back to the point where we messed up so we can fix it.

Jonah caught the right ship this time (3:3). He went to Nineveh and made this proclamation: "Forty more days and Nineveh will be overturned." (3:4)

Isn't the grace of God wonderful? God not only had patience with Jonah's rebellion, but He reinstated Jonah to his ministry as a prophet. Most of us would have given up on Jonah long before this. This is why I believe in the possibility of reinstatement even for a fallen minister, after he has gone through the full restoration process.

But that's not all. From that simple sermon, God gave Jonah one of the greatest revivals in human history. There is no revival either in the Bible or in the days since that can compare with this revival. Read Jonah 3:5-10 and you'll see what happened. God shook that evil city, from the king's palace to the sheep pen.

I mean, Jonah's message went right to the top of the government. The king himself put on sackcloth and ordered everything that moved in Nineveh to be covered in sackcloth. These wicked people became prayer warriors, fasting and praying and calling on God in repentance. And according to verse 10, God turned away from his anger. The city was spared.

God did all of that through Jonah. He forgave and restored His prophet and energized Jonah's message in an amazing way. God can restore and re-energize you, but you must come back to Him. You must do it His way. You must obey His Word. He is not going to change (Malachi 3:6).

The Bible says that God has elevated His Word alongside His name (Psalm 138:2). Now you can't get higher than that because God's name is above every name. If God's Word is as exalted as His name, then you are messing with unchangeable territory here.

TIME FOR AN ATTITUDE CHECK

So God sent a great revival to Nineveh. "But Jonah was greatly displeased and became angry." (4:1) It seems that the book of Jonah should have ended with chapter 3. But Jonah still had a major problem. He was like the little boy we talked about earlier who was sitting down on the outside, but standing up on the inside.

Jonah 4:1-2 tells us Jonah wasn't preaching this sermon with the right heart attitude. He was saying, "Forty more days and Nineveh will be overturned." He was thinking, "Good. I hope it *is* overturned. I hope these people don't repent." He was mad because God was gracious.

You say, "I thought we dealt with Jonah's rebellion when he was swallowed and vowed to obey God." Well, we did. Jonah obeyed God. But he still had an attitude problem. He was glad God sent a fish to save him. But now he's saying, "I don't want the Ninevites to get the grace I received. I don't want God to save them. They're our enemies."

What Jonah needed was a little lesson in who was in charge. He needed to know that this is God's world and He loves everyone in it. Jonah needed to know that God can show His grace to anyone He chooses. And Jonah needed to know that since he wasn't the Creator, he had no say in how God runs the world.

To teach Jonah all of that, God prepared a nature object lesson for him:

> Jonah went out and sat down at a place east of the city. There he made himself a shelter, sat in its shade and waited to see what would happen to the city. Then the LORD God provided a vine

and made it grow up over Jonah to give shade for his head to ease his discomfort, and Jonah was very happy about the vine.

—4:5-6

So here's this rebellious prophet now pouting. Let me tell you right here, I know why I'm not God. If I were God, this is the conversation old Jone and I would be having by now:

"Jonah, boy, I called you to preach. You can't preach, but I called you. I sent you to Nineveh, but you ditched Me. I had to send a fish after you. You finally obeyed, and you delivered your little old short sermon. I empowered your sermon so that it did something, and you got mad. You want to die because I'm good! What color coffin you want, boy?"

If I had been God, this would have been one dead prophet. This dude would have gotten on my nerves. But our gracious God says, "Jonah, it's a little hot outside today, isn't it? Why don't I provide a plant to give you some shade?"

Let's stop here and update our list of all the things and people in this story that obey God. The wind obeys, the sea obeys, the sailors obey, the fish obeys, the Ninevites obey, and the plant obeys. Then God appointed a worm the next morning, and the worm obeyed by chewing and withering the plant (verse 7).

So the worm attacked the plant, and Jonah lost his shade. "When the sun rose, God provided a scorching east wind." (verse 8) Do you get the impression that the book of Jonah is really a book about God?

It's really not about Jonah, and it's certainly not about a prophet being swallowed by a whale. The book of Jonah is about a God who touches nature and nature obeys; a God who can touch people, and they obey.

Now that's comforting on one hand because that means we serve a God who can do something when we get on our knees. It means we can talk to God about anything because all He has to do is say the word, and it happens. Whether it's a wind or a worm, God can touch it.

But this also tells me how foolish and dangerous it is to defy and rebel against a God like this. How could Jonah possibly expect to escape, let alone prosper, by running away from God? There's no way—and there's no way you and I can run from him either.

What we men call self-reliance or doing it our way or being our own man is really the grace of God letting us have a little rope until we get hung up and discover, like Jonah, that God is the One in charge. He's calling all the shots.

So it's not as if a man can say, "Well, I may be rebelling against God, but at least I'm doing what I want. At least I'm enjoying my rebellion. I guess I showed everybody who's boss." No, you just don't understand the kind of God we have. You don't realize that all He needs to bring you low is a little worm and a little scorching east wind.

That wind scorched Jonah and the sun beat down on his head, and our man was miserable again. He was ready to die all over (verse 8b). So here was Jonah, fuming about the loss of a little plant while he wished for a city full of people to be wiped out. He had a big lesson to learn.

Now the story ends with God verbally spanking Jonah for his twisted value system (verses 9-11). God was saying, "Jonah, what kind of preacher are you? You want Me to wipe out a city with 120,000 people who don't even know their left hand from their right hand yet? Jonah, I even care about the cattle in Nineveh."

YOU MAKE THE CALL

Then the book ends. But I want to know what Jonah did. I want to know the rest of the story. Did Jonah die? Did He commit suicide? Did he say, "I'm sorry, Lord. You're right"?

Why does the story of Jonah end there? Because God is asking you and me the same question He asked Jonah. The question is, "What are you going to do with My compassion?"

Jonah had to decide that first for himself, and then for the people of Nineveh. The rebel prophet decided to accept God's grace and turn back. But he couldn't extend that same grace to the Ninevites. Now it doesn't really matter what Jonah finally chose because that's history. (And anyway, the Bible doesn't record what his choice was.) The question is, what are you going to do now?

Are you going to come back to God's will if you are rebelling against Him? And if you see someone else not in God's will, what are you going to do? Are you going to say, "Let him have it, God. Lower the boom on him"? Or are you going to reach out and try to bring that person back, the way God reached out and brought you back?

So the issue on the floor is pretty clear. What are you going to do with the grace of God? Remember, you don't deserve what you have. I don't deserve what I have. If it weren't for the grace of God, we would have been swallowed up a long time ago. But God in His grace has appointed circumstances that give us the opportunity to return to his perfect plan.

The story of Jonah actually ends in the New Testament. In Matthew 12:40 Jesus said, "For as Jonah was three days and three nights in the belly of a huge fish, so the Son of Man will be three days and three nights in the heart of the earth."

Jesus' point was that if the people of Nineveh repented at the preaching of Jonah, His generation had no excuse for not repenting at His preaching because He was greater than Jonah (Matthew 12:41). In other words, we don't have any excuse for running from God when He has given us His Son to save us.

So let me come back to the original question. Are you rebelling against God? Are you using your masculinity or your personality bent or any other reason as an excuse to say no to God? If so, the bad news is, it will never work. You can't run from the presence of God.

The good news is that if you'll get off the boat going to Tarshish and get on the boat going to Nineveh, God will give you a second chance like He did with Jonah. In fact, you'll discover He's the God of the second, third, fourth, fifth, and one-hundredth chance. This is the magnificent grace of God. What are you going to do with an offer like that?

SIX

NO MORE COMPROMISING YOUR INTEGRITY

"EVERYBODY'S DOING IT."

ntegrity is a hot issue today. In a society where people feel like they can't trust anyone anymore, integrity is a big deal.

It's a big deal for the businessman who is looking for employees he can trust. It's a big deal for the church that is looking for godly leaders they can follow. And it's a big deal to a generation of young people who need some role models they can follow without winding up in the ditch.

When we talk about integrity, we are talking about a person's trustworthiness. The word *integrity* means to be "complete" or "whole." It means that what you say and what you mean are the same thing. It means that when you make a promise, you intend to keep it. It means that when you say you will do something, that is exactly what you plan to do.

YOUR DAILY DECISION: COMPROMISE OR INTEGRITY

Now, one reason integrity is at such a premium in our culture is that it's so easy to excuse our lack of it. On some of the issues we are dealing with in this book, you are more or less alone if you try to excuse yourself.

But when it comes to compromising integrity, you will have no lack of company. When you hear someone say, "Everybody's doing it," you know that's not too far from the literal truth.

Another reason integrity is hard to find these days is that it can be compromised in so many different ways, large and small. We can compromise it by *lying*, saying something we know isn't the truth; by *lusting*, inappropriate relationships with the opposite sex; by *loitering*, hanging out with the wrong crowd; and by *looting*, taking something that is not ours.

All of us know what it is like to talk one way and act another. All of us know what it feels like to appear to be a man of integrity, yet to have things in our lives that don't add up.

It's like the story of the man and woman in Los Angeles who went to a fast-food chicken restaurant one night. The man went in and ordered a box of chicken. He took the box and drove off, only to discover that the box was full of cash. It seems the manager of the restaurant had put the night's receipts in a chicken box to camouflage them so he could take the money to the bank. The man was mistakenly given the box that had cash rather than chicken in it.

Well, the man looked at the box and said, "I can't keep this money." So he took it back to the restaurant and gave it to the manager. Of course, the manager was elated that there was still an honest man around. He told the man he was going to call the newspaper to report the story, because he wanted people to know there were still honest folk in the world.

"Go get your wife," the manager said, "and bring her in here so we can get a picture of you two. Let's let the community know what kind of man you are."

But the man said, "No, I can't do that. I'm married, but that lady in the car is not my wife."

So it is easy to appear that you have integrity. It's easy to appear to be one way and actually be another. And Satan is always getting us in the perpetual squeeze play between what's right and what's more convenient.

If you watch baseball, you've seen the squeeze play. The runner on third breaks for home as soon as the pitcher goes into his windup. The batter has to bunt the ball, because if he misses, the runner is left hung up between third and home with noplace to go. He's trapped, just as Satan tries to trap us and cause us to compromise our integrity.

Now, I am sure there is not one man reading this who has not compromised his integrity on at least one occasion. It may have been at a newsstand or the gift shop at the airport, when you looked around and made sure no one was watching before you picked up that magazine. You may even have tried to spiritualize it by telling yourself you were just keeping up with the trends of the day in *Playboy* or *Penthouse*. But the fact that you had to look around first says something.

It's also possible to compromise your integrity in your hotel room by watching a movie you know you should not be watching. The temptation is especially strong if the movie is free or if no one knows what will show up on your hotel bill.

Or it may not be anything you are doing. It may all be in your mind, but it's still an issue of integrity because integrity has to do with more than just your outward behavior.

When we talk about integrity, we are not talking about your reputation. Your reputation is what other folks think of you. Integrity goes beyond that, to what you are really like on the inside. It has to do with your character.

DANIEL: A MAN WHO STOOD OUT FOR THE RIGHT REASONS

But rather than trying to define and dissect the quality of integrity, I want to show you a man who incarnated integrity. Daniel had more reasons to excuse compromise and conformity than most men will ever have. But the fact that he refused to compromise makes his life all the more incredible.

Daniel illustrates what it takes to be a man of integrity rather than a man of compromise and conformity. Let's meet him now in the book that bears his name.

> It pleased Darius to appoint 120 satraps to rule throughout the kingdom, with three administrators over them, one of whom was Daniel. The satraps were made accountable to them so that the king might not suffer loss.
>
> —*Daniel 6:1-2*

Darius was king of the vast Medo-Persian empire, which had conquered the Babylonian empire. Daniel had been brought to Babylon many years earlier as a Jewish captive. He had served the Babylonian king Nebuchadnezzar, and now he was an official of the Persian empire.

To administer his kingdom, Darius appointed satraps or managers to run things. But because he knew there would be great temptation and great opportunities for fraud and corruption, and because he could not watch 120 men, Darius also named three commissioners—vice-presidents, if you will—to oversee the satraps. Now for obvious reasons, these commissioners had to be men Darius could trust implicitly. In other words, they had to be men of integrity, of impeccable trustworthiness, beyond question and reproach. Daniel was chosen as one of the three.

How does a man achieve such a position of trust? Well, Daniel was about eighty years old by this time, so he had been around for a while. But he didn't just wake up one morning as an eighty-year-old man of integrity. It began way back in the first chapter, when he was carried to Babylon as a teenage captive from Israel.

You may remember the story. Daniel was ordered to eat meat that had been offered to idols. But he refused, because it would violate his commitment to God. Daniel was vindicated in his stand, and his integrity of heart was established early on.

Men like that are hard to find, so Daniel rose fast during the reign of Nebuchadnezzar, until he became one of the leading officials in Nebby's empire. And when the Medo-Persians conquered Babylon and established their own empire, Daniel still had a job.

There is always a job for a man of integrity, because everybody is looking for trustworthy people. If a man lacks ability, you can teach him job skills. But if a man lacks integrity, no amount of job training will make him a trustworthy person. Integrity has to come from within.

Now Daniel was not only one of the three most trusted men in Darius's kingdom, but according to 6:3, "Daniel . . . distinguished himself among the administrators and the satraps." Why is that? What did Daniel have that set him apart? He possessed "exceptional qualities," verse 3 continues, and "the king planned to set him over the whole kingdom."

SERVING WITH DISTINCTION

This verse tells you the first thing you need to know about integrity. That is, a man of integrity has "exceptional qualities," a spiritual frame of reference. Even non-Christians who have integrity operate from a spiritual frame of reference, because honesty and faithfulness and dependability are all spiritual, biblical principles.

Daniel took it one step further, because he also had a relationship with God. The man who lives with integrity at home and in the marketplace will always stand out. People will begin to see that he is not like everybody else. In fact, the more wicked a culture becomes, the more a man of exceptional qualities will become obvious.

When you are the only one who's not stealing from the company, when you are the only one who's not swearing with every other word, when you are totally honorable and dependable, you will look very extraordinary in this culture.

Daniel had that kind of a witness. Turn back to Daniel chapter 5, the night that King Belshazzar saw the handwriting on the wall and was frantic to know what it meant. The queen came in to him in the banquet hall and told him, "Don't be alarmed! Don't look so pale!" (5:10)

Why? Because "there is a man in your kingdom who has the spirit of the holy gods in him." (verse 11) She was talking about Daniel, of course. Notice in verse 12 that the queen said he possessed "a keen mind and knowledge and understanding." The queen of Babylon didn't know that Daniel belonged to the true God, the God of heaven. She just knew that there was something very extraordinary about this man and that he had served Nebuchadnezzar with great distinction.

Belshazzar said the same thing when Daniel was brought before him (5:14). And by the way, Nebuchadnezzar was Belshazzar's grandfather, which means that Daniel had already been serving with integrity for many years.

A man of integrity is one who looks at life through spiritual glasses. He doesn't follow the crowd. Daniel could have easily blended into Babylonian culture and adopted Babylonian ways on the excuse that he didn't ask to be there in the first place. He could have taken the attitude that he was just a teenager anyway, so it would be okay if he gave in. But Daniel had spiritual insight and spiritual wisdom and said no to the easy way.

When you have spiritual insight, it affects your attitude. Do you work with someone who has a bad attitude? A bad attitude reflects a warped perspective. Now, everybody has a bad day. That's not what I am talking about. I am talking about folk with a bad life, where something is wrong every day.

That person doesn't have the right perspective. He or she doesn't have spiritual insight. But when you see life through spiritual glasses, you realize that it is the Lord Christ you are serving (Colossians 3:24).

Therefore, you don't have to get jealous or worried when you see so-and-so playing up to the boss and being political. Chances are the boss knows what's going on anyway, because business owners are looking to protect their investments, and to do that they have to have people they can trust. So instead of playing the game, hold on to your integrity and look to God to take care of your promotion.

You say, "Yeah, but I'm just an ordinary guy." That may be, but if you know God, you have extraordinary spiritual insight. Even ordinary guys can have extraordinary spirits and keen minds.

A number of years ago I went to China with a group of professional basketball players for an outreach ministry. While we were there we visited the Great Wall of China, a massive and awesome structure. It was built to keep out China's enemies from the north.

But even though the Great Wall is so thick and high and long that no enemy could deal with it, China's enemies were still able to invade because they were able to bribe the gatekeeper. If you can move a man away from his integrity, it doesn't matter how high or how thick or how long you build the wall. The enemy will still get through.

Daniel had integrity. He had it as a teenage slave in Babylon, and he had it as an eighty-year-old ruler in Persia. His three Hebrew buddies had it too. Shadrach, Meshach, and Abednego had come to Babylon with Daniel. Nebuchadnezzar was going to throw them into the fiery furnace for refusing to worship the image he had made.

Their answer reflected extraordinary insight: "If we are thrown into the blazing furnace, the God we serve is able to save us from it, and he will rescue us from your hand, O king. But even if he does not, we want you to know, O king, that we will not serve your gods or worship the image of gold you have set up." (Daniel 3:17-18) They saw something that nobody else in that situation could see, because they were looking at it from a divine perspective.

If you are in a bad job, a bad marriage, or any bad situation, are you looking at it through spiritual glasses? Or, as I like to ask, do you have cable?

If you don't have cable television, all you have is ABC, CBS, and NBC. You can't get CNN or CBN or TBS or ESPN, so you don't have continuous, twenty-four-hour-a-day access to the news, weather, and sports that are happening around the world.

A lot of Christians are like that spiritually. They get ABC on Sunday morning, CBS on Sunday night, and NBC on Wednesday night, but in between they don't have twenty-four-hour-a-day access to God because they don't look at life from a spiritual perspective. They're not tuned in.

PUBLIC INTEGRITY: IT DOESN'T JUST HAPPEN

Back in Daniel 6:4, we see that another aspect of Daniel's integrity was his spotless record of service in the public arena. As often happens when confronted with someone like Daniel, his fellow government officials became very jealous and tried to find a way to bring him down. They tried to dig up a little dirt on my man.

They tried to drum up charges against Daniel, "but they were unable to do so." (verse 4) Even a little bit of dirt in the carburetor can stop a big truck from climbing a mountain. If Satan can find just a little bit of dirt, he can keep a man from climbing spiritual mountains. But there was not even a little bit of dirt to be found under Daniel's rug.

I used to work at the bus station in downtown Dallas when I was going through seminary. I worked the graveyard shift on the weekends, from eleven o'clock at night until 7 in the morning. What I soon discovered was that the workers on my shift had a system going whereby they would punch each other's time cards in and out and grab an extra hour or two for lunch without getting caught. So if someone clocked out at three o'clock and was due back at 4, someone else would clock him back in at 4 while he would go somewhere and sleep for an extra hour.

When I started working there, the other employees began educating me to the system. They told me that I would cover for somebody else one day, and then the next day that person would cover for me. That was the way it worked.

I said, "I can't do that."

"No, you don't understand. Everybody does it."

"But I can't do it."

"Why not?"

"Well, I'm a Christian," I said. "The Bible tells me this is dishonest. It's lying and cheating and I can't do it."

From that day on, I was disdained among my fellow bus station workers. They did not like me. I was not fitting into their system. It was working fine until I came along.

Little did I know that the company had hired people to come to the station at night, posing as passengers, to see what was happening with the different shifts. They soon caught on to the employees' scheme.

So after I had been there about two months, the head of my area called me into his office. "Evans, we are going to make you the head of your shift."

I was surprised. "I have only been here two months."

Then he said, "Yes, but we can trust you. We have been watching, and we know that people are being gone two and three hours. We need somebody we can trust." If the other people on my shift didn't like me before, you can bet they loathed me now.

My point is that integrity was the issue. Daniel had integrity in his public life, and so his enemies couldn't find a thing to accuse him with.

Now please notice how these men teamed up on Daniel. We have 120 satraps, along with Daniel's two fellow commissioners, plotting together against him. That's 122 top government officials sniffing around, and they come up empty.

Today if there's suspicion of corruption in government, they usually hire a special prosecutor and dig up all kinds of stuff. But Daniel came up clean. One hundred and twenty-two to one, and Daniel wins. That is integrity in public life!

A pastor got on a bus one Monday morning and paid his fare. The driver handed him his change, and when he sat down and looked at it, he realized the driver had given him too much. Well, the pastor had just preached the day before on honesty, and the sermon was still fresh on his mind. He knew the right thing to do, so he took the money back to the bus driver and said, "You gave me too much change when I got on the bus."

"I know," the bus driver said. "I did it on purpose. I was in church yesterday, and I wanted to see if you were really what you said you were." You never know when people are testing your integrity.

PRIVATE INTEGRITY: A DAILY DISCIPLINE

Daniel was also faithful in his private life, and the other government officials knew it. They knew he would be true to his God no matter what. So when they realized they had nothing on him in his public service, they decided to set him up another way. They said, "We will never find any basis for charges against this man Daniel unless it has something to do with the law of his God." (Daniel 6:5)

These men decided to attack Daniel at the point of his spiritual life. They said, "He is completely devoted to his God. Let's get him there." So they came up with an idea.

The idea they came up with was an ancient version of that 1950s television program, "Queen for a Day." Except their program was called "God for a Month." They drew up a plan they knew King Darius would go for; then they brought it to him for his signature (6:6-9).

The plan was fiendishly simple. Darius would sign a statute decreeing that no one in the kingdom could pray to any god except him for thirty days. Failure to abide by the statute would result in the offender being tossed into the lions' den.

Darius liked the sound of that. He was flattered that his subjects thought so highly of him. So he signed the law. Now, in the Medo-Persian empire, once a law was enacted, it could never be changed or revoked (verse 8). So this thirty-day ban on praying to any other god was now an unchangeable law.

That put the issue in Daniel's court, because we learn from Daniel 6:10 that daily prayer was his habit.

> Now when Daniel learned that the decree had been published,
> he went home to his upstairs room where the windows opened
> toward Jerusalem. Three times a day he got down on his knees
> and prayed, giving thanks to his God, just as he had done before.

How did Daniel become a man of integrity? Here is the secret. If we found out that a law like this had been enacted, a lot of us would say, "Well, I guess I'll just have to stop praying. It's now against the law, and the Bible says to obey the authorities. Can't fight City Hall, you know." Well, that might sound like a pretty solid excuse to some, but it wasn't good enough for Daniel. He just continued on with his daily prayer life. He didn't call a special prayer meeting to pray for wisdom on what to do. His life *was* a prayer meeting. He had developed a consistent, personal walk with God, and that became the source of his integrity.

If you and I are going to be men of integrity rather than looking for an excuse to take the easy way out, it will boil down to our personal walk with God. Daniel didn't stop praying, he didn't panic, and he didn't use the excuse that as the executive vice-president of a nation, he was too busy to pray anyway. The real deal is he was too busy *not* to pray. Daniel prayed like you and I eat—three times a day.

It is interesting that the windows in Daniel's prayer chamber were open when he went home. After that law was passed, I probably would have at least closed the windows. I'd spiritualize it, thinking, "No one really needs to know I am praying. Prayer is private anyway. It's not for show."

Maybe Daniel could even have argued, "I'm a government official, so I need to keep my official and private lives separate. I need to keep my religion out of my work. After all, I'm serving an ungodly king in an ungodly nation. He wouldn't understand."

But Daniel was not about to be a "secret agent saint." He prayed publicly like he always did. He had a consistent witness, and he wasn't about to change it. His enemies were banking on Daniel's integrity and courage, because they showed up with their Polaroids to catch him praying by his open windows. And they weren't disappointed. They found Daniel on his knees (6:11).

So they ran to Darius with their evidence and reminded him of the statute he had signed. Then they threw down their snapshots and said, "Guess what, dear king? Your Jewish slave boy, Daniel, is ignoring you and the law you signed." (verse 13)

Now the minute Darius heard that, his heart sank. He wasn't a believer in Daniel's God, but neither was he crazy. He wanted a government led by people he could trust. Darius knew the kind of man Daniel was, and I think he really loved Daniel. When it dawned on him what this meant for Daniel, the king was deeply distressed (verse 14).

Darius spent all day trying to figure out a way to save Daniel from the lions' den. But after some hemming and hawing by the king, Daniel's enemies in the government got a little testy. They went to the king and said in effect, "Come on, Darius, what are you waiting for?

We're talking about the law of the Medes and Persians here. Daniel broke that law. You know what has to be done." (verse 15) So into the lions' den went Daniel.

Your integrity is severely tested in adversity. If you want to know the level of your integrity, measure it at a time when things are not going well. What you are really like can only be measured when your life is falling apart.

Well, Daniel's life seemed to be falling apart here. The next morning, Darius hurried to the den to see if Daniel was still alive. Notice what the king said:

> When he came near the den, he called to Daniel in an anguished voice, "Daniel, servant of the living God, has your God, whom you serve continually, been able to rescue you from the lions?"
>
> —*Daniel 6:20*

Darius was saying, "Daniel, is the God you talk about at the office every day real? Is He working for you? Does He have the power you say He has?"

How did Darius know about Daniel's God? Because Daniel lived a life of integrity before everyone and did not hide his witness. So God joined him in the lions' den, and the lions became Daniel's pillows for the night. His enemies had counted on the lions taking care of Daniel. What they hadn't counted on was his God taking care of Daniel.

HOW TO INTERNALIZE INTEGRITY

By now I hope you're asking what it takes to get the kind of integrity Daniel had. Let me make a few suggestions.

First, *don't wait around* for your boss or your wife or your environment to get better before you make a move. Integrity has to do with who you are on the inside regardless of what is happening on the outside. Don't blame others if your level of integrity isn't what it should be.

Second, *set your standards in advance*. Decide on the things you won't compromise on before you find yourself in the middle of a problem. You and I cannot become men of integrity on the spot. We cannot wait until the action gets hot and heavy to make our decisions about integrity. Establish your guidelines in advance.

Third, *develop a daily devotional life*. Make spending time with God the rule, not the exception. As we saw in the case of Daniel, cultivating your walk with God will do as much or more than anything else to help you to become a man of integrity.

Fourth, *find some friends who will hold you accountable for living up to your standards*. Find the friends who will ask you the hard questions about what you're doing and not doing.

Fifth, *major on God and not your circumstances*. If Daniel had majored on his circumstances, he would never have maintained his integrity. He would have become just like everybody else. He would no longer have been extraordinary. God did not save you so you could become like everybody else. God saved you to be extraordinary.

THE DIFFERENCE INTEGRITY MAKES

You say, "OK, Tony, I am willing to become a man of integrity. But what good is it going to do me?" The answer is, it's going to do you all the good in the world. Let me show you.

Daniel told Darius, "My God sent his angel, and he shut the mouths of the lions. They have not hurt me." (Daniel 6:22) The first thing that being a man of integrity will do for you is give you God's presence in the midst of your trials.

Do you want to see God's power operating on your behalf? Become a man of integrity who refuses to make excuses. It may not keep you from going into the lions' den, but it will keep you from going there alone. There may be lions in your life waiting to devour you. You cannot shut their mouths, but God can.

What else will becoming a man of integrity do for you? Let's continue reading in verse 22, where Daniel said, "[The lions] have not hurt me, because I was found innocent in [God's] sight. Nor have I ever done any wrong before you, O king."

Because Daniel stood by his integrity, he not only experienced

God's presence—he enjoyed God's protection. He had done what was right both in the sight of God and in the sight of the king, and God vindicated him by protecting him from the lions. When a man maintains that kind of testimony, he can ask God to intervene in his situation.

As the story in the sixth chapter of Daniel winds down, we can see another benefit of being a man of integrity. After Darius rejoiced in Daniel's safety and had him hauled out of the lions' den, he had a little administrative matter to care for.

The picture was now clear to Darius if it wasn't before. His real problem was not a disloyal Daniel, but a scheming bunch of government officials who had maliciously accused Daniel. The king had them and their families thrown to the lions, and this time there was no one around to shut the lions' mouths.

When you are a man of integrity, God deals with your enemies for you. "'It is mine to avenge; I will repay,' says the Lord." (Romans 12:19) God fights your battles for you. You just keep doing the right thing and resist the temptation to hide behind excuses, and God will vindicate you.

Another benefit of living with integrity is that God is glorified.

> "I issue a decree that in every part of my kingdom people must fear and reverence the God of Daniel. For he is the living God and he endures forever; his kingdom will not be destroyed, his dominion will never end. He rescues and he saves; he performs signs and wonders in the heavens and on the earth. He has rescued Daniel from the power of the lions."
>
> —*verses 26-27*

Darius got a lesson in theology that day. He learned more about God in one day than most people do in seminary. Daniel changed the spiritual nature of a country without even preaching a sermon. He was simply a man of integrity.

But because of that, Darius issued a decree that the God of Israel would be feared throughout the kingdom. And by the way, *this* decree was unchangeable too.

There is one more thing integrity will do for you: it will make you successful (verse 28). Daniel enjoyed success not only under Darius, but under the next king, Cyrus. Now, even if he had been eaten by the lions, Daniel would still have been successful. No matter how you measure success, one thing is sure—you won't achieve it in God's eyes unless you live with integrity.

Now you may say, "Tony, I've already compromised. My wife doesn't trust me. My kids don't respect me. My boss knows I am not dependable at work. It's too late for me."

No, it's not. God can take lemons and make lemonade. Think back to some of the men we have already studied. Moses definitely lost his integrity when he killed the Egyptian. But God gave it back to him at a burning bush and called him to lead Israel. Moses became, says Scripture, like God to the people.

David lost his integrity with Bathsheba, but he confessed his sin, and God restored him. In fact, David went to his grave with God saying of him, "David is a man after My own heart."

In the next chapter we'll see that Peter also lost his integrity when he denied the Lord three times. But he got his integrity back when he humbled himself. Before this, Peter was a prideful man. He said, "These others may leave you, Lord, but I'll never leave you." But he found out different.

These men experienced the forgiveness and grace of God. We need it too. If just some of the things we have thought and said and done, if just some of the places we have gone, were projected on a screen, there isn't a man alive who would have any integrity left.

But the good news is that Jesus is in the editing room working with the videotape of our lives. He can edit out things you wouldn't believe once they are confessed, forgiven, and cleansed by His blood. He can splice the tape back together so that you and I can be men of integrity. Whatever is keeping you out of Jesus' editing room, don't excuse it. Bring it to Him, let Him take care of it, and live with integrity.

SEVEN

NO MORE SIFTING THROUGH THE RUBBLE

"IT'S TOO LATE. I'VE ALREADY MESSED UP AND
BLOWN IT. THERE'S NO USE TRYING
TO GET IT BACK TOGETHER."

If you've ever seen a building being imploded, you know what a spectacular sight it is to see a ten- or twenty-story high-rise collapse in on itself and disappear in a few seconds.

Dallas had an implosion not too long ago, and it was enough to draw local television coverage. Those who got up early to watch the 7:00 A.M. event weren't disappointed, because it was an amazing thing to watch. One reason I think men like implosions is that it appeals to the little boy in us, imagining being the guy who gets to push the button and set off all that dynamite.

It's amazing to see a building that stood for years get reduced to a pile of rubble in a few seconds. Sadly, the same thing can happen to us as men. At just the wrong moment, Satan or circumstances or other people can hit the button and bring our lives crashing in on us.

More often than not, it's some combination of the above factors that does the destruction, and we can even do this to ourselves. Whatever the cause, the result is usually the same: a massive collapse of some kind.

If your life has ever imploded, you know what I'm talking about. It may have been a marriage or some other relationship that caved in. It may have been a circumstance you never thought would happen to you. It could be a business or some other interest that you spent years carefully building, only to see it come crashing down in a heap of rubble.

I don't want to overstate the case, because obviously not all men experience the big crash. But even if your implosion was relatively small, it's still a mess to clean up the debris. And if you can say, "Tony, so far nothing in my life has really crashed," then I say, praise God and keep reading. Because the reality is that all of us face the potential for a spiritual implosion.

What I want you to see is that no matter how devastating your collapse may have been, it doesn't have to be an excuse to give up, to throw in the towel, to decide that God wants nothing more to do with you.

The beauty of God's grace is that he can put Humpty Dumpty back together again. Even if your life has imploded and is lying in a heap, God has something better for you to do than just sifting through the rubble. Failure at one point or in one area in your life is not an excuse to give up the whole ball game.

PETER: A CASE OF MISPLACED CONFIDENCE

How do I know that? Because I know Peter. I know the man who should have worn peppermint socks since he loved to put his foot in his mouth so much. I know the guy who would speak or act on impulse, who would just say or do whatever came to mind, right or wrong. I know the disciple whose life caved in on him so bad he thought it was over between him and Jesus.

I don't know how well you know Peter, but I want to show you some things about his life you may not have realized were true. Most of all, I want to show you how God took the debris of Peter's life and did a magnificent rebuilding job.

We probably wouldn't know so much about Peter's big mess-up if he were not the leader of the twelve disciples. But he was. His denial of Jesus, which will be our focus, probably wouldn't have gotten so much space in the New Testament if Peter hadn't bragged that he would never let the Lord down.

Even with all of this, though, Peter's failure probably wouldn't have looked so bad if his timing hadn't been quite so rotten. But it was. For you see, Peter denied Jesus while Jesus was on His way to Calvary to die for Peter—and for all of us.

It was Peter who had said just hours earlier, "Jesus, even if everyone else deserts You, You can count on homeboy here to stick with You through thick and thin" (see Matthew 26:33). Jesus then prophesied the explosives that would soon go off in Peter's life when he said, "I tell you the truth, this very night, before the rooster crows, you will disown me three times." (verse 34)

That's the central plot of the story. But I want to stop here a minute, because I believe a lot of us Christian men are like Peter. There was nothing wrong with Peter's intention. His promise was a good one. His vow of faithfulness was solid.

A good many of us men have been challenged by movements like Promise Keepers, and we have responded in a very genuine way. We have good spiritual intentions, we make well-meaning spiritual promises, we vow great spiritual vows, only to find that we can't carry them out. Things may even implode when we try.

Why? One reason may be that, like Peter, we try to pull off spiritual goals in the power of the flesh. Peter had a lot of self-confidence. He just knew that he couldn't and wouldn't fail. But his confidence was misplaced.

Another reason we sometimes fail even in our spiritual efforts is that we underestimate the weakness of our flesh. If Peter overestimated his courage, he underestimated the weakness of his flesh and the power of temptation. Right after Jesus' prophecy about Peter, He took Peter, James, and John into the Garden of Gethsemane and asked them to pray (Matthew 26:36). But they all fell asleep. Notice, though, that Jesus addressed Peter (verse 41), warning him of the ease with which we fall to the temptation to spiritual lethargy. By the way, it's interesting that Peter failed to pray three times here (see also vv. 43 and 45), and then he denied Jesus three times.

A Bomb Waiting to Explode

So now that we can all identify with Peter a little better, let's pick up the story in John chapter 18. Jesus and the three disciples were still in the Garden, only now they weren't alone. Judas had come with soldiers to betray Jesus.

Jesus said in John 18:8, "I told you that I am he. If you are looking for me, then let these men go." I take that to mean that Jesus was telling Peter and his pals, "Leave right now. Don't stay around here. You are not to be a part of this." This was not just a nice gesture on Jesus' part. He was fulfilling His own prophecy (see John 17:12 and 18:9).

But Peter disobeyed and took the most famous swing in Bible history (verse 10). This brother didn't play. He was saying, "How dare you come to take Jesus Christ!"

Now most men would applaud Peter. We would say, "Hurrah for Peter! That took guts. You mess with Peter, you go earless." That's a good macho reaction. But Jesus corrected Peter (verse 11). Our boy Pete had missed the point completely. This was the Father's will for Jesus.

Here is a fundamental issue we all have to face when it comes to keeping our lives from imploding. We need to make sure we are not analyzing the events in our lives from a secular, human, worldly point of view rather than from a divine, spiritual, godly point of view.

We are quick to adopt the world's methods. Some guy gets in our way, we take him out. I don't mean that we use violence, but we are quick to strike out against apparent obstacles. However, Jesus said to Peter, "I'm supposed to drink this cup."

A "cup" in the Bible often stands for suffering. The world awards cups to honor suffering and hard work in the achievement of a triumph, like the World Cup given to soccer champions. Jesus said, "My Father has given Me a cup of suffering to drink, that I might achieve what he wants Me to achieve." So if you take out the sword of human methodology when God wants to give you his cup, you interfere with his plan for your life.

The Apostle Paul put it this way: "The weapons we fight with are not the weapons of the world. On the contrary, they have divine power to demolish strongholds." (2 Corinthians 10:4) But Peter chose the way and the weapons of the flesh.

By the time we get to John 18:10-11, Peter was a walking implosion device waiting to go off. He failed to pray, he disobeyed when Jesus told him to leave the Garden, and he acted with a worldly perspective. When one is prayerless, disobedient, and worldly, that is a lethal combination.

The Bomb Goes Off

The soldiers arrested Jesus and led Him away (John 18:12-13). Peter followed, which he was not supposed to do, because Jesus had told him to stay out of this (verse 15). But Peter and John were kind of sneaking around wondering what the officials were going to do with their Master.

In verses 16-17, we hear the first charge of dynamite being set off in Peter's self-implosion. "'You are not one of his disciples, are you?' the girl at the door asked Peter. He replied, 'I am not.'"

Wait a minute. Is this homeboy, the one who had said, "Even if I have to die with you, I will never disown you" (Matthew 26:35)? A little girl says, "Excuse me, but you look a lot like one of those guys who were hanging out with Jesus." Peter says, "Who, me? No, you've got me mixed up with someone else. You've seen one Galilean, you've seen them all. It wasn't me."

Denial number two came as Peter warmed himself by the fire with the slaves and soldiers (John 18:25). They were all standing by the fire, kind of rapping and taking it easy. Then they turned to Peter and said, "You are not one of his disciples, are you?" He denied it, and said, "I am not."

Now the slave girl and these guys by the fire weren't sure about Peter's identity. But notice verse 26. A slave who was related to Malchus, Peter's victim in the garden, said, "Didn't I see you with him in the olive grove?"

This guy was a lot more confident, so Peter had to make his point very clear. John simply says that Peter denied Jesus again (verse 27). But Matthew 26:74 says, "Then he began to call down curses on himself and he swore to them, 'I don't know the man!'" Then the rooster crowed, and Peter "went outside and wept bitterly." (verse 75)

PETER GETS LEVELED

Peter's collapse took less than twenty-four hours. He couldn't even keep his promise for a single day. Have you ever made a promise to God in the morning that you broke that afternoon? Well, that was Peter's situation. This guy had been hanging out with the world long enough to adopt the world's way of thinking.

Peter had neglected the warning of Psalm 1:1, "Blessed is the man who does not walk in the counsel of the wicked or stand in the way of sinners or sit in the seat of mockers." He had made his bed with unbelievers, and now to protect himself he denied his Lord.

What Peter did is called apostasy, a definitive denial of the faith. He publicly renounced any commitment to God, one of the worst sins anyone could commit. Pete had now hit rock-bottom. You can't get any lower than this.

To let you know that this is not just some little clear-the-throat, I-don't-think-I'm-familiar-with-this-Man kind of denial, Matthew records that Peter denied Jesus with a curse. Now this wasn't just sailor-language. Peter took a special oath, something like we do when we go to court, put our hand on the Bible, and swear to tell the truth.

The oath Peter took is called a "self-maledictory" oath, an oath taken against oneself. That is, you swear you're telling the truth—and you invite judgment upon yourself if you are lying. In the courtroom today, if you commit perjury you become liable for judgment based on the oath you made to tell the truth. We do something similar in an informal way when we say, "If I'm lying, may lightning strike me!" I don't know if any liars have ever been killed by lightning, but making a self-maledictory oath in Bible days was very serious and could cost you your life.

So with Peter, we are talking about a bold-faced liar. We are talking about a man who wanted to make it absolutely clear that he had nothing to do with Christ. He didn't know Him, had never known Him, and even if it cost him his life, he didn't want to be associated with Him.

I would say that Peter strayed pretty far in twenty-four hours. I would say that he'd gone pretty low. He had denied the faith, and yet this is the same man who earlier had confessed concerning Jesus, "You are the Christ, the Son of the living God." (Matthew 16:16)

This is the same man who had helped Jesus feed the five thousand. This is the same man whose name Jesus changed from Simon to Peter, because he was going to be a rock for the church (Matthew 16:17-18). This is the same man whose name was always at the top of the list of disciples, because he was the leader of them all.

The fact that you were okay yesterday has nothing to do with whether you are going to be so today. The fact that you were close to God yesterday has nothing to do with whether you are going to be close to God today. All Satan needs is an opportunity. You don't even have to open the door for the devil. Just leave it unlocked; he knows how to turn the knob.

Remember that Peter didn't plan on denying Jesus. He thought he had the stuff to stay in there. He even contradicted Jesus when the Lord predicted his denial. But the human will is no match for Satan when he gets hold of you.

Too bad Peter forgot that. He was so sure of himself that he didn't even remember what Jesus had said until after his three denials. He forgot Jesus' word. Whenever you forget the Word of God, you open yourself up to the work of men or of Satan. In fact, Jesus had to turn and look at Peter before he remembered (Luke 22:61).

Lord, have mercy! Can you imagine Peter denying Christ and then having Christ look straight at him? No wonder he ran out and wept bitterly.

Have you ever messed up so badly you had to cry? It takes a lot to make most men cry. But if your life has ever imploded to the point that it drove your face into your hands and you were distraught and destroyed because you blew it, then you know how Peter felt.

Some men have blown it in ways that only they know. But the

implosion is just as devastating. As far as we know, Jesus never told anyone else what Peter did. It may have been their secret, just as your own problem may be your secret. But a secret sin can break up hearts and homes just as easily as a public sin. And Peter was a broken man.

A Brand-New Day for Peter

But don't stop there, because the rooster crowed. Why? Because Jesus said it would. Nature reacts when Jesus speaks. Jesus also knows the future, because He prophesied Peter's denial as well as the rooster's crowing. Jesus also knew Peter's future, and that's where our hope lies. Let me show you what I mean.

When do roosters crow? Roosters crow at the beginning of a brand-new day, right? Peter was about to get a brand-new opportunity, despite the fact that he had a weak prayer life, a worldly perspective, and a disobedient spirit.

Actually, Jesus had given Peter a glimpse of his future restoration back in Luke 22:31-32:

> "Simon, Simon, Satan has asked to sift you as wheat. But I have
> prayed for you, Simon, that your faith may not fail. And when
> you have turned back, strengthen your brothers."

Do you know what would happen to us if Jesus weren't praying for us? Peter went very low, but he would have gone a lot lower if Jesus had not prayed for him. The same is true for us. None of us knows how low we would go if Jesus' prayers hadn't kept us from going there.

I don't know what your low point is, but you probably have not done what Peter did, which was to publicly renounce any association with Jesus Christ. That's about as low as any man can go.

Why do we need to know that? Because if there's hope for Peter, there's hope for you and me. If Jesus wouldn't let Peter use his failure as an excuse just to walk away and forget it, then he won't let us just walk away either. Let me say it again. God has something better for us than sifting through the rubble of a collapsed life.

Peter's forgiveness and restoration are recorded in John chapter 21, but the scene opens in an unusual way. Now Jesus has been crucified and has risen from the dead. So things are different now. Peter and six other disciples were sitting around when Peter said, "I am going fishing." They said to him, 'We will also come with you.'" That's generally how it was. Whatever Peter did, the rest followed.

Now you probably know that Peter was a fisherman. He was fishing one day when Jesus borrowed his boat to teach from and then told him, "Put out into deep water, and let down the nets for a catch." (Luke 5:4)

Peter protested that they had caught nothing all night, but he obeyed anyway. They let down the nets and caught a miracle load of fish, and then Peter realized who Jesus was. He fell at his feet, and Jesus called him to be His disciple (Luke 5:5-11).

Now go back to John 21:3, and what do you find? The same thing happened again. "So they went out and got into the boat, but that night they caught nothing." Peter was so messed up he was all the way back to where he was when he first met Jesus, catching nothing.

When you are out of the will of God, you catch nothing. When you are out of the will of God, you cannot produce. Peter's life had collapsed, so he went back to his old job. He figured he had blown it, so why try anymore?

Jesus had said to Peter, "*From now on* you will catch *men*." (Luke 5:10, emphasis added) But Peter had lost his vision for ministry, his vision for his calling. He was saying, "God can't use me. Might as well go fishing."

Have you ever felt that way? "Aw, what's the use? I've already blown it once. I'd probably just blow it again if I tried to do anything."

That was Peter. But please notice that the next morning, grace showed up. Here was Peter's brand-new day. Jesus came and stood on the shore. Then the same thing happened that had happened in Luke chapter 5. Despite his night of futility, Peter did what Jesus asked and let the nets down once more. And once more, they hauled in a miraculous boatload of fish (Luke 5:4-6).

You can't get started at all without Jesus. And when you have messed up, you can't get back to where you were without Him. But the good news is that when you get right with God, you begin to be productive again.

Now Peter at least had a good memory. When he saw all the fish, and when John said, "Hey, Pete, that's the Lord talking to us," the head of the disciples dove into the water and did his Johnny Weismuller thing all the way to shore.

So Peter swam to shore while the other disciples rowed in. When they got there, they found that Jesus had made breakfast for them (John 21:9). This is good stuff. This is grace. Jesus saw Peter in his despair, having gone back to his old life. He called Peter and told him, "If you let Me, I can still make you a successful fisher of men." Then he fed Peter and the others with fish He already had. He didn't need their fish.

When you are in the will of God, you don't have to worry about the fish. When Jesus tells you where to cast your net, the fish come looking for the net. The beauty of being in God's will is that He brings his plan to you. He brings His purpose to you.

Verses 12-14 of John chapter 21 describe an amazing scene— Jesus serving a meal of fish and bread to His disciples just like he had fed the five thousand and the four thousand in their presence. They must have watched in wide-eyed wonder, especially Simon Peter.

Once the meal was over and the dishes were done, Jesus got down to the reason for His appearance that day. John 21:15-19 is one of the greatest demonstrations of the grace of God you will ever see.

PETER'S RESTORATION: IT BEGAN WITH "I LOVE YOU"

"Simon, son of John, do you truly love me more than these?" Jesus asked in verse 15.

What a way to start an after-breakfast conversation. Who are "these"? The other disciples. Remember that Peter had said, "These other guys may forsake You, but not homeboy. I'm going to stick with You. I'm going to stay with You. You don't have to worry about a thing because You can count on me. I love You more than these others. I'm more committed to You than they are."

Never measure your spiritual life by your neighbor. Never measure your spiritual walk by how well or how badly everyone else is doing. Some men want to say, "Well, at least I don't do what Joe does. So I must be a better Christian than him."

The moment you start thinking like that, pride will trip you up. Peter had bragged himself right off the deep end, so Jesus was going to bring him back the way he left. He had denied Jesus three times, so Jesus was going to give him three opportunities to confess his love and loyalty.

To understand what is going on in this exchange, we need help from the Greek text, because you don't see it as clearly in English. I want you to see the interplay between two Greek verbs for love, *agapao* and *phileo*. Let me plug these words in at the appropriate places and show you what's going on.

Verse 15: "Simon, son of Jonah, do you *agapao* me more than these?" He said to Him, "Yes, Lord; you know that I *phileo* you." He said to him, "Feed my lambs."

The word *agapao* is the verb form of the Greek word *agape*, which is God's sacrificial love, the love that seeks the highest good of the one loved. It's John 3:16 love. Jesus was saying, "Peter, do you love Me sacrificially? Do you love Me supremely?"

But Peter answered with *phileo*, the word for "brotherly love," a word of affection. Peter was saying, "Yes, I like you." What happened here? Well, reality had set in. When Peter's life imploded, he found out that he wasn't as spiritual as he thought he was. All of a sudden, top dog wasn't top anymore. Big dog had become little puppy.

Peter was saying to Jesus, "I can't say that I love You supremely. I would never have denied You if I really loved You like that. So the best I can say is that I like You. I'm not going out on that limb again."

If you say, "I would never do that," but then you go ahead and do it, you are never going to say never again. Why? Because you've learned that in this flesh, you have the capability of doing anything on any given day. We all do.

But even though Peter was reluctant to say he loved Jesus supremely, Jesus still said, "Feed my lambs." He was inviting Peter back into the ministry, back into the Lord's service. Now we may want to ask Jesus, "Are You really going to give this guy another shot at the ministry when he can't even say he loves You supremely?"

I think Jesus would say, "Yes, because for the first time he can tell Me the truth." A lot of us flat-out lie to God. We say, "I love You more than anything," but we don't live it.

Sometimes we lie when we pray. We get on our knees and we say all the right words, but God shuts his ears because it's not the truth. It would be much better to go before God and say, "I think I like You," or even "I'm angry with You."

Someone will say, "Well, I would feel uncomfortable saying that." Would you feel more comfortable lying? But God will not sanction our theological lies.

If your world has imploded, don't go around saying, "Everything is fine," because it's not fine. If you've collapsed, you are not OK. If your life has caved in, you need more than the standard three-minute prayer: "Lord, thank You for this. Thank You for that. Bless me with this. Help me do that. In Jesus' name. Amen."

God says, "I'm tired of that. That's not really the truth. Your family is falling apart. You've got a pornographic mind. You're not loving your wife. That's what I want to talk about. I want to talk about those hurts and those sins. I want to get down to the nitty-gritty. Do you really love Me?"

When you come clean with God, He can come clean with you. But some men are living out an inauthentic, fake Christianity, while others are living out a proud Christianity that says, "I'm better than these other guys."

Peter came clean with Jesus. He was authentic. And Jesus said, "I have a place for you. Feed My lambs."

That's grace. So even if your world is broken, if you will be authentic with God, He can use you and bless you and guide you to do all the things you've been wanting him to do.

Let's go back to John chapter 21 and notice verse 16: "Jesus said to Peter again a second time, 'Simon son of John, do you *agapao* me?' He said to him, 'Yes, Lord; you know that I *phileo* you.' He said to him, 'Take care of my sheep.'"

Now the first time, Jesus added "more than these?" This time, however, he dropped the second part of the question. He simply wanted to know if Peter loved Him.

But notice that both Jesus and Peter used the same two Greek words they used the first time. Peter was still basically saying, "I like You."

With this question, Jesus seemed to be pressing Peter a little more to declare his level of commitment. "Come on, Peter, you must love Me. I'm Jesus."

But even though Peter answered with *phileo*, Jesus told him to care for his sheep. Before it was lambs. They have grown up now. Jesus has just increased Peter's ministry, and he hasn't even started it yet. They're still sitting around the fire.

The reason, I think, is the same as it was the first time. Peter was authentic. He was for real. When we are real with God, He can expand us and do things with us before we have even moved. All Peter did was tell the truth. That's grace.

Now in the third exchange, described in John 21:17, things changed. "The third time he said to him, 'Simon son of John, do you *phileo* me?' Peter was hurt because Jesus asked him the third time, 'Do you love me?' He said, 'Lord, you know all things; you know that I *phileo* you.' Jesus said, 'Feed my sheep.'"

What has happened? They're both speaking the same language now. Guess what Jesus did. He came down. Before, He was using that awesome word *agape*. Peter was saying, "Lord, I'm not there yet. I'm struggling. I'm hurting. I'm in pain. I'm still at *phileo*." So Jesus came down to meet Simon.

YOUR RESTORATION: IT BEGINS WITH THE TRUTH

Isn't that what Calvary is all about, Jesus Christ leaving heaven and coming down? Isn't it about the God of the universe condescending to our level so that we can be raised to His level? Now we need to remember that this was not the end of the story between Jesus and Peter. It was actually a new beginning.

I'm sure if you asked Peter afterwards if he loved Jesus supremely, he would have said an emphatic yes. He was ready to give his life for Jesus at that point, and church tradition says that he eventually did in fact give his life.

The good news for today is that no matter how bad your life has collapsed, Jesus will come down and help you rebuild it. He will come down to you, but you've got to tell Him the truth. You need to come clean with Him.

Jesus once told about a proud Pharisee and a despised tax-gatherer who went into the temple to pray:

> "The Pharisee stood up and prayed about himself: 'God, I thank you that I am not like other men—robbers, evildoers, adulterers—or even like this tax collector. I fast twice a week and give a tenth of all I get.' But the tax collector stood at a distance. He would not even look up to heaven, but beat his breast and said, 'God, have mercy on me, a sinner.'"
>
> —*Luke 18:11-13*

Jesus then said the tax-gatherer went away justified because when he honestly admitted his sin and cried out for mercy, God reached down to him and lifted him up.

Peter was hurt when Jesus asked him the third time about his love. But think what those three exchanges did for Peter. They reminded him of the three times he had denied Jesus. Asking him to declare his love three times wasn't too much. This represented God's grace. Jesus met Peter on the shore, reached down to him, and rebuilt his collapsed life. He even reinstated him into a larger ministry—something many contemporary Christians are unwilling to do for their fallen leaders.

The same thing can happen to you if you will come to God and tell Him the truth about your need or your sin. If you will come clean with him, He will say to you what Jesus said to Peter: "Now I can use you." This means you have hope. It means that even if your life is a pile of debris, Jesus can put it back together.

My wife Lois is an exceptional cook. She can literally razzle and dazzle you with her culinary excellence. But Lois is also extremely frugal. She doesn't believe in throwing anything away.

Most Sundays, she prepares a large meal that we enjoy together after church. But rather than throw the scraps away, she puts them in Tupperware. Then on Monday she will take the leftovers from Sunday and reconfigure them. She will dice, chop and grate them, remix them, put some cream of mushroom soup over them, give theis meal a new made-up name, and we think we're eating some new delicacy we've never had before, when in actuality all it is is leftovers reconfigured in the hands of a master.

So it is with God. You look at your past failures, your broken relationships, or your present circumstances and conclude you are a heap of leftovers deserving only to be thrown away.

But if you will commit yourself to God, He will chop you, dice you, grate you, remix you, and then pour a little cream of the Holy Ghost over you, turning your leftover life into a spiritual delicacy that looks great and brings spiritual benefits to others. God can take the leftovers of your life and turn you into something special. All you must do is let Him.

As we saw, the proof that Jesus restored Peter was that he told him three times to shepherd his sheep. If you want to know whether the restoration "took," turn to Acts chapter 2 when you have time, and read the story of Pentecost again. When nearly incredible things started happening and the people accused the believers of being drunk, notice who stood up to declare the truth (Acts 2:14).

It's Peter. Yes, the same Peter who so often put his foot in his mouth. The same Peter who kept messing up; who made promises he couldn't keep; who was scared to death of what the Jews would say; who was scared of going public with his faith; who actually denied the Lord.

Peter not only stood up, he spoke up. His sermon on the Day of

Pentecost brought three thousand people to faith in Christ. And listen to this very public confession: "Therefore let all Israel be assured of this: God has made this Jesus, whom you crucified, both Lord and Christ." (Acts 2:36)

Then in Acts chapter 5, the Jewish authorities ordered Peter to quit preaching in the name of Jesus. And to underscore the threat, they beat him and the other apostles on their backs with straps (5:40). But verse 41 says Peter went out rejoicing that he was considered worthy to suffer disgrace for Jesus.

Something had happened to our boy Pete! Does this sound like a man who was looking for a way out, who was using his hour of failure and defeat as an excuse to check out of Christ, the ministry, and the Christian life? You can answer that for yourself.

My Christian brother, may I urge you one more time? If you're sifting through the pile of rubble that was your life, looking for something you can salvage; if you're shoveling out the debris in an attempt to clean up the mess, put your shovel down and come to Jesus. He can reverse implosions!

EIGHT

NO MORE GIVING IN TO TEMPTATION

"I CAN'T HELP IT. I'M JUST NOT VERY STRONG WHEN IT COMES TO RESISTING TEMPTATION."

D o you remember an old B-grade movie called *The Blob*? As I recall, a meteor came hurtling in from outer space, crashed to earth in a wooded area, and split open. As it lay there glowing, a man came up to it and poked it with a stick. Suddenly and violently, this cosmic goo slithered up the stick and onto the man's arm.

The man began screaming and running, doing all kinds of things to try and get this glue-like substance off his body. But as we watched, the blob began to consume him. The harder he worked to shake off the blob, the more completely he was consumed until finally, he was gone. This blob-like creature had devoured him.

As the movie went on, the blob got bigger and bigger by consuming everything in its path. Pretty soon, it was eating everyone in town. People were running around screaming because the blob was taking over.

TEMPTATION: A LITTLE GOES A LONG WAY

When I think about temptation, I am reminded of *The Blob*. Like the blob, temptation is pervasive. It didn't matter whether the people in the movie wanted to deal with the blob. It was there, and it was coming for them. Their only choice was to run or get blobbed.

That's the way it is with temptation. If you're a man and you're alive, you're on the list. It's that simple. Temptation will find you.

Now, the blob started off small. It was just an interesting-looking lump of glowing goo. The man who poked at it with a stick didn't really feel threatened at that point. He was just curious to see what it was.

Temptation usually starts in a small way too. It's in just one little area. We reach out to touch it and get a little bit of it on us. But when we try to shake it off, we find out it's sticky. No matter what we do, it doesn't let go. In fact, it starts moving up our arms, eating away at us until it consumes us.

When this process goes beyond a certain point, the temptation becomes an addiction. We're all aware of the more obvious addictions to things like drugs, tobacco, and alcohol—or the various sexual addictions. But a lot of addictions are not so obvious. A man may not be immoral in his actions, but if we could peer into his mind, we might be very surprised at what we see. In fact, some of us do with our minds what most people would never do with their bodies, because we become addictive in our way of thinking.

Now, addiction is at the far end of the scale. It's what happens when temptation is allowed to wander out of control, like the blob. An addiction is something that has gained such complete mastery over us that our ability to resist has been all but destroyed. Like the blob, this thing is consuming us and perhaps even rubbing off us and destroying other people around us as well.

Obviously, not every man is addicted. But temptation is a fact of life for all of us, Christians as much as unbelievers. The difference is that if you are a son of God, you have supernatural power available to you to say no to temptation and to live a life that pleases our Creator.

A nonbeliever may whimper and roll over in the face of temptation, excusing it by saying, "I just can't help myself." But that doesn't have to be your story.

Since temptation is an ever-present reality, we need to know how it works and why trying to conquer it in our flesh won't work. To help us get past the excuses, we are going to learn from a brother in Christ who thoroughly understood the lusts of the flesh and the wiles of Satan, and who struggled in this area more than you might think. I'm talking about Paul, the Apostle to the Gentiles.

If you know your Bible, you're probably not surprised that Paul spoke so frankly about his struggles with temptation and sin. He was open and forthright about everything, and since he wrote more books of the New Testament than anyone else, it's more likely that we would have his teaching on the subject.

Paul had a realistic view of himself. We tend to think of him as playing in the "Super Bowl" of righteousness, and he did. But he was also a man, and he knew what his flesh was capable of. In fact, he had been a Super Bowl-caliber sinner before he came to Christ.

That's why, for example, he said in 1 Corinthians 15:9 that he was "less than the least of all God's people." In Ephesians 3:8, he called himself "the very least of all saints." And in 1 Timothy 1:15, he classified himself as "the worst of all sinners."

So we are talking about a follower of Christ who continued to struggle with sin. Paul was a man with passions just like ours. Some Bible scholars even think he was married at one time. The point is, he was not living in a monk's cell or ivory tower. When he looked in the mirror, he saw a man who knew what sin was and who realized that it was an all-encompassing "blob" seeking to control his life.

Now in case you don't already know, let me give you two pieces of news right up front. The first is that the Bible never condemns you for being a man and having a man's desires. God made you that way. Your desires are normal. You'll take them to the grave with you. So the answer to temptation is not denying who and what you are.

The second piece of news is that the Bible never allows you to make excuses for sin based on your maleness and your normal, God-given desires. Why? Because your *temptations* to sin are not from God (James 1:13-16). And because God has made provision for victory over temptation. Let's talk about it.

If you've ever read Romans chapter 7, you know that Paul had a constant struggle with sin. This is a difficult chapter because it sounds like Paul wrote it before he became a Christian. That's the view some people take as a way around all the problems. They say there's no way this material could have been written by a Christian.

EVERY TRUE BELIEVER'S BATTLE

But I think Paul is speaking here as a believer, because only a believer could say what he says. For example, in Romans 7:17 he says, "As it is, it is no longer I myself who do it, but it is sin living in me." Paul makes the distinction between sin in his life and his true self.

Look at verse 19: "For what I do is not the good I want to do; no, the evil I do not want to do—this I keep on doing." Paul says he's doing things he doesn't even want to do. Does that sound familiar? He goes on to say in verse 22: "For in my inner being I delight in God's law." Only a Christian has an "inner being" that can rejoice in the law of God.

But it's the last verse of this chapter that validates Paul as a believer: "Thanks be to God—through Jesus Christ our Lord! So then, I myself in my mind am a slave to God's law, but in the sinful nature a slave to the law of sin." Only a Christian could make a statement like that.

Paul isn't trying to tell us what he was like before salvation. He is writing from personal experience to help us understand what it is that causes the habit of sin and the addictions that bring us under their control. And he wants us to know what to do about it.

Let me try to clear up a common point of confusion here. A lot of people think that once you become a strong, spiritual Christian, the kind of Christian Paul was, you sort of rise above the problem of sin. You aren't bothered by it anymore.

If you've been a Christian for any length of time, you know better than that. The truth is that the greater your spiritual development, the greater your sensitivity to sin. The more you grow in Christ, the more you will be aware of your propensity to sin.

The reason Paul was so conscious of the war going on within him was because he *was* a mature, spiritual man. Once you realize that you are in a spiritual battle with the forces of evil, you will become very sensitive to sin's attempts to conquer you. In a war, only a fool is not on constant alert for the enemy.

The man who goes around thinking that temptation is no problem may be right, because he has probably been conquered by it so often and surrendered to it so consistently that he no longer feels any conflict. Paul knew he would struggle with sin as long as he was in the flesh.

FREEDOM IN CHRIST

The discussion in the seventh chapter of Romans centers on the Mosaic Law and a Christian's relationship to it. Paul opens the chapter with the illustration of marriage (verses 1-6). In this scenario, the law is the husband and the believer is the wife (sorry, brother).

It's obvious that as long as a husband is alive, his wife is bound to him. But if he dies, she is free to marry another husband. Paul is actually talking about a double death here, for in Christ the law became dead to us and we became dead to the law. The bottom line is that the law is no longer the standard by which we are judged—and we can be glad for that.

Why? Paul answers that in verses 7-13. The law of God is good and perfect, but it is powerless to help us obey its commands. All the law can do is make us aware of sin and condemn us for not being faithful children of God. Remember, if you want to try and obey God's law, you have only one standard—perfection!

Paul illustrates what he means with the law against coveting: "I would not have known what coveting really was if the law had not said, 'Do not covet.'" His point is that knowing the tenth commandment didn't help him stop being a covetous person. It just made him painfully aware of how covetous he really was. I remember once walking downtown in Dallas and seeing a sign that said, "Wet paint. Do not touch." There were fingerprints everywhere. Why? Because when people see the law, it brings out their lawlessness.

The Ten Commandments were never written with the expectation that you would be able to keep them. They were written to show you that you *can't* keep them. But the only way you would know that is by having the commandments in front of you. Otherwise, being human, you and I would continue to deceive ourselves into thinking we were doing fine. That's doubly true for men, because we all want to think we can do it ourselves, that we don't need any help.

So the law comes along and says, "You shall not lie." All of a sudden, lies jump out everywhere. "You shall not commit adultery," says the seventh commandment, and Jesus says that includes lust (Matthew 5:27-28). With that commandment before us, lust becomes a major problem.

That's because the law is like a mirror. All your mirror does in the morning is show you the junk in your eyes, the yellow on your teeth, and your unruly hair. You don't take the mirror off the wall and wash your face or comb your hair with it. A mirror can't fix what's wrong. It only shows you what's wrong.

By the way, the sin Paul chose to mention in Romans 7:7 is one that no one can get away from, because we all have coveted. Coveting means wrongfully wanting something that belongs to someone else, something you should not have, desiring it so much that you scheme to get it or will even hurt the person who has it. Everyone covets on some level. Even if a man isn't a drug addict, for example, he may still be a coveting addict.

WINNING THE WAR AGAINST SIN—STEP 1: CLEAN HOUSE

Verses 1-13 of Romans chapter 7 set the stage for the discussion on which I want to focus, and that is the issue of how to resolve the struggle with sin that we all must face (verses 14-25).

Let's look first at Paul's condition as a spiritual Christian. We know that he's a believer, so that issue is settled. But we also know from this chapter that he's got a real battle going with sin. Paul states his condition in three verses that I want us to consider together:

> We know that the law is spiritual; but I am unspiritual, sold as a slave to sin.
>
> *—verse 14*

I know that nothing good lives in me, that is, in my sinful nature.
For I have the desire to do what is good, but I cannot carry it out.

—verse 18

So I find this law at work: When I want to do good, evil is right
there with me.

—verse 21

Paul's condition is such that the "new Paul" is still locked up in
the "old Paul," his flesh. When you came to Jesus Christ, He put a
brand-new *you* inside your old flesh. Now by "flesh" or "sinful nature,"
Paul doesn't mean the meat on your bones. He's talking about your
humanness, your body and its appetites outside of Christ. "Flesh" is
the term the Bible uses for the human in contrast to the divine—for
the things that are material as opposed to the things that are spiritual.

Before we became Christians, our flesh was well trained in evil
by the devil and the world, and we developed sinful appetites. Some
men may have a propensity for drugs because that's what they were
around in their days in the flesh. Others may have a problem with sexual immorality for the same reason.

The flesh is like a magnet that attracts what is evil and against God.
What you were exposed to in your life helps to determine what your
"magnet" attracts. Some men are worse off than others in this regard
because they received Christ at a later age and had a lot of years to indulge
their appetites for evil. Even among those who turned to the Lord at a very
early age, the flesh still has plenty of chances to express itself. This is true
because we all sin every day in the things we say, do, and even think.

Now this is important to understand. Paul is saying that even
though he is saved from the consequences of his sin, and even though
his desire is to please God, his flesh is still a magnet attracting sin.
When God redeems and justifies us, He does not repair our flesh. He
never disconnected the magnet, if you will.

That is the problem with trying to please God in the flesh and
making New Year's resolutions and such things. Those are just human

attempts to fix the flesh. God has already consigned the flesh to the grave. Someday it will be worm food. Our flesh is so corrupted by sin that it is actually beyond repair.

Now once you understand this, it will save you from trying to solve your struggle with sin by trying to make your flesh behave. Again, the flesh is terminally diseased and destined for the graveyard. Instead of trying to repair the old house, God is going to give you a brand-new one at the resurrection.

But in the meantime, becoming a Christian and living like one is like moving into a house where the old inhabitants were dirty and grimy and their filthy things were thrown all over. You move in and start cleaning. You paint the walls, get new carpet and appliances, and eventually the place looks totally different on the inside. It's the same house outside, but it's brand-new on the inside.

That's what God did to our inner person when we became heirs to salvation. You are a brand-new person inside. You may look the same physically, but spiritually the story is different: "If anyone is in Christ, he is a new creation; the old has gone, the new has come!" (2 Corinthians 5:17)

None of this minimizes the new birth. Paul is a new creation in Christ. The problem is what he calls indwelling sin, the fact that "evil is right there with me." Paul battles this sin that tries to bring him under its control.

WINNING THE WAR—STEP 2: OWN UP TO YOUR PROBLEM

In this sense, we Christians are true dual personalities. Our redeemed inner self wants to please God, while our sin-contaminated, unredeemed flesh seeks to enslave us again. How did Paul know that this was his condition? Well, after each of the three statements of his condition he gives the evidence that verified it.

> I do not understand what I do. For what I want to do I do not do, but what I hate I do.
>
> *—verse 15*

For what I do is not the good I want to do; no, the evil I do not
want to do—this I keep on doing.

—*verse 19*

For in my inner being I delight in God's law; but I see another
law at work in the members of my body, waging war against the
law of my mind and making me a prisoner of the law of sin at
work within my members.

—*verses 22-23*

Paul knew he had a problem with sin because he was doing some
things he didn't want to do, and not doing other things he really wanted
to do. That ought to sound familiar. What Christian hasn't felt that
struggle?

Your inner person, which has been made brand-new in the image
of God, doesn't want to sin. But your outer person, your old fleshly
nature, is used to sinning and doesn't want to stop.

Paul knew there were times when he fell short of pleasing God.
There were times when he lost the battle, because he says in Romans
7:23 that sin made him its prisoner. He's being very real and honest
about this struggle with sin, and yes, even his defeat at the hands of
sin. But because Paul has shared his struggle with us, we know how
to wage war against sin and win.

Now you may read this chapter in Romans and say, "Man, Paul
sounds like he was deep into some terrible sin that really had him tied
up." The least that can be said is that Paul certainly recognized our
human capacity to become addicted to sin. He knew how easy it was to
be enslaved to the sins that nobody sees, hidden sins like coveting or lust.

We tend to categorize sin. To us, being a drug addict or a wife
beater is real bad because sins like these are so visible and the destruction they cause is so terrible and so obvious. But God sees all sin as
equally horrible.

That's why you can never say you are better than the next guy.
You may be less public with your sin than the next guy, and the con-

sequences of your sin may not be as obvious as the next guy's, but you're no better. Paul declares that we are all "sold as a slave to sin."

This is our problem as much as it was Paul's. We are believers, but our new natures are engaged in a very real struggle with the old flesh for control of our appetites and actions.

But notice that Paul does *not* try to excuse himself or make allowances for sin. He doesn't say, "I just can't help myself. I'm not strong. Everybody else is doing it. I'm a Christian anyway, so one little sin won't hurt."

Instead, he says he knows what the flesh is up to; he knows it's out to trip him up and enslave him. And he knows he needs to oppose the flesh because he says, "I've got this other law within me that hates what the flesh is trying to do. In my mind and heart, I want to serve God."

WINNING THE WAR—STEP 3: DEVELOP SPIRITUAL SENSITIVITY

Notice Paul's spiritual sensitivity to sin, which I mentioned before. It's the immature Christian who thinks he can handle temptation. It's the carnal Christian who says, "That could never happen to me. I would never fall for that."

The Apostle John wrote, "But if we walk in the light, as he is in the light . . . the blood of Jesus, his Son, purifies us from all sin." (1 John 1:7) That's a continuous action. Jesus' blood keeps on cleansing us.

How can the blood of Jesus keep on cleansing us from sin as we walk in the light? Because it's only when we walk in the light that we can see our sin. For example, a Christian who is not walking in the light may say that adultery is bad, but that lust is normal. But a Christian who is walking in the light of God's Word says adultery is bad and lust is equally hideous. His sensitivity to sin has grown because he has God's point of view on things. The more of God you see, the more of your own sinfulness you see. A man may not be a drug addict, but he may see that he's a pride addict or an arrogance addict.

The more you grow in Christ, the bigger the war against the flesh is going to get. Why? Because Satan will try to entice the flesh to keep the Spirit from controlling you. But here is the good news. While your struggle with sin definitely verifies that you are in the same condition as Paul, your awareness of the struggle may signal your *growth* in grace, not your lack of it.

I see an example of that in Psalm 119, David's great poem in praise of God's Word. After spending 175 verses telling God how much he loves His Word, David says in the last verse, "I have strayed like a lost sheep. Seek your servant, for I have not forgotten your commands."

In David we have a man who was close to God. But David's closing prayer in the psalm was a recognition of his propensity to stray. The more of the Word you see, the more of your own sin you realize. God called David a man after His own heart, because David had a divine perspective.

THE SIN THAT LIVES WITHIN

We will look at the answer to the problem of temptation and sin, but first we should discuss the source or cause. Paul also mentioned this three times in Romans chapter 7, just as he talked about his sinful condition and its verification three times:

> As it is, it is no longer I myself who do it, but it is sin living in me.
>
> —*verse 17*

> Now if I do what I do not want to do, it is no longer I who do it, but it is sin living in me that does it.
>
> —*verse 20*

> What a wretched man I am! Who will rescue me from this body of death?
>
> —*verse 24*

That's like saying you have a cancer that has metastasized. The indwelling principle of sin is akin to a spiritual cancer that has spread and taken over every part of your flesh. Sin owns the flesh. That's why Paul makes the distinction between the real him and the sin that indwelt him.

Paul's image of having a dead body clinging to him may come from the practice of some in that day of tying the body of a murder victim to his murderer. They would tie the two together, nose to nose and eye to eye. The murderer would have to carry that dead body around until the decay from it entered his own body and killed him.

The question is, what is controlling you? Paul says, "It's not my inner man at work when I sin. It's the principle of sin that is promoting the flesh." It was Paul's realization of this struggle and the power of sin that caused him to issue his famous lament, "What a wretched man I am!"

Until we realize how wretched we are, God can't help us. Does it sound to you like Paul was a man saying to himself, "Come on, kid. You can do it. Remember the power of positive thinking. I'm just not going to touch that person. I'm not going to pick up that bottle"? No, this is a man saying, "I can't help myself." You and I have been contaminated by sin. We dress it up with suits and ties, but given the right circumstances it will pop up like a jack-in-the-box. We keep stuffing it back down in the box and closing the lid, but every time that old song hits the right note, out it comes.

If you are trying to overcome temptation or to deal with a sin addiction, you'll never make it by human effort. Now don't misunderstand me. There is a time and place for seeking help, and sometimes we need counseling and guidance and someone to walk with us. I am not denying any of that, but I am rejecting a perspective that says you can retrain and restrain your flesh.

It's amazing how contradictory we can be. We say, "Jesus is sufficient," but then we do the exact opposite of what Jesus tells us to do to fix what's broken. It's like going to the cafeteria, loading your plate down with fattening food and rich desserts, and then looking for a can of diet pop.

It's a contradiction. You can't feed the flesh with calories and saturated fat and hope to escape any weight gain with a diet drink. But that's often what we do spiritually. We try to feed and starve the flesh at the same time.

Victory—Once and for All

What's the answer to this problem of temptation and sin? How can we get victory over it rather than constantly caving in and excusing our failure?

THE LONG-TERM SOLUTION: RESURRECTION!

Actually, there are two answers, one for the short term and one for the long term. Let me give you the long-term answer first. It's in Romans 7:25: "Thanks be to God—through Jesus Christ our Lord!"

You say, "Oh yeah, I know what Paul means. He means that Christ's victory over sin at the cross and our salvation in Him provides us the victory we need over sin." Yes, but the fact is that what Paul is talking about here is not victory over sin in the here-and-now. Rather, he is talking about the consummation of this age, when Jesus Christ is going to return, totally dismantle our corrupt flesh, and give us brand-new bodies. If you want to see what Paul is talking about in more detail, look ahead to Romans 8:19-23. There he anticipates the liberation that all of creation will experience when Christ returns.

Note particularly 8:23: "Not only so, but we ourselves, who have the firstfruits of the Spirit, groan inwardly as we wait eagerly for our adoption as sons, the redemption of our bodies." (See also 2 Corinthians 5:1-4.)

This is what Paul was looking forward to in Romans 7:25. This is what he was groaning for, to be set free from his body that was carrying around in it the sentence of death. What he is saying in Romans 8:23 is that this problem of sin won't get completely solved until we get to heaven.

We will carry our propensity to sin with us to our grave because our flesh is beyond repair. But when Christ returns, we will know complete liberation. Listen to Paul in another place:

> When the perishable has been clothed with the imperishable, and the mortal with immortality, then the saying that is written will come true: "Death has been swallowed up in victory."

"Where, O death, is your victory? Where, O death, is your sting?" The sting of death is sin, and the power of sin is the law. But thanks be to God! He gives us the victory through our Lord Jesus Christ.

—1 Corinthians 15:54-57

This last verse is an echo of Romans 7:25. So victory over sin will ultimately be realized at the resurrection of the dead, when God does away with this body of lust and degradation.

I believe this is one reason God allows Christians to get sick and sometimes even to die in pain. He doesn't want us falling in love with this body so that we start serving it. He wants us to be willing and ready to shed this body, to hurt enough that we will cry out, "Lord, take me home." Then God will say, "That's what I wanted to hear. Come on up. I want to get rid of that old body of sin anyway. I'm not going to bring it up here. I've got a new one for you."

THE HERE-AND-NOW SOLUTION: THE HOLY SPIRIT

Now that's in the future, the long term, but God has something good for you in the meantime. Look at the rest of Romans 7:25: "So then, I myself in my mind am a slave to God's law, but in the sinful nature a slave to the law of sin."

Paul says, "I've got two laws working in me. I've got the law of sin telling me, 'Come over here. Do this. Try this. Touch this.' And I've got the law of God saying, 'No, come over here. Do this. Don't do this. Don't touch this.' Where am I going to get the power to obey God since I've got this other law of sin that I can't shake?" Well, keep reading:

> Therefore, there is now no condemnation for those who are in Christ Jesus, because through Christ Jesus the law of the Spirit of life set me free from the law of sin and death. For what the law was powerless to do in that it was weakened by the sinful nature, God did by sending his own Son in the likeness of sinful man to be a sin offering. And so he condemned sin in sinful

man, in order that the righteous requirements of the law might
be fully met in us, who do not live according to the sinful nature
but according to the Spirit.

—Romans 8:1-4

Learning to walk or live in the power of the Holy Spirit is the key
to victory over sin and temptation. Paul said it this way in Galatians
5:16: "So I say, live by the Spirit, and you will not gratify the desires
of the sinful nature." Now let me remind you once more, this does not
mean you will no longer have the desires of the flesh. We've established that they are a reality.

But notice the new law Paul introduces in Romans 8:2: "The law
of the Spirit of life." This law or principle, the power of the indwelling
Spirit, will keep you from having to obey the law of the flesh. It won't
keep you from feeling the desires of the flesh, but it will keep you from
having to act on those desires. You may feel like taking illegal drugs,
but you don't have to take them. You may feel like practicing immorality, but you don't have to act on that temptation. You may be tempted
to be prideful, but you don't have to yield to the flesh.

Remember our movie *The Blob*? They tried every which way to
get rid of that pile of cosmic goo. They shot it and bombed it, but every
time they split it into a thousand little pieces it just grew back together
again—that is, until someone haphazardly put some ice on it. They
discovered the blob couldn't handle the cold.

So they started spraying the blob with cold things. The cold didn't
destroy it, but it did hold it at bay until they could move it to a place
where it was perpetually cold. That way, it could never cause trouble
again. While they couldn't get rid of the blob, they controlled it by
changing its environment.

That's what God wants us to do with our "blob," our propensity
to sin. We need to change its environment. We cannot feed the flesh
and expect to be victorious in the Spirit. We need to starve the flesh
and feed the spirit, because when we do that, the law of the Spirit will
transcend the law of the flesh.

There is no one forcing us to sin. The devil is a powerful being, but all he can do is tempt and influence us. If you are feeding the spirit within you through prayer, the study of God's Word, and worship participation in a Bible-teaching church, you can overcome the law of sin and death. If you will starve your flesh by denying it the magazines, books, movies, and other enticements it craves, you can tame your wrong desires.

LIVING BY A HIGHER LAW

You say, "Yeah, Tony, I really want to please God. But I'm a man, and you know, there are all these things around me. The world, the flesh, and the devil are really pulling me down."

Well, there is a law called gravity that says, "What goes up must come down." But many years ago the Wright Brothers came up with an idea. They said, "If we can make something go at a certain speed with enough thrust and create an aerodynamic force, we can transcend the law of gravity."

Every time you get on an airplane, those two laws, gravity and aerodynamics, are at work. Guess which one wins? If you're still here, the law of aerodynamics must have overcome the law of gravity. Notice I said overcome, not get rid of. The law of gravity is still very much in force.

But if you'll get moving with the Holy Spirit at the right speed, the law of grace will overrule the law of sin and lift you high so you can be victorious in Christ Jesus. I want to fly; how about you?

No More Second-Rate Marriages

"I'D DO A LOT BETTER IF MY WIFE WOULD JUST
DO WHAT SHE'S SUPPOSED TO DO. SHE'S
CAUSING THE PROBLEM."

One of the first things mamas teach their little kids is, "It's not polite to point." Adam didn't have a mama, but he sure needed to learn that lesson. The first thing Adam did when God confronted him about his sin was point at Eve and say, "She gave me the fruit and told me to eat it; it's her fault." (See Genesis 3:12.) Men have been tempted to blame their wives ever since.

But if there is any area where we as Christian men need to move beyond excusing and blaming to loving and blessing, it's in our marriages. This is where most of the enemy's attacks will come, because Satan's long-term goal is to destroy the whole human race, not just men.

Satan didn't bother Adam before Eve was created. But as soon as Eve came on the scene, the attack was launched. Satan focuses his attacks on the husband-wife relationship because by destroying that, he destroys children and families too. He who controls the family controls the future.

What that means, my brother, is that if we can learn to relate to our wives with love and sensitivity while providing the godly leadership we're responsible to provide, we'll start winning a lot of spiritual battles that Christian men are now losing. And we'll be happier and more fulfilled in the process.

ADJUSTING OUR ATTITUDES

But to get there, we're going to have to change our thinking. We're going to have to stop pointing our fingers at our wives and saying things like, "If I hadn't married you, I'd be successful and important by now." We're going to have to stop buying Satan's lie that it's normal for marriages to go downhill from ecstasy to agony as the years pass.

Some men feel like they made a mistake in getting married. They become disenchanted because their wives turn out to be different than what they thought they were. The story is told of a man who fell in love with an opera singer. He heard her sing and was so enchanted by her voice that he was convinced he could live happily ever after with a woman who could sing like that.

The man was so infatuated that he didn't notice she was considerably older than he, and he didn't seem to care that she walked with a limp. After a whirlwind romance and a hurried ceremony, they were off on their honeymoon.

As the man watched his new bride prepare for their first night together, his chin dropped to his chest. She plucked out her glass eye and dropped it into a container on the night stand. She pulled off her wig, revealing a bald head. She rubbed off her false eyelashes and took out her dentures. Then she unstrapped her artificial leg and took out her hearing aid. Stunned, the man hollered out, "Sing, woman, sing!"

That's how some men feel about their wives. That feeling often comes because men subscribe to the popular version of love and marriage that goes like this: Two young people fall madly in love. They feel chills, thrills, and butterflies in their stomachs. With eyes only for each other, the infatuated pair promise undying love and rush to the altar to seal their vows.

Unfortunately, soon after they say, "I do," they don't anymore. Their relationship looks as if they were married by the secretary of war instead of the justice of the peace. They're like Winston Churchill and his nemesis, Lady Astor. One day she said to him, "Sir, if I were your wife, I would put arsenic in your tea."

Churchill replied, "Madam, if I were your husband, I would drink it!"

Someone has captured this downward spiral in a humorous little scenario concerning the successive stages of the "married cold":

Year One: "Sugar dumpling, this cold is making you mighty uncomfortable. Won't you let your lover boy take his baby to the doctor to get rid of that nasty cough?"

Year Two: "Darling, that cold seems to be getting worse. Call Dr. Miller."

Year Three: "You'd better lie down, dear, and rest with that cold before the baby wakes up."

Year Four: "Be sensible now and take care of that cold before it gets any worse."

Year Five: "You'll be all right. Just take some aspirin. By the way, how about ironing these pants for me to wear today?"

Year Six: "Would you do something about that cough instead of barking like a seal?"

Year Seven: "Woman, do something about that cold before you give me pneumonia!"

That's so close to the truth it hurts. As a marriage decays, the partners start to shift their focus from concern for each other to concern for themselves.

Now since this book is addressed to men I'm going to approach things from the man's side of the issue. But don't get the idea that I'm blaming everything on men or that this is a one-sided problem. It's just that as men, we are called to take the lead in our marriages and not sit around waiting for our wives to get their act together.

Why do so many marriages deteriorate as the years pass? Why do so many marriages fail after ten, fifteen, or even twenty or twenty-five years? I think the answer is that many men simply never learned how to be married. They have never grasped God's design and purpose for them in marriage. So let's start there, which means going back to the beginning of the creation.

WHAT GOD EXPECTS

In Genesis 2:15, God made His will clear to Adam right up front when He put Adam in the garden and appointed him to "work it and take care of it." Then God told him to enjoy all the fruit of the garden, with one famous exception—the tree of the knowledge of good and evil (verses 16-17).

In other words, God taught Adam about work and following instructions before He ever created a mate for him. But these verses point out a major weakness in many homes today: husbands who don't know what God has said. Ask the average man what God has said about his responsibility to his wife, to his children, and to himself as the head of the home, and he will either admit he doesn't know or give an answer that reveals he doesn't know.

And instead of looking to God for answers as to who they are, many men adopt the standards of the culture and base their identity on clothes, cars, cash, or romantic conquests. That reduces manhood to a primitive and degrading level.

But God's definition of manhood is the ability to put divine truth into action at home and on the job. No amount of strength, good looks, or liquid assets can improve a man's performance—not from God's perspective.

So God didn't bring a woman into Adam's life until he had a job and divine insight. Only when Adam had met those two requirements was he ready for marriage. Only then did God say, "It is not good for the man to be alone. I will make a helper suitable for him." (Genesis 2:18)

Creating a mate for Adam was God's idea, not Adam's. That reminds us that all of God's plans are perfect. If you're in a bad marriage, it's not because God had a bad idea. Marriage is His ideal. It's the partners in a marriage who turn it from an ideal into an ordeal, causing them to look for a new deal.

So Adam was a responsible, godly man when the Creator brought him Eve to be his helper. That word *helper* gives you a woman's basic responsibility. She was created to come alongside the man to assist him. She was never meant to bear the burden of responsibility for the home and family.

God laid the responsibility for the home on Adam, not Eve. That's why, even though it was Eve who plucked the forbidden fruit and gave it to her husband, God came looking for Adam. And when Adam tried to pass the blame to Eve, God wasn't buying it.

Whenever a husband shifts the burden of leadership to his wife, he makes a serious mistake. Generally speaking, that gives the wife a level of responsibility God never planned for her to have. God intended and still intends for the husband to carry the weight of the responsibility for his home.

By now you may be saying, "Boy, Tony, you sure are hard on men." You're right. But that's only because men are to be the leaders. As leaders, we are held accountable for our marriages in the same way that Adam was called to account for Eve's surrender to the serpent.

We are also commanded to love our wives the way Christ loves the church. Paul writes:

> Husbands, love your wives, just as Christ loved the church and gave himself up for her to make her holy, cleansing her by the washing with water through the word, and to present her to himself as a radiant church, without stain or wrinkle or any other blemish, but holy and blameless.
>
> —*Ephesians 5:25-27*

Why does God command men to love their wives? Because we are to take the lead in demonstrating the nature and power of unconditional love, the kind of love Christ demonstrated for His church. A husband's love is meant to be so powerful that it transforms his wife into what she should be, just as Christ's love for the church transforms us into what we should be.

That means if our wives have blemishes, it is our job to correct them. But because we men don't understand the theology of marriage, we want to bail out when the going gets tough. However, the weaknesses of our wives provide the perfect context for revealing the reality of God and how powerful the Holy Spirit can be in transforming people. When we demonstrate this kind of sacrificial, servant love, we will see our wives transformed from what they were into what they should be.

A lot of men don't realize that when they married their wives, they married their wives' histories as well. Some women enter marriage deeply bruised and broken from abuse or neglect from previous relationships. Although these scars may be hidden, they are there and sooner or later they will reveal themselves. Drawing on the analogy of Ephesians chapter 5, it is the husband's job to be his wife's "savior" and sanctifier; to bring deliverance that frees her from the pain of the past and leads her into the joy of a glorious new future, just as Christ does for us.

Now make no mistake; this kind of love is tough for many men to pull off. One man said to me, "Man, this stuff is so hard. My wife is crucifying me." To which I responded, "You said you wanted to be like Jesus, didn't you?" Remember that after the crucifixion comes the resurrection.

None of this absolves women from responsibility. God did not command women to love their husbands, maybe because that seems to come naturally to them. But God did command women to respect their husbands (Ephesians 5:33).

Just as women have a need to be loved, men have a need to be respected. That is why Peter tells wives not to use their tongues to turn disobedient husbands around, but rather to use reverence (1 Peter 3:1-2). If each spouse follows the command God gave specifically for the male and female, a couple can become the unit He intended.

Respect is particularly needed by men in the black community. Often black males don't receive respect at their jobs. In a society where many black men are still regarded as "boy" no matter what their age, there needs to be a place where they *know* they are respected. That place should be the home.

The mate God gave you was created to fit together with you in marriage. When God created Adam, He knew that the man was in need of someone similar to himself. Eve was created to make Adam complete, to help him fulfill God's intentions for his life.

Whenever a man says, "I have achieved so much," he ought always to include, "because I have a wife who has enabled me." A godly man will acknowledge his wife's contribution to his success. On every rung of the ladder of success, there is ample room for two sets of feet!

WANTED: A LIFELONG PARTNER

Back in Genesis 2:19-20, notice how God showed Adam that he needed companionship. God set him to work naming the animals. Before long, Adam noticed that for every ram there was a ewe, and for every rooster there was a hen. All of the animals had mates, but for Adam there was no one who could fulfill his needs.

A MATCH MADE IN HEAVEN

Do you know what that means to us as men? It means that *manhood is not the ability to make it alone*. God planned for man to be made complete through marriage. Dedicating yourself in lifelong marriage to one woman is more than a prerequisite for marital survival. It is essential to your complete growth and development. Recognizing your need for your wife isn't a sign of weakness; in fact, it is quite the opposite.

This also reminds us that sexual activity and manhood are not synonymous. Every animal is capable of reproduction. How much "manly strength" does it take to surrender to animal-like urges? Genuine manhood is the ability to see your need for a specific helper and to commit yourself to her alone.

As Adam named species after species of animal, he began to experience a new emotion: loneliness. Then "the LORD God caused the man to fall into a deep sleep" so he could open up Adam's side and remove a rib (Genesis 2:21).

Then God built a woman from Adam's rib. He purposely constructed a woman that man would consider well-fashioned and pleasing. Having done this, God brought Eve to Adam—an example of excellent matchmaking.

MAKING MAN COMPLETE

When Adam awoke and saw God's choice for him, he said, "This is now . . ." (2:23) That seems like it might have been a lame thing to say until we understand that the spirit behind the Hebrew words is joyous astonishment. This could be translated, "Ooooweee!" Here was the solution to his loneliness. Now Adam was like God's other creations, complete with a suitable mate.

After he calmed down, Adam returned to his job of naming God's creatures, calling God's new creation "woman, for she was taken out of man."

From that day on, Adam had a rib missing and Eve had the rib that belonged to Adam. Marriage gave Adam the companionship he missed, and it gave Eve a relationship she had not previously possessed. In God's perfect plan, they made each other complete.

In light of God's plan for wholeness in marriage, one of the most uninformed statements a husband can make is, "My wife and I are not compatible," or "We are as different as night and day." Of course that's true. That's the way God created you. If you were the same, one of you would be unnecessary! The reason you need each other is *because* you are so different.

MAKING MARRIAGE WORK

Adam recognized immediately how distinctly different Eve was from him, and he was excited about those differences. He also knew that Eve was part of him; she made him complete and drove his loneliness away. He called her "bone of my bones and flesh of my flesh." (Genesis 2:23) Since this was a match made in heaven, God went ahead and performed the wedding. And in one verse, the Bible captures the essence of marriage. "For this reason a man will leave his father and mother and be united to his wife, and they will become one flesh." (verse 24). That is marriage in a nutshell: leave, cleave, and become one. The tragedy is that most people have heard these words many times but don't know what they mean.

LEAVING: CLOSING THE DOOR ON THE PAST

The first step in marriage is for the man to "leave" his father and mother. If you are going to marry, you must be willing to sever other ties. Marriage means demonstrating a willingness to give up everything because, as Adam said, "This is now!"

A lot of men today don't have any problem leaving Mom and Dad when they get married, but they aren't really willing to leave behind their former way of life. For example, they want to be married but still do all the things with their buddies they did when they were single.

I think a lot of guys get married with the idea that now they will have to work a wife into their schedule. They don't understand what it means to "leave" in the biblical sense, to sever any and all ties that would come ahead of their wives.

Now obviously, we don't have to dump all of our friends when we get married. But the man who goes into marriage without planning to sever any ties, cut back on any activities, or give up anything for his wife doesn't know what marriage is about.

God asks a man to give up his closest ties because one of a woman's greatest needs in marriage is security. Often when a wife asks her husband to hold her, he misinterprets that as a request for physical intimacy. But if the need for security is on her mind, she is not thinking about physical desires.

Because a wife needs to feel secure, a husband must leave his parents and his other former ties. There must be something he gives up for his wife to demonstrate to her how deep a commitment he is willing to make. When he does that, he will begin to understand what marriage is all about.

CLEAVING: LOVING TO THE LIMIT

Second, a husband must "cleave" to his wife. This word means to stick like glue, or to attach oneself in a vise-like grip.

In marriage, this is more than a physical attachment. It is not only union with a physical body; it's union with a whole person, body and soul. Too often a man's "Let me love you" means "Let me please me." To cleave to a woman is to work toward pleasing her, not yourself.

To some men, this sounds more like slavery than mere sacrifice. But there is a special way in which leaving and cleaving provides exactly what most men want in their marriages. Look at the end of Genesis 2:24: "They will become one flesh." The pronoun has changed from "he" to "they."

God says if a man will leave and cleave, he and his wife will become one flesh. That's a promise. If a husband leaves and cleaves the way God intended, his wife will respond the way he (and God) wants her to respond.

God made the woman to be a responder. He made her a little softer, a little warmer, a little more emotional in order to respond to the man. In other words, when a husband leaves his other ties and cleaves to his wife, she will join him and begin to respond to him so that the very thing the husband wants will be received by giving rather than by demanding.

God does not want a wife to love her husband and respond to him because the man demands it. God wants her to do it as a response to her husband's overloading her emotional circuits with tender loving care. I tell many men who come to me for marital counseling, "Stop pushing so hard, and start loving a little more. Stop complaining so much, and start loving a little harder."

If a husband lets his wife know she is loved, and if he makes her feel secure, he won't have to worry about her fulfilling her responsibility at home. He won't have to worry about their physical relationship. She will be right there, responding to his needs.

Now you may be saying, "I'm trying. How come my wife isn't

responding?" Well, it may have to do with the different emotional "wiring" of men and women. A man can become angry with his wife at 10:00 A.M. and be ready to kiss and make up by 10:30. But if a wife becomes angry with her husband at 10:00 A.M., she may still be angry at 10:00 P.M.—and maybe at 10:00 P.M. a week later! Her emotions take much longer to stabilize.

A husband can shorten that recovery time significantly if he takes the time to learn how it can be done. It requires a decision to love with or without response, no matter how difficult the process. For many husbands, love like that will require an apology: "I've failed. I haven't loved you the way I am supposed to love you, and I know it has affected our relationship. I'm going to change. I'm going to love you the way you need to be loved."

It's going to take that kind of commitment to succeed in marriage. For some men, that will be a new decision; for others it will be a continuation of a commitment already made. But whether the decision is new or old, it will be worth it.

Now if you think this idea of cleaving puts too much weight on our shoulders as husbands, remember that the responsibility is already ours, as we saw in Ephesians 5:25-27. And never forget that we benefit immensely when we become one flesh with our wives. Leaving and cleaving beats blaming and excusing any day of the week!

BECOMING ONE: GETTING BACK TO WHERE YOU WERE

God concludes the description of marriage by saying, "The man and his wife were both naked, and they felt no shame." (Genesis 2:25) This is much broader than just physical nakedness. Adam and Eve were transparent, open to one another in friendship.

You may say, "Yeah, that's the kind of marriage I'd like to have. I'd love for my wife to be my best friend. I wish we could share our total selves with each other. But it may be too late for us. Can my marriage be revived?"

The answer is a resounding yes! In fact, the formula for success is quite simple, although the application may be difficult. It is the same formula Christ gave to the church at Ephesus, which had lost its zeal for one another and for the Lord: "Remember the height from which you have fallen! Repent and do the things you did at first." (Revelation 2:5)

The relationship between Christ and the believers in that church had become so dead that He was ready to walk out and leave them to their loveless rituals. That's the way a lot of husbands and wives feel about their marriages. But Christ offered them a formula for reviving their first love: remember, repent, and repeat.

First, the Ephesians were to remember their previous situation. They needed to reflect on the early days when love ruled their lives. Can you remember that time in your marriage? Do you remember how you used to open the car door for your sweetheart? Now she's lucky to get in before you drive off. We tend to forget the things we did in those early days of marriage. Then we wonder why our wives don't respond to us as the caring, loving, and thoughtful men we think we are.

The point is, if you will go back and remember how your marriage was at one time, you're taking the first step toward making it that way again—or even better.

Second, the formula calls for repentance. To confess that you are wrong is tough, especially when words are not enough. To repent means not only to change your thinking, but to change the actions that result from your thinking. To repent is to turn and go in the opposite direction, the right direction.

In this case, the right direction is probably back to the early stages of your marriage. The right direction is the one in which your wife takes precedence over your career, your friends, your own interests, and anyone or anything else on earth.

Finally, the church at Ephesus was told to repeat the works it did at first. For you and me as husbands, that means bringing the works of the past into the present and the future simply by repeating them in a consistent, loving fashion.

We've already talked about some of those "first works" in terms of leaving and cleaving. They may also include starting to date your wife again, sending her those special notes, flowers, and cards you sent when you were trying to win her. It may mean giving her time away from the kids.

I often tell husbands to quit being so boring, so predictable. Remember how spontaneous you were when you were dating your wife? You were always doing the unexpected, springing little surprises on her. Now you say, "Where do you want to go tonight?" That's not very creative.

For a lot of men who have become insensitive to the need for courtesy toward their wives, the first works of marriage may include opening the car door, helping her up the steps, or complimenting her. Granted, it may be a little tougher now, since you're out of practice. But it's a question of how much you want the feelings of love back. The prize is worth the effort.

I know some men will say it's their wife's fault, and that therefore she should do the remembering, repenting, and repeating. That's probably not altogether true, since it usually takes two to mess up a marriage.

But even if that were 100 percent true, it's still no excuse for us as husbands to do nothing. Why? Because our model is Jesus Christ, who bore the penalty for our sins even though He was innocent. Following His example may take a willingness to go to the limit to win our wives back.

I realize that following this formula will not be easy. That's where your dependence on the Holy Spirit comes in. Without the enabling of God's Spirit, you are merely trying by human effort to produce a supernatural response. But God can give you the power to accomplish whatever He commands through the Holy Spirit's work.

We husbands are to love our wives whether we feel like it or not, because God commands it and the Holy Spirit can accomplish it in us if we will yield to His power by faith.

How to Love Your Wife

We've talked about the importance of understanding and loving and supporting your wife, so let me bring this down to a final focus.

In 1 Peter 3:7, the apostle gives husbands some very important insight into their wives and how to treat them:

> Husbands, in the same way be considerate as you live with your wives, and treat them with respect as the weaker partner and as heirs with you of the gracious gift of life, so that nothing will hinder your prayers.

THE PERFECT EXAMPLE

Whenever the Bible says "in the same way" or "likewise," you know the writer is building off of something that came before. Peter does the same thing in 3:1 when he says to wives, "In the same way be submissive to your husbands." What Peter is referring to is the end of chapter 2, where he paints a magnificent portrait of Christ as our suffering Redeemer.

Notice especially how relevant these verses are to the marriage relationship. Christ "suffered for you, leaving you an example, that you should follow in his steps." (2:21) So husbands who are suffering with their wives can't go around thinking, "Yeah, well, that's Jesus. If I were Jesus I could live with her too."

No, no, my brother. We are to follow "in his steps." It gets even better in verse 23: "When they hurled their insults at him, he did not retaliate; when he suffered, he made no threats."

Jesus could have said, "I'm not going to have any human beings talking to *Me* this way. I'm not going to *have* them treating Me this way. Don't they know who I am? I could take them out with a word." Jesus could have done that, but when He was messed over, He didn't retaliate or make threats.

Instead, He "bore our sins in his body on the tree . . . by his wounds you have been healed." (verse 24) Notice that He got the wounds or stripes, but we get the healing.

SACRIFICE, SACRIFICE

Now when you put this all together in relation to the way a husband is to treat his wife, what you get is an incredible picture of an amazing sacrificial, selfless, and gracious love.

Could it be that the only way some husbands will win back their wives is by the stripes these husbands are willing to bear? When you are willing to bear stripes for someone else, that's when you start to understand the meaning of love.

Now you are not going to hear that on the street, I guarantee you. No one is going to go on a TV talk show and tell about how he was willing to suffer to love and nurture his wife. The word on the streets to men is, "You give the stripes, you don't take them."

TO KNOW HER IS TO LOVE HER

Peter also says we are to be understanding toward our wives. What he means is that we should study them. The Bible tells men to study the Word and their wives. Both can be difficult to interpret and understand, but both richly repay the effort! I'm afraid we give very little time to really getting to know our wives.

Women are very complicated and often hard to understand. When they are experiencing the emotions and mood swings that come with changes in their bodies, it's easy for a husband to react with irritation and anger, especially when his wife doesn't respond the way he thinks she should. I'm not saying it's easy to deal with that, but then it's not easy for your wife either. You'll get a lot further with understanding than you will with the kind of irritation that pushes her away and says, "I don't want anything to do with you when you're like this." Peter says to study your wife, to learn to read her movements and emotions so you can respond with understanding instead of rejection.

LOVE, HONOR, AND CHERISH

Peter continues by saying we husbands are to grant our wives honor. That means lifting them up, pampering them the way we did when we were dating. Notice that Peter doesn't say, "Work at changing your wife." If you are trying to change your wife instead of honoring her, you are messing up.

You may be saying, "Oh, I get the deal. I'm to honor my wife so she will change into being the person I want her to be."

No, that's not the deal. True love, *agape* love, does what is needed for the person loved whether or not the one doing the loving receives anything in return. Besides, our ultimate goal should be to help our wives become what God wants them to be, not what we want them to be.

Now if you truly love and honor your wife, it will change her. But don't expect it to happen in a week. If it took you five years to mess up your marriage, it may take you five years of pampering to fix it. I don't know.

What I am saying is that you need to be willing to love your wife the way Christ loved you, and that may involve taking some stripes and some abuse in order to put things back on track.

Peter calls the wife the "weaker partner" or the "weaker vessel." When she has to work and then come home and cook and take care of you and the kids, her emotional circuits get overloaded. Then you get mad because she is not loving and available to you at bedtime.

But that's saying your desires and needs are more important than hers, which is not treating her as an equal, as a fellow heir of the grace of life. You are the leader in the home, but your wife is every bit your equal in essence and in worth before God.

One reason we are to live with our wives in a loving, understanding, and sacrificial way is so that "nothing will hinder [our] prayers." (1 Peter 3:7c) If we are not honoring our wives, if we are not willing to take stripes for them, if we are not loving them as Christ loves the church, then we may as well get off our knees.

But what a reward we have when we learn to love our wives as our own bodies. Remember, God doesn't take our love and give us nothing in return. As we love and honor our wives, they will blossom and develop into women of grace and true beauty. Then we will experience the kind of fulfilling love that a lot of married people think is beyond their grasp.

A Perfect Union

The Trinity is made up of three co-equal Persons. One God who makes Himself known to us as God the Father, God the Son, and God the Holy Spirit. Marriage is an earthly replica of this divine trinity, three persons who are "three-in-one": a man, a woman, and God. You cannot leave God at the altar and expect to have a happy marriage.

Christ's resurrection power operating in your life is the only power that can save your life, your marriage, and your home. When Christ arose from the dead, He gave you access to the power of His resurrection. That power can enable you and your wife to love one another, trust each other, and share life together until death parts you. God alone can give you the ability to do that.

It's the power of God operating in your life that makes marriage work. If you haven't made that personal decision to turn the totality of your life—including your marriage—over to Jesus Christ, you don't have that resurrection power.

But you can have that power if you believe Christ rose from the dead to help you be the kind of husband He has called you to be. When you give Him your life, then you will experience marriage as God intended it to be. He made marriage, and He can make it work.

I challenge you, as one brother to another, to commit yourself without reservation to the Lord. Give Him your marriage, and let Him remake it in His image. Then you won't need any more excuses.

· TEN ·

NO MORE PASSIVE FATHERING

"HEY, I PUT FOOD ON THE TABLE AND TAKE MY
KIDS TO CHURCH. WHAT ELSE CAN I DO?
THEY'LL TURN OUT ALL RIGHT."

The story is told of an eagle flying over a river in the wintertime and noticing a large chunk of ice floating down the river. The eagle landed on the ice to relax for a minute, even though there was a steep waterfall ahead. He knew he had plenty of time to fly away before the ice chunk plunged over the fall.

But as the eagle stood on the ice, his feet froze to it. Then, as the chunk of ice got near the waterfall and the eagle tried to fly away, he discovered that he was stuck. So over the waterfall went the ice and the eagle, because he waited a little too long to do something about his situation.

That's a pretty accurate picture of American fatherhood today. Most dads are content to ride the ice chunk as long as things seem to be going along all right.

Here's a very common scenario. Mom goes to Dad and says, "You need to talk to your son. He's getting real sassy and giving me a hard time." But Dad doesn't want to confront Junior and have one of those knock-down-and-drag-out emotional brawls. He figures as long as Junior's not getting suspended from school or arrested, he'll be fine. Every kid lips off to his mother once in a while.

So Dad hides behind the paper or goes back to channel surfing, while Mother is left to deal with Junior. Then when the call comes that Junior is in trouble at school or with the law, Dad finally gets stirred out of his recliner because now he has to go down and bail his offspring out of the clink. Dad's also very frustrated because he's wondering, "What happened?"

If that scenario more or less describes your situation with your kids, I want to show you a better way from God's Word. I want to help you get beyond the excuse that you're too busy or too tired or too whatever to keep up with what's going on in their lives.

I also want to disabuse you of the notion that raising children is really kind of the woman's thing anyway. After all, women are made for that nurturing stuff, aren't they?

SILENT NO MORE

Yes, they are, but so are you! In fact, we're going to see that when God's Word addresses the issue of raising and nurturing children, the instruction is given *primarily* to fathers.

Ephesians 6:1-4 is a classic example:

> Children, obey your parents in the Lord, for this is right. "Honor your father and mother"—which is the first commandment with a promise—"that it may go well with you and that you may enjoy long life on the earth." Fathers, do not exasperate your children; instead, bring them up in the training and instruction of the Lord.

Paul is writing in the context of a Roman society completely dominated by men. Wives were like slaves at the fathers' feet, and so were the children. A father in ancient Rome had the right to get rid of his child at birth if he didn't want it for any reason whatever. The father could take his baby to the forum and lay it on the ground, where someone might come along and buy the infant to raise as a prostitute or slave. That's the context in which Paul is writing.

Now you say, "Hey, wait a minute. That was terrible. I would never do that to my children." I didn't think so. I would never do that either. But a lot of Christian fathers who would never harm their children physically are discarding them emotionally and spiritually by being the silent partner in their nurture and training.

Dad is too busy out working or playing. And even when he's home, he doesn't really want to be bothered with the details. It's easier to let the kids watch TV, because too often Dad is watching TV too.

It's like the father who took his son to the toy store. He asked the salesman to help his son find a toy he would like and that would keep him quiet and out of Dad's way. The salesman showed the boy every toy in the store, and the kid turned up his nose at every one of them.

The father got frustrated and started complaining to the salesman about his inability to find what the boy wanted. The salesman looked at the father and said, "Mister, we don't sell what your son really needs. He needs a dad."

With this kind of uninvolved fathering, what we are getting is a generation of children being raised on the world's values. Now a father may say, "Well, I tell them what to do." That's fine, but it's not enough just to say it. The reason it's not enough is because children are born in sin, just like you and me. Given the opportunity, apart from Jesus Christ they will do what they are not supposed to do. Their bent is toward sin.

That's why you *never* have to teach a kid how to lie or be selfish. He's already got that down.

INSTRUCTION "OF THE LORD"

Now you may read the first three verses of Ephesians 6 and say, "Amen, brother, preach it. I want my kids to read this stuff." Paul does tell children to obey their parents, but he tells them to do it "in the Lord." That means you have to instruct them in the things of the Lord if they are going to do what is right.

Your children need the right information and the right application. You can't leave them to themselves and expect someone else to teach them. If it isn't you, it will be the TV or their peer group or a secularist educator or someone else out there. But make no mistake, they will learn about life somewhere.

Now you can't know what is right until you know what God said about it. So you need to be hanging around where the Bible is being taught and be in the Word yourself. Our assignment as fathers is to instruct our children in how they ought to live under God's authority, to submit to Him. This is what "submit" means—to put yourself under someone else's authority.

That's important because remember, even though they will move out from under our authority someday, they will always need to be under God's authority. In fact, this is the first problem we face. No one wants to be under anyone's authority.

Kids used to say, "You ain't my mama. You ain't my daddy. Don't tell me what to do." Problem is, in today's world kids don't want their mamas or daddies telling them anything either. Our children are living in a world that models and encourages rebellion.

If that bothers you as much as it bothers me, let's find out what we can do about it as fathers. In fact, just recognizing the problem and committing ourselves to counter it is half the battle.

HONOR STARTS WITH YOU

Ephesians 6:2 instructs children to honor their parents. There isn't much mystery about the word *honor*. It means to hold in high esteem, to treat with reverence and respect.

My father has always commanded my respect. Today, even though I'm a grandfather too, I do *not* go home and get overly familiar—"Say, Arthur, what's happening?" I just can't do it. The man would just stare at me. It's "Dad" or "Sir" or some other term that tells him I respect his position.

Kids need their fathers to help them understand that you are the adult and they are the child, and that they are to respect adults. In time, they are going to get that right. But what we dads need to do in the meantime is be consistent, teach it, expect it, and encourage it.

In teaching our children to honor us we are teaching them ultimately to honor God. Why? There are several good reasons for it, according to our text.

First, "for this is right." (Ephesians 6:1) God says, "I'm not telling you something wrong. When you teach your children according to My ways, it pleases Me. And when I am pleased, I will bless you." Since God Himself is the standard of what's right, it's right to teach our children His ways because He commands us to do it.

Second, there's a promise of long life attached to this. Paul is going back to Exodus chapter 20, where the Ten Commandments were given. Read the list, and you'll see that the first four commandments deal with our relationship to God: "You shall have no other gods before me," "You shall not make for yourself an idol," and so on. Then the fifth commandment becomes a transition because it deals with family: "Honor your father and your mother" (Exodus 20:12). The promise is then stated, "so that you may live long in the land," and the rest of the commandments deal with personal relationships.

Why did God make a special promise to children who obeyed their parents? The reason, I think, is this: God knew that children properly nurtured in a home would become the strengthening fiber in society. If respect for authority, reverence, and honor did not start in the home, it would never get to the street. And if it never hit the street, it would never touch the community. And if it didn't touch the community, it wouldn't affect the city. And if didn't affect the city, it would never move on to the state. And if didn't move on to the state, it would never permeate the country.

Eventually a whole country undergoes a collapse that started because some kid didn't want to do what Dad said. Now we don't look at it that way because we are like the frogs in the pot, neither knowing nor caring that the water is slowly being brought to a boil under us.

We say, "Well, one kid not obeying his parents isn't going to bring down the United States of America." Maybe, but try fifteen or twenty million disobedient young people!

The Ephesians 6:2-3 text reminds us that honor isn't just some nice little concept we teach to help polish our kids' manners and keep them from being rude. Literally, honor has the power of life and death in it.

But let's turn this around for a minute, because if we're going to be worthy of honor as fathers, we'd better take a reading of our "honor quotient" toward *our* parents.

For us, honor means two basic things. We've already mentioned the first one, to hold our parents in high esteem and treat them with reverence. So we have no right to speak to them any way we want just because we're adults ourselves. That doesn't mean you have to agree with them, but it does mean that you have to disagree in honor.

The second thing honor can mean is financial help and/or personal care. I believe we as Christian men are responsible to support our parents. It will be our turn soon enough.

A LIFE-CHANGING PURPOSE

Before we go on to Ephesians 6:4, I want to go back for a minute and pick up the thought of a nation's destiny being determined in large measure by the quality of spiritual instruction in the home. I want to show you the larger purpose God had in mind when He commanded fathers to instruct their children in His truth.

Deuteronomy 6:4 may be the single most important statement of this truth in the entire Old Testament. It's the declaration of the utter uniqueness of Israel's God: "The LORD our God, the LORD is one." The next verse is indispensable too, according to Jesus (see Matthew 22:37), "Love the LORD your God with all your heart and with all your soul and with all your strength." But notice the very next thing God commands in verses 6-9. Let me summarize:

"Now, fathers, go home and train your children in My truth. Train them when they wake up. Train them when they lie down. Train them in between their waking up and lying down. Train them formally. Train them informally. I want My truth tied on their foreheads. I want them to bump into My truth when they come into the house and when they leave the house."

Why? Because God wanted Israel to be different from all the other nations. He wanted Israel to be a people built on truth and righteousness, love and respect, and on worshiping God as opposed to the world around them.

But that's not the way things are today. We have even Christian kids acting like all the other kids in the neighborhood. We have parents saying, "I love Johnnie, so I don't spank him." Excuse me, but with that attitude you hate him. Do you know what the Bible says about God? "Whom the Lord loveth, he skins alive." That's another Evans rendering of Hebrews 12:6. It means that God lights your fire if He loves you.

My father would tell me, "I want you home at 10:00 P.M. That's not 10:01. You be in here at 10:00, or it's fire!" I would get upset and say, "Why do I have to be in here at 10:00? My friends are making fun of me. They can stay out until 2:00 and 3:00 in the morning." And Dad would say, "Well, maybe their parents don't care. But I care. Be in here at 10:00."

When I go back to Baltimore where I grew up, guess where many of those guys are? Still hanging out on the corner until 2:00 and 3:00 in the morning. I can trace where I am today back to a father who had a hold on me, who disciplined me, and who would not let me have my way all the time.

I'm in love with Jesus Christ today because of it. I didn't get involved in drugs and all of those things the other guys were getting involved in because I had become accountable to my father at home.

YOU EITHER BUILD THEM UP—OR BREAK THEM DOWN

Now we're ready to talk about verse 4 of Ephesians chapter 6. Good fathers don't let their kids run things, but they also know they can't provoke or exasperate children and expect them to come out right.

As a father, I think I know why Paul spoke to fathers. All things being equal, Dad's the first one to get mad and the one most likely to react by coming down hard. So we dads need to ask, what are some ways we can provoke or anger our kids?

One way is by overparenting or smothering them. This is not a problem fathers are usually guilty of as much as mothers, but it is a possibility and needs to be mentioned.

Favoritism is another spirit-killer for your kids: "Why can't you be more like your brother?" This sort of constant comparison can be a real temptation, for example, if you have one son who is athletic and another who is more artistic. Depending on your own preference, you can end up frustrating the son who doesn't meet your idea of what a man should be and do.

You can also anger children by forcing your unfulfilled dreams on them. "I didn't get to be an entomologist, son, but you are going to be an entomologist." But what if your son doesn't like bugs?

Discouragement, criticism, and the withholding of approval are several other prime ways we can exasperate our children. Be careful not to puncture your kids' hopes and dreams. Try not to focus too much on what they're *not* doing. Don't be afraid of words of approval and affirmation. In fact, affirm them often. You rarely hear a man say his mother never once affirmed him when he was young. But the men who say that about their fathers are legion.

I've got to mention one more way we provoke our children because it's a biggie in the 1990s: failure to sacrifice. By that I mean fathers who send the message to their kids that "I need fulfillment now. You are in my way." For a lot of modern fathers, their kids *are* in their way. They are stopping Dad from doing what he wants to do.

Often we fathers are called upon not only to choose between our children and our work, but between our convenience and the inconvenience of keeping a promise. I remember one occasion when I promised my son I would be there for his final football game of the season. I knew how important it was to my son that I be there, but on the day of the game an emergency arose that demanded I leave Dallas and go to Houston. I was between a rock and a hard place. So I decided to inconvenience myself. I went to Houston, flew back to Dallas for the second half of my son's game, and then flew back to Houston for the rest of the emergency meeting.

Now thankfully, Ephesians 6:4 has a flip side. If you're not to anger your children, what do you do? Two things: you train and discipline them (same idea), and you instruct them.

Train means you give your children rules with resultant rewards and punishment. The expectations are clear, and you create an environment where the kids are helped to succeed, not set up to fail.

Instruct is the teaching of God's Word. This means, as I said above, that dads have to be in the Word and living the Word themselves.

My brother, I believe that most Christian fathers sincerely want to build good Christian homes. They want to keep their promises to their wives and children. I remember the story Howard Hendricks, my prof at Dallas Seminary, always told about the guy who heard him talk about having family devotions and a family altar. This man decided that's what his family needed. So he asked Professor Hendricks if they sold those family altars at the bookstore.

At least that dad was willing to invest some bucks in building a Christian home. You'll never have a home that is Christian if you are not willing to invest your time in your children. You can't have it if all you want to do is watch television. You can't have it if you don't want to learn God's Word and find out how to teach it to the kids.

Dad, you cannot have children who will honor you and obey God if you don't want to invest time and energy in them and in the ministry of your church, where your efforts are supported and enhanced by the work of God's people.

But if you're willing, God has given you a staggering promise. It will be well with your children, and well with you.

GOOD MAN / BAD DAD

Let me shift gears and go from precept to example by looking at the story of the Old Testament priest Eli and his two boys (1 Samuel 2–4). But you can tell from the subhead that this is not a happy-ending kind of story. Eli did a bad job of fathering, and we can learn a lot from his bad example.

The sad story of Eli and his sons is set in contrast to the story of little Samuel, who was sent to live with Eli and serve the Lord at a very young age.

If you remember the story, Samuel's mother, Hannah, was barren and cried out to the Lord for a child. If God would give her a son, she promised to give her boy back to God to serve Him all of his life.

When Samuel was weaned, Hannah brought him to Eli at the temple in Shiloh. So here was little Samuel, serving the Lord. But right down the hall were the bedrooms of Hophni and Phinehas, the no-good, wicked, grown-up sons of Eli who had no regard for the Lord (2 Samuel 2:12). They were the preacher's kids, messing around while Dad faithfully served the Lord. Ouch!

A Passive Father Produces Out-of-Control Kids

By the time we meet Eli's family, his boys were assisting him in the ministry of the temple. They were going to church with him every Sunday. They were wearing the veneer because Dad was the holy man of Israel.

But these brothers had a racket going. They were dipping their hands in the offering plate; only it wasn't money they were taking. They were taking more of the sacrifices than the priest's rightful share. If anyone called them on the scam, he would be threatened by force. And that's not all; the sons were also seducing the women who served at the entrance to the temple.

By now you are probably saying, "Please, tell me what Eli did or didn't do as a father so I can run as far and as fast the other way as possible." Well, Eli was a man of God. No question about that. But evidently he didn't take a strong hand in training his sons. Maybe they ran wild around the temple, getting into trouble. We don't know.

How many times have you been in the grocery store or mall and heard a parent say to a screaming, obnoxious two-year-old who's pitching a fit, "Now, now, don't do that, dear. Here, let's stop that."

Meanwhile, the kid is wreaking havoc. I don't know if that's how Eli got started with Hophni and Phinehas when they were young. We're not given any details of their childhood. What we have here in 1 Samuel is the bottom line, which is this: Eli's sons were vile before the Lord, and he did absolutely nothing about it.

Now it's true that he did speak to them:

> So he said to them, "Why do you do such things? I hear from all the people about these wicked deeds of yours. No, my sons; it is not a good report that I hear spreading among the LORD's people. If a man sins against another man, God may mediate for him; but if a man sins against the LORD, who will intercede for him?" His sons, however, did not listen to their father's rebuke, for it was the LORD's will to put them to death.
>
> —2:23-25

Eli heard about the terrible things his sons were doing and said, "Now, boys, you ought not do that. No, no. Bad, bad."

And the boys said, "Yes, Daddy," then went right back to robbing the people who came to the temple and misusing the women. And from all indications, Eli just turned away from it (look ahead to 3:12-14).

DON'T JUST STAND THERE—DO SOMETHING!

The issue was not that Eli didn't tell his children the right things, for clearly he did. It's that he didn't *enforce* the right things he was telling them. I don't know any parents who go out and tell their kids, "Go rob a bank. Go find someone to kill. Ten or twenty years in prison will do you good." I suspect you don't know any parents like that either.

No, the parents we know probably say the right things, just as Eli did. A lot of prison inmates' parents probably said the right things too. But what is missing in so much of our well-intentioned parenting is enforcement, which represents the strength of our convictions.

Eli was not enforcing the truth. He was only stating it. He didn't pull his sons from their posts; he didn't strip them of their privileged access to the temple and to the people of Israel. He knew what they were doing, but he let them keep on doing it while mouthing platitudes that they should stop.

Discipline includes more than telling your children what they *ought* to do. We talked about that earlier. The reason that telling isn't good enough is that our kids are born in sin. And you do not leave sinners to decide things for themselves because they will inevitably go the wrong way.

When my son was little and decided he wanted to touch a fire, I told him, "Don't put your hand in the fire." Not only that, but as he approached the fire I restrained him from touching it. Now that does not mean that at some later point, he might not touch the fire anyway. But in my love for him, I enforced my telling with some concrete restraint.

It takes more than saying the right thing to get the job done. If we are going to get the results God wants, we must lovingly discipline our children. Discipline is one test of God's love, as we learned in Hebrews 12:6. One way you know God loves you is that He doesn't just let you go on in your sin without doing anything about it.

Now I can't stop all the neighbors' kids from messing up because they are not part of my family. But my kids, that's a whole different story because I love them. If you want to love your children the way God loves His children, chastening and correcting have to be part of the equation.

Love means you'd better say something. And if that doesn't take care of the problem, you'd better *do* something. If you love me and you see that I'm destroying myself, yet you keep quiet, you're killing me. The most loving thing a parent or any spiritual leader can do is chastise in love.

The writer of Hebrews drives home his point about fathers and discipline in the home in Hebrews 12:8—"If you are not disciplined (and everyone undergoes discipline), then you are illegitimate children and not true sons."

Have you ever had kids in the neighborhood who come to your house and act like they live there? Your kids bring some kids home to play and it's fine at first. They come in and all they want is a little glass of water. But after a while it gets out of hand, and mom has to make it known that this is not a hotel and she's not a bellhop. The reason you do that is because the neighbor's kids don't have legitimate rights to that freedom. Your children have the right to partake of your home because they are part of your family. But then they also get to partake of your discipline.

DISCIPLINE OR DESTRUCTION

One of the Bible's inescapable principles is that when you walk away from the will and the Word of God, you walk toward death. Now I don't necessarily mean you are going to die and go to the grave. That's a possibility, but what I'm talking about is spiritual death. The "Father of our spirits" (Hebrews 12:9) is responsible for spiritual life. When you walk away from Him, then you move toward the realm of spiritual death.

One thing that can bring us closer to God or push us away is His discipline. When He chastens us, we have two options. We can say, "I'm not serving You anymore." Or we can say, "I get the message."

If we choose option one, God has some work to do. There comes a time when He has to say like any good father, "If you don't want to abide by My rules, you cannot live in My house."

My brother was a Maryland state wresting champion in the unlimited weight division. He was a pretty big fellow, basically all muscle. My father chastised him one day, and my brother got hot. He decided he was a state wrestling champion and he didn't have to take that.

So my brother decided to leave home. He didn't want any more of his father's discipline. He wanted to come in when he wanted to come in and to do what he wanted to do. He didn't want anyone telling him how high to jump.

My father told him, "As long as you are in this house, I set the rules. So you can either stay here and live according to my rules, or you can go out there and make it on your own."

My brother said, "I'm leaving! I don't have to take this!"

Then he packed and left. About fifteen hours later, he was back on the porch wanting to come home, because after he got out there on the streets it occurred to him he didn't have anywhere to go. He had no money, no job, and no car. He tried a couple of his buddies, who talked bad about not taking anything from the old man, but they weren't there to help him.

So my brother came back home and submitted to our father after he found out that home was where life really was. The message he got on the streets was that real life was on the streets. But it wasn't. It was at home, where he had a father who loved him and disciplined him in the Lord. Life is where God's Word is being obeyed and applied.

God decided that since Eli's sons were not living by His rules, they could no longer live in His house. But their discipline was much more severe than simply being put out on the street.

They went too far, and God said it was time to get rid of them. Their deaths were prophesied (1 Samuel 2:34), and they did in fact die when the Philistines captured the ark. Unfortunately, they took their father Eli with them (see 4:17-18).

Eli's failure as a parent led to the destruction of the whole family, including the in-laws (verses 19-21). And if you read all of 1 Samuel chapter 4, you'll see that this became much more than the saga of one family. It became a case of national disaster for Israel, showing how sin entering one house can destroy everything. The name of the boy born to Phinehas's wife says it all: Ichabod, "The glory has departed from Israel" (see 1 Samuel 4:21).

LEADING THE WAY TO A GODLY HOME

So what do we do as fathers in light of all this? We enforce the truth in love, we discipline, and we chasten. We do our best under God to be consistent, not like the mother I heard of who kept calling her son. Every time she called, he ignored her. This went on for a while until finally his playmate looked at him and said, "Your mother's calling you. Aren't you going home?" "Not yet," the boy responded.

This mother had trained her son to know that she didn't really mean "come in" the first time she called. She meant, "I am now start-ing a process that will ultimately lead to your coming in sometime in the future." Wrong message.

The last chapter in the life of a failed father often isn't pretty, as Eli shows. He lived to see his sons die and the ark of the covenant, the symbol of God's presence among His people, captured by the Philistines. And that was the last thing he lived to see.

In case you may be feeling a little overwhelmed by now, let me draw a spiritual parallel that I hope will encourage you. The world is still doing to us the same thing the Philistines were successful in doing to Israel. The world is trying to take the ark of God—His glory, His presence, His power—out of our homes. The weapons are not swords and spears, but the battle is just as intense. Using weapons like the media and popular entertainment, the forces of darkness are seeking to make our kids reflect the values not of God but of the world.

The good news is, this doesn't have to happen. You may not be able to change Hollywood, but you can do something just as effective. You can turn off Hollywood in your home!

What Christian fathers like you and I need to do is to step for-ward in our homes and claim them for Jesus Christ. We need to write over our houses not "The glory has departed," but "As for me and my household, we will serve the LORD." (Joshua 24:15) Like they tell the men at Promise Keepers rallies, "Men, we're in a war, but a lot of us have not been *at* war."

Read Ephesians 6:10-17 and realize that we've got the right weapons and that we're on the side that's *already* won.

Now if we're going to fight a good fight for our kids, we need to get our own act together. Children don't mind following someone who's showing by example how it's done and who's doing it with them. Dad, are you ready to lead the way? Then let's get after it!

· ELEVEN ·

NO MORE
SISSIFIED MALES

"SOCIETY AND THE FEMINISTS HAVE TAKEN
AWAY MEN'S LEADERSHIP ROLE, AND
THEY WON'T GIVE IT BACK TO US."

Men, we face a crisis. The very concept of manhood has been taking a beating. In their attempts not to appear Neanderthal about the whole thing, a lot of men have rolled with the punches and played dead when it comes to their manhood. The political and social climate has become an excuse not to exercise their God-given role of leadership.

Any way you look at it, manhood is in a crisis. But the crisis I'm talking about has little to do with what you see and hear. The crisis of manhood is a theological crisis.

MISUNDERSTANDING WHAT IT MEANS TO BE MALE

By theological crisis, I mean that we have misconstrued what God has said on the topic of gender, and in particular the meaning of maleness. And having misconstrued God's intentions for the genders, we have misconstrued how the world works. Then when we try to make the world work according to our faulty view, we find that it doesn't work.

The Apostle Paul made this foundational statement: "Now I want you to realize that the head of every man is Christ, and the head of the

woman is man, and the head of Christ is God." (1 Corinthians 11:3)
Paul says that God has designed creation to function by means of a
hierarchy—that is, a chain of command.

The last part of that verse helps us out a great deal, because it
says that Christ is subordinate to God the Father. So it's not a matter
of inequality, because the Son is equal in essence to the Father. Instead,
it's a matter of function, of the management of creation. God the
Father calls the shots, and Christ the Son is obedient to the Father.

When Christ was on earth, He said over and over that He came
to do the Father's will (see John 4:34). Jesus never made a decision or
a plan, never purposed a direction, that was not in keeping with the
Father's will.

Now when Paul says that "the head of every man is Christ," he is
talking to Christian men. We know this because he is writing to the
church. Obviously, the unbelieving world is not under Christ.

For believers, therefore, authority flows from God the Father to
Christ, and then from Christ to the man. If Jesus Christ had disobeyed
his Father, there would have been no plan of salvation. And if those
of us now under Christ had disobeyed the Lord, we would have no
salvation.

Then Paul says in 1 Corinthians 11:3 that "the head of the
woman is man." This is what I call God's covenantal chain; that is, this
is how authority is supposed to flow in creation. That's why in the second chapter of Genesis, God created the man and then from the man's
side he created the woman. The order of creation established a divine
chain of authority.

But what has happened is something like the concept of the old
chain letter. Chain letters always come with a threat that if you break
the chain, something bad will happen to you. Well, that's the idea here.
When you break God's chain, you lose His blessing.

Many of us are already experienced in breaking God's chain. We
men have, as a whole, done this passively by abdicating and surren-
dering our role of spiritual and marital leadership. A whole generation
of women has been taught to aggressively seize that role. The culture,

and sometimes even the church, has contributed to the breaking of God's covenantal chain.

The result? Today's men know little of biblical male leadership. So we are not giving our boys an example to follow. At home, dad may be present in body, but he's missing in action. At school, boys are in a system dominated mostly by women. At church, the pulpit may be filled by a man, but the rest of the church program is often largely under female leadership. Most of a boy's Sunday school teachers are women. And now that homosexuals have come out of the closet, boys are getting an even more feminized picture of what it means to be male.

All of this leads to what I call "sissified" men who have relinquished their leadership roles in the home, at church, and in society at large. Now don't misunderstand. I am grateful for every godly and gifted woman God is using in the home, at church, and at school. We'd be in even worse shape than we are without these talented and committed women.

But over the last thirty years or so, this role reversal has given rise to a feminist movement specifically designed to assert the role of women. Now a lot of women don't like to hear me say this, but I believe that feminists of the more aggressive persuasion are frustrated women unable to find the proper male leadership. If a woman were receiving the right kind of love and attention and leadership, she would not want to be liberated from that. But Satan has successfully detoured many of us men and duped us into pouring most of our energy and attention into other areas that allow us to feed and assert our maleness, such as our careers.

After we pour ourselves into these other areas, we have little energy and attention left to claim and live out our roles as godly leaders in the home and church and society at large. The result is a culture in shambles, particularly among the generation we are supposed to be raising to follow us.

Today's children are sometimes referred to as a lost generation. But I think that our children, especially our boys, are the *product* of a lost generation. They are being raised in an environment that does not model biblical manhood and certainly doesn't hold them accountable to that standard.

THE WORLD'S DEFINITION OF MANHOOD

The definition of what it means to be a man has undergone a revolution over the last few years. The new male model is the Rambo-type superman who can slay dozens and never go down, who carries out his one-man vendetta of violence without shedding a tear. His job is to kill the enemy at all costs and feel nothing while doing it.

I hope you realize that we now have a generation of boys and young men with exactly this mentality. They are quick to deal out violence, and that's scary enough. But what's even more scary is that they can deal out violence and feel absolutely nothing. They seem to be completely without normal human sensitivity. That didn't just happen. These violent kids were nurtured on a culture of violence.

They've been bombarded by television programs and movies and peer pressure that have reshaped their thinking and redefined their priorities. But what I suspect they haven't been overwhelmed with is healthy male examples to override the negative input. So these boys are growing up uninformed as to what a real man is.

And the effect of this dearth of biblical manhood on young girls is just as devastating. We also have a generation of girls who don't know how to identify the right kind of man because they haven't seen enough of them. We are talking about two handicapped groups of kids.

Guess what happens when these boys and girls marry each other or produce children outside of marriage? They produce a new generation of children who will not get the care and nurture they need. The undisciplined male who fathered them is not interested in taking that responsibility, and the young woman who bore them is not well prepared to raise them.

What we are doing as a society is perpetuating a system that was unworkable. Since President Lyndon Johnson instituted the "Great Society" programs in the early sixties, some five trillion dollars have been spent to address these problems, particularly the problem of families with dependent children.

I think most of us will agree that these social programs have been an utter failure. Although they were well intentioned, they did not address the core problem. This has to do with the set of values transferred from one generation to another. One of the reasons God created the family unit was to give us a system for perpetuating and transferring values.

Now, our children will not always buy our values. Our children may rebel against our values, but at least there are explicit values there to react against. Today, many children don't have to rebel against parental values because there's nothing there.

If you grew up in a home that had a system of values, even if you rebelled against those values, you had to work at it. You had to climb over Mother whispering in your ear even if you were many miles from home at college, because that influence was always there.

Parents love to quote Proverbs 22:6: "Train a child in the way he should go, and when he is old he will not turn from it." But this verse assumes that a body of biblical data has been transmitted that God can use to quicken a young person.

Unfortunately, that is not happening today, and we are paying the price. Our schools have metal detectors, the media are redefining the family, and homosexuals are not only coming out of the closet, but they're parading down Main Street. In fact, some of our many legislators are trying to find ways to make homosexuality fully acceptable.

I believe the future of our children and our nation lies primarily in the hands of our men. I do not mean by this that women are not important and crucial to the process. But I am suggesting that if we men do not step up to the plate and stop giving excuses for our failure—if we do not own the problem—then we will not be able to fix the problem. What we need is a generation of men who have a proper—that is, a theological—perspective on what it means to be a real man.

Without that theological viewpoint to which we adjust our lives, we are going to see the moral slippage in our society reach the catastrophic stage. And we won't be able to throw enough government money at the problem to keep the lid on. Government doesn't have any more money to spend on any more programs to solve any more of our problems.

That means that we must own the problems ourselves, and the responsibility for dealing with them falls primarily at the feet of today's men. Whether it is personal problems, family problems, church problems, or community problems, we must own them and step up to the plate to do something about them.

GOD'S IDEA OF A REAL MAN

What is the Bible's definition of a real man? What is God's idea of a real man? How does God define maleness? If God were to draw a picture of a real man, what would he look like? Would he be bulging with muscles because he works out at the health club five days a week? Most of us better hope not, because most of our bulges aren't muscles!

Is a real man somebody who can get girls pregnant? No, my dog lives like that. Is a real man someone who slaps his wife and shows her who's boss? Obviously, we know the answer to that. We know what a real man isn't, but what is he? And where is he? We'd better be finding him fast, because we have another growing problem in the church, particularly in a minority-led church. This is the problem of a generation of very godly women with no men to marry who have the spiritual qualities they are looking for.

That is because of the absence of men in the church. And that is the result of the absence of leadership in the home. If you're a messed-up man, you're going to help make a messed-up family. And if you are a messed-up man leading a messed-up family and your family goes to church, then your family is going to help make a messed-up church.

And if you're a messed-up man leading a messed-up family, resulting in a messed-up church, and your church is supposed to be a light to the neighborhood, then you're going to have a messed-up neighborhood.

And if you're a messed-up man leading a messed-up family,

resulting in a messed-up church, causing a messed-up neighborhood, and your neighborhood is in the city, then you're going to have a messed-up city.

And if you're a messed-up man, leading a messed-up family, making a messed-up church, resulting in a messed-up neighborhood, causing a messed-up city, and your city is in a county, then you're going to have a messed-up county.

And if you're a messed-up man, causing a messed-up family, resulting in a messed-up church, causing a messed-up neighborhood, leading to a messed-up city, resulting in a messed-up county, and your county's in the state, then you're going to have a messed-up state.

And if you're a messed-up man, leading a messed-up family, resulting in a messed-up church, causing a messed-up neighborhood, leading to a messed-up city, resulting in a messed-up county, causing a messed-up state, and your state is in a country, then you're going to have a messed-up country.

And if you're a messed-up man, causing a messed-up family, resulting in a messed-up church, leading to a messed-up neighborhood, resulting in a messed-up city, producing a messed-up county, causing a messed-up state, leading to a messed-up country, and your country is in the world, then you are going to have a messed-up world.

So if you want a better world, made up of better countries, composed of better states, filled with better counties, composed of better cities, made up of better neighborhoods, influenced by better churches, inhabited by better families, we had better start by becoming a generation of better men.

That's where it starts. So where can we go to get God's portrait, God's idea, of what makes a real man? Job chapter 29 gives us what I think is a portrait of a real man. If anyone in the Bible can tell us something about what makes a real man, it's this suffering patriarch of the Old Testament.

I won't try to review all of Job's story for you. You are either already familiar with it, or you can read it for yourself. The early chapters of the book of Job detail his unbelievable trials. Job was hurting, but his circumstances weren't controlling him. Now he was crying out to God, trying to understand what was happening. But Job was not a whiner in the sense that he was blaming everybody else and not accepting responsibility himself.

In the course of Job's discourse with the three men who came to be with him, we come to chapter 29. And there we find five traits or qualities that help us see what a real man looks like.

A REAL MAN CONSTRUCTS—AND HANDS DOWN— A SPIRITUAL LEGACY

First of all, a real man is one who has a spiritual legacy to leave behind. This is a man who cultivates and develops a spiritual foundation in his life so that he can leave behind a spiritual legacy. Look at verses 1-5 of Job 29:

> Job continued his discourse: "How I long for the months gone by, for the days when God watched over me, when his lamp shone upon my head and by his light I walked through darkness! Oh, for the days when I was in my prime, when God's intimate friendship blessed my house, when the Almighty was still with me and my children were around me."

Notice how Job traced his relationship with God in past days, when he was in his "prime." What man can't identify with that feeling! Now Job is not saying here that his faith was a thing of the past. In fact, he is saying just the opposite.

Remember, Job was going through the kind of suffering and loss most of us will never know, and he was looking back to happier days. But because God had illumined Job's way in days past, he had a history, a legacy, of God's presence to help him hang in there when his whole world collapsed.

Notice also that Job shared his spiritual pilgrimage with his children when they were still alive. Even though they were now dead, Job's children had been given a spiritual legacy. One reason children are directionless today is that fathers are not leaving a legacy behind for them to hang on to.

If you don't have a history with God, if you can't see the footsteps of grace in your life, then a slice of your life is missing. If God didn't do anything in your yesterday, you won't have what you need to hang on to in your today so that you can make it to your tomorrow. And you won't have a spiritual legacy to pass on to your children.

The Israelites would often build a memorial of stones to mark the place where God had done something great. Then when a son said to his father, "What do these stones mean?" (Joshua 4:6), Dad could tell Junior the story of God's deliverance.

Here's a convicting question, so I'll direct it to myself as well as to you, my reader. What if our son or daughter said to us, "Dad, has God ever done anything really special in your life?" Would we be able to recount stories of God's grace in our lives? Could we talk about the time God made a way when there was no way?

Our grandparents and great-grandparents could. They could tell how, when there was no bread, Jesus was their bread; how when there was no doctor, he was the doctor. When you don't have that spiritual legacy and you run into a brick wall, you're quick to quit.

But when you have a legacy and run into a brick wall, you think twice before you quit because you've seen God work in your yesterday. When you get into Job's plight and your world collapses, you are willing to trust God in your today and hope in Him for your tomorrow.

Recently I asked the people of our church in Dallas how many were made by their parents to go to church when they were children. The majority of hands went up. But that legacy is quickly fading. By and large, that is no longer true for the next generation. The parents don't have it, so they don't care if the kids get it.

The problem is, the brain is not neutral. It will be attracted like a magnet to whatever is available to it. So if we are not instilling a godly legacy in our children, they will get their mind-set from a generation that has no connection with God.

And when the brain and the heart are unplugged from spiritual reality, kids lose their conscience. They have no moral compass to tell them right from wrong. As I said before, today's kids can do evil and not even feel a twinge of conscience about it.

And when a bunch of kids like this get together, we call it a gang. For these kids, gangs are alternative families. The reason gangs are growing, and the reason that children are committing violence at younger and younger ages, is because kids are ceasing to feel pain or remorse or regret or fear.

When that happens, these kids are dangerous. A person who is not afraid to die is very dangerous, because he doesn't care about the consequences.

When I was growing up, I cared about consequences because my father wore me out. He gave me "sessions" when I did something wrong. I remember once I got suspended from Garrison Junior High School for fighting. There was a regular old rumble in the cafeteria, and I was getting it on too. I don't remember whether I won, but I was in there. And I got suspended.

My father was called up by the principal and told to please come get me because I was suspended for fighting. Dad had to leave his job at the waterfront, and he only got paid if he was there. So he was losing money to come to my school to escort me home because I had, in his words, "cut the fool in school."

I'll never forget my father's words to the principal. He looked at him and said, "Thank you," and then he added, "You'll never have to worry about Tony ever being suspended again." Lord, have mercy! That was the longest ride home in my life.

When we got home, Dad said, "Now go up to your room." So I went up to my room, but he didn't come right away. He didn't come in thirty minutes. He didn't come in an hour. He didn't come in two hours. You know what he was doing? Mental torture! He was making me think about it.

And then I heard the creaking of his footsteps on the stairs of that old Baltimore house as he began to walk ever so slowly, step by step toward my room. And he came in with Old Faithful. Let me tell you what Old Faithful was. Old Faithful was a barber's razor strap. No switch, no regular belt like most people used. My father used a razor strap, one of those thick bad boys too.

He came in, sat on the side of the bed, and said, "Are we going to fight any more at school?"

I said, "Heavens, no, no, no!"

He said, "I know." He then proceeded to administer the physical discipline I fully deserved. He said, "Now I ask you, are we going to get suspended any more?"

I said, "Dad, I told you, no!" Then he brought Old Faithful down again. Brother, I woke the neighborhood up!

Then Dad said, "I didn't hear you. Are we going to get suspended again?"

At the top of my lungs, I said, "No, Daddy, no, Jesus is my witness, I am not going to be suspended again!" Then Dad came down with Old Faithful several more times. That was enough.

My dad had rules, and we were going to follow the rules or suffer the consequences. After a whipping he would say, "Better I spank you than the cop down the street."

My daddy could only do that because he was there. If he hadn't been there for me, he couldn't have disciplined me and kept me on the right path.

Now we have a generation of boys who, once they hit thirteen or fourteen, are entirely out of control. Their mothers are too weak physically and too burned out emotionally to handle them, and Dad is not there.

So there must be a spiritual legacy, a divine frame of reference, that's transferred. We fathers need to start with our children first. If you aren't building a spiritual legacy, you can either fret about it or you can start building one today.

You can say, "I'm going to begin establishing a spiritual legacy for my children. I want to see God at work in my life starting today." Bring Him to bear on your circumstances now. Begin the legacy today.

Let me show you another thing about Job's legacy. Look at Job 1:5:

When a period of feasting had run its course, Job would send and have them [his sons and daughters] purified. Early in the morning he would sacrifice a burnt offering for each of them, thinking, "Perhaps my children have sinned and cursed God in their hearts." This was Job's regular custom.

What a picture of a father acting as family priest. When was the last time you knelt by your child's bed and said, "I want to talk to God about you"? That leaves a lasting impression.

I'll never forget opening Dad's bedroom door because I heard this noise coming out of the bedroom. It was my father wailing in prayer for his children. Just wailing in utter spiritual anguish.

It wasn't easy for him to do that. He had to do back-breaking work on the waterfront. He had to tote that barge and lift that bale for thirty-five years. Talk about being tired. My father would come home dragging, but he was never too tired to wail for his kids. I'll never forget that.

A REAL MAN EARNS RESPECT

A second truth I want to show you from Job 29 is that a real man earns respect. Look at verses 7-10:

> "When I went to the gate of the city and took my seat in the public square, the young men saw me and stepped aside and the old men rose to their feet; the chief men refrained from speaking and covered their mouths with their hands; the voices of the nobles were hushed, and their tongues stuck to the roof of their mouths."

Look at the respect Job had. The young men stepped aside. "Job's here, let's go. We can't be doing this out here when Job is around." How many kids do you know who treat adults with this kind of respect today?

One of our members was at the bowling alley where some teenagers were cutting up and messing up everybody else's game, using all manner of profanity. They didn't seem to care that they were surrounded on all sides by adults.

One person said, "Why don't we go over there and tell them they have to cut this out?"

The answer came back, "You're crazy." This person was afraid of these kids and what they might do.

There used to be a time when kids were scared of adults. Now what happens? We see a group of teenagers coming, we cross to the other side of the street because we are scared of them. What happened?

Someone says, "Well, kids today don't have any respect for anyone." But why not? Could it be that we haven't earned it, haven't insisted on it, and so, therefore, they don't give it? Job said, "When I showed up, the kids scattered because Mr. Job was there."

There also used to be a time when you would at least get a little respect if you were a preacher. You'd show up and the men would say, "Ole rev's here, we can't cuss anymore."

What happened? The men saw too many preachers on TV get caught with their hands in someone else's pockets or sleeping in someone else's bed. Maybe they heard too many preachers cussing. So why should they run and hide when the preacher shows up?

Mr. Job said his influence was such that even the older men stood up when he showed up. And "the chief men" or princes paid him respect too. They stopped talking when Job sat down at the city gate. That's respect.

Now Job didn't get this kind of respect by chance or by accident. He lived in a pagan world just like we do, but he lived in an environment that had been influenced by his character. If we want our young boys to respect women, they must see us respect women. They shouldn't hear the way some men talk about women.

If your wife is your "old lady" to you, then why shouldn't the girls the boys hang out with be someone's "old lady"? You can not only earn respect for yourself by being a real man, but you can teach others, especially boys, the same kind of respect.

My son gets ticked off at me because when we're ready to go

through a door I'll say, "Just a minute, back up, let your mother and your sisters in first." He gives me the old line, "But, Dad, they's just my mother and my sisters." But if our boys never see us insisting on these kind of things, then they're not going to do them. We often forget to show respect ourselves, and when you don't show respect, you don't earn respect.

In many cultures, you have to earn your manhood stripes. If you're Jewish you get a bar mitzvah, a time of recognition that you are entering the status of manhood. In some African cultures, you have to go on the hunt and bring back the meat to demonstrate that you're now a man.

In other words, you have to prove yourself. You can't just say that because of your physical size, chronological age, and overactive libido, you are now a man. Perhaps we need some kind of initiation rite that our boys go through so they can earn their manhood and earn respect. Job earned respect because when he showed up, a higher standard entered the scene.

MERCY AND JUSTICE

A third trait of a real man is that he is a person of mercy and justice. Job says in 29:12-16:

> "I rescued the poor who cried for help, and the fatherless who had none to assist him. The man who was dying blessed me; I made the widow's heart sing. I put on righteousness as my clothing; justice was my robe and my turban. I was eyes to the blind and feet to the lame. I was a father to the needy; I took up the case of the stranger."

A real man hurts with people who hurt. A real man helps people who need help. A real man isn't cold and hard and insensitive and calloused. A real man is like Jesus; he weeps if he needs to. Job was a successful businessman, but he was compassionate.

I like that last phrase in the *New American Standard Bible* ("I investigated the case which I did not know"). Job got the facts of the case. No, every problem isn't racism or classism or culturalism. A real man is a man of justice who doesn't allow people to threaten him because they bait him or use other illegitimate means to make their point. Sometimes charges like racism can be legitimate. But then, that's part of getting the facts. The Bible says only a fool speaks before he hears the whole matter. Job blended justice and mercy, and so must we.

A REAL MAN IS ROCK-SOLID IN ALL HIS WAYS

Fourth, a real man is a man of stability. "I thought, 'I will die in my own house, my days as numerous as the grains of sand. My roots will reach to the water, and the dew will lie all night on my branches." (Job 29:18-19)

What Job was talking about was stability. When the world shook around him, he was rock-solid. When I think about my dad, stability is what comes to my mind. We were in the heart of the ghetto in Baltimore. It was bad. We saw drug deals going down when we were home.

I said, "Dad, aren't you going to move?"

He said, "No."

I said, "Dad, they're shooting out here in the daytime. Why aren't you going to move?"

He said, "Because God kept me here this long, I believe He can keep me until He's ready to call me home." I didn't like his answer, but I sure respected it. Why? Because he went on to tell me, "Whenever you want to come home, as long as I live, I want this to be the home you come back to." What stability! Can your loved ones count on you like that?

A REAL MAN HAS WISDOM

Finally, a real man is a man of wisdom. "Men listened to me expectantly, waiting in silence for my counsel. After I had spoken, they spoke no more; my words fell gently on their ears." (Job 29:21-22)

Job said, "People came to me for advice. I was their counselor." Why? Because of the wisdom coming forth from his lips and his life. A wise man is a man who has been with God, who knows His mind.

Wisdom is the ability to apply truth to the issues of practical, day-to-day life.

Think about the everyday, "sanctified common sense" kind of wisdom that used to pour forth from our parents and grandparents. Kids today don't have it. They have plenty of "street-smarts," but that's another thing altogether. Kids need wisdom for living, but a lot of them aren't going to get it because the people they are turning to don't have it either.

RETURNING TO YOUR ROLE

What's a real man? One who has a spiritual legacy to leave behind. One who earns respect and teaches respect to others. One who balances mercy and justice and who is rock-solid in his stability. One who has godly wisdom to share.

Are you frustrated because it seems that the world has robbed you of your biblical manhood? Don't use that as an excuse for not being a real man. Take your role back—not by acting tough or strutting around claiming, "I'm the man around here," but by being the man God wants you to be. Do that, and your wife and children will follow your leadership gladly.

TWELVE

NO MORE PLAYING THE LONE RANGER

"I'M TASK-ORIENTED. I SET GOALS AND GO FOR
THEM. MEN DON'T NEED ALL THAT 'TOUCHY-
FEELY' RELATIONSHIP STUFF TO MAKE IT."

This excuse could have been written about me. Once I set a goal, my passion is to reach it. Now there's nothing wrong with setting goals and then moving ahead to reach them, but often that becomes a convenient excuse and camouflage for not building relationships along the way.

So when it comes to helping men get past the excuse that they don't need relationships with other people to make it, I am a fellow traveler with you down this road. I'm learning, and God's Word has been very revealing to me on this subject. But I still have a way to go in balancing the need for quality relationships with my task- and goal-oriented makeup as a man.

I got off to a bad start in learning how to build relationships because one of my favorite TV programs as a kid was *The Lone Ranger*. His face was always hidden behind that mask, and the only time the mask was off was when his back was turned or when he disguised himself as an old prospector or something like that. But he *never* revealed his true identity.

The Lone Ranger and Tonto would just ride into town and get rid of the bad guys. Then as they rode off into the distance, someone would always ask, "Who was that masked man?" All we knew was that it was The Lone Ranger.

That describes the way a lot of men live today. It's easy for them to put on the mask and play a role, leaving people to wonder, "Who is that masked man?" In fact, there are a lot of wives who could ask that very question even about their husbands, because a lot of men hide out when it comes to authentic relationships.

OVERDOSING ON INDEPENDENCE

We men have a problem that I call an overdose of male independence. I say overdose because there is nothing wrong with being independent per se. But there is everything wrong with an overdose of independence that leaves us with a relationship deficit.

In our culture, men have acquaintances rather than real relationships. Too many of us are content to pass people by as we continue toward our goals. We don't really worry about it if we're not able to stop long enough to build significant relationships along the way.

That's why it's not unusual for a man to reach midlife and not have much of a relationship with his wife. His children are ready to leave home, but they don't really know him and he doesn't know them. Maybe the company's been built, the salary has been made, the position in the corporation has been achieved. But there are relational casualties along the way.

Granted, women are much more oriented to relationships. It seems like they have been structured in such a way that it is natural to them. All of us married men have had our wives come to us and say, "I just want to talk." We want to say, "Well, it's OK to talk if I can do this or that too." But when the wife slips that word *just* in there, we know they want to do some focused, undistracted talking. And that makes us uncomfortable.

Men tend to be much more competitive. We want to win. We want to make sure that we're out in front. I am so competitive by nature that I can't stand to lose to my son Jonathan in basketball. He's pretty good, so you know if he's ahead and the game is on the line, it will become a football game. Dad will make the necessary adjustments so he doesn't lose.

This competitive side of our nature makes it hard to admit when we're wrong. A man might be driving and make a wrong turn. He's as lost as a skunk. His wife says very humbly and submissively, "Dear, honey, why don't you ask for directions?"

"I know where I am."

"But you took a wrong turn."

"Yeah, but there's another way to get there. This is a shortcut."

This kind of thing is evidence of our desire not to lose. A competitive nature is not bad because that's the way God made men. But we can carry it way too far.

When our passion for our businesses or hobbies or churches or whatever leaves damaged relationships along the way, we have misappropriated God's unique gift to us as men.

Some of us are leery of deep relationships because we have been burned. We tried it one time, and it didn't work. Now we have the Julius Caesar Syndrome. Caesar thought Marcus Brutus was his friend until Brutus came up to him as one of his assassins and stabbed him.

Once you've been stabbed, you don't want to go through that again. You decide you're better off being self-reliant, so you buy into the media myth that real men are tough guys who don't need anybody.

My wife has only seen me cry a few times in twenty-five years of marriage. The reason, I think, is that I have this mentality a lot of men have that big boys don't cry, or at least they don't let anybody see them crying. So if you don't want to appear unmanly, it's better not to take the risk of a relationship that might reveal your more emotional side.

Now, I'm getting better. I'm not where I want to be, but I'm not where I was. God has brought some very good people into my life to help me begin the process of learning to build relationships. I'm learning, and I want to learn more. But this process doesn't come easy to most men.

However, it is critical that we learn to build relationships, because I have discovered from God's Word that you can never be what He wants you to be apart from relationships. If we let the world's philosophy of male independence dominate us, we are courting spiritual, personal, and family disaster.

CREATED FOR RELATIONSHIP

Do you remember what God said about Adam before the creation of Eve? "It is not good for the man to be alone." (Genesis 2:18) God's first comment on the state of human beings was that Adam needed a helper.

But modern men have changed that. We say it is better that we should be alone; not unmarried, but alone as far as relationships are concerned. So we are flying in the face of God's Word when we insist on our independence to the detriment of those around us. God said aloneness is not good.

Not only this, but Philippians 2:4 says, "Each of you should look not only to your own interests, but also to the interests of others." Not only do you need good relationships for yourself, you need to provide them for others.

Failing to build a strong relationship with your wife because you don't think you need one yourself is to deprive her of her need. The same thing goes for your children.

When we do this as husbands and fathers we say, "I count, and you don't." That's selfishness, my brother. If God tells me it's not good for me to be alone, but I insist on being a loner, then I deprive others who are in desperate need of what I have to offer. And I also hurt myself, because although I may not know it, I'm in desperate need of what they have to offer too.

RELATIONSHIPS: A TOP PRIORITY IN GOD'S PROGRAM

We can see how important relationships are in God's program by looking at the way He has constructed His church. The Bible's favorite metaphor for the church is "the body."

INTIMATELY RELATED AND ABSOLUTELY NECESSARY

A body is not just a bunch of parts that are mere acquaintances. Drop a brick on your bare toe and your brain will instantly let you know how intimately related the parts of your body are! Your head and your neck are not just neighbors. They are intricately related.

If an acquaintance moves away, it may bother us for a while, but it doesn't usually tear us up. But when it comes to the parts of our bodies, we don't want any member packing up and taking off on us. I like my arms and legs just where they are. I need each one of them to be whole.

It's the same in the body of Christ. In 1 Corinthians 12:12-27, Paul uses the analogy of the body to let us know that as members of the body of Christ, we need each other desperately. No member can say to another member, "I don't need you." It staggered me a little to realize that when I preach about the church, I am preaching on the need for relationships. This gives a lot of passages new meaning.

For instance, Hebrews 10:25 tells us not to neglect meeting together as the church. But in verse 24, we find that the context for this exhortation is our need to "spur one another on toward love and good deeds." So we don't come to church just to show up and be counted. We come because we are related.

Satan has been able to keep the races apart and keep a brotherhood from developing between men because he has kept us from understanding how the body works. I appreciate the Promise Keepers organization for their emphasis on quality relationships among men, and also the need to leave our comfort zones and build bridges to men of other ethnic backgrounds.

I believe every man should intentionally reach out and develop a meaningful relationship with another man from a different race, culture, or social class. Hey, even the Lone Ranger had Tonto!

JESUS AND RELATIONSHIPS: AN IMPORTANT INVESTMENT

In John 15:14, Jesus looked at the disciples and said, "You are my friends." Remember that He had a Judas in the bunch. One of the

Twelve was bad. And Jesus knew it, being God in the flesh. But He still invested His earthly life in building vital relationships with those men.

Judas betrayed the Lord anyway. So if Jesus Himself lost a friend, then not all of our relationships are going to work out either. But it was worth it for Jesus because the other eleven men were so committed that they gave their lives for Him.

PAUL AND RELATIONSHIPS: AN ESSENTIAL ENCOURAGEMENT

Relationships were certainly important to Paul. In 2 Corinthians 7:6-7, he told the church that during a period of tremendous affliction he was greatly comforted by the coming of his coworker Titus. And when Paul learned that Titus himself had been comforted by the Corinthian believers before his arrival, Paul rejoiced even more.

Later in his ministry, Paul wrote to Timothy, "May the Lord show mercy to the household of Onesiphorus, because he often refreshed me." (2 Timothy 1:16) Then Paul urged Timothy himself to "get here before winter." (2 Timothy 4:21) Paul was saying, "I'm lonely in this prison cell. It's cold. I need your fellowship." To Philemon, Paul wrote, "You, brother, have refreshed the hearts of the saints." (Philemon 7)

OUR NEED FOR RELATIONSHIPS

Sometimes I come into church on Sunday morning needing a word of comfort from someone. Sometimes I am so spent emotionally or physically, I just need a word. But my ego won't let me say so, because I'm a man. I'm the pastor. I'm supposed to be lifting *others* up. So I often don't say how much *I* need to be encouraged. That's to my detriment.

But as I said, I'm learning. And I'm not suggesting that no men care about forming solid relationships. The fact that you're reading this book says something about your commitment. But in general, men have a hard time forming bonds with one another and with loved ones.

I know there are men who are struggling in this area because I've talked to them. I know there are men making an effort to improve their relationships with their wives and children. We need to encourage and help each other in this area. If a man is struggling morally, for example, and he doesn't feel he knows anyone well enough to ask for help, he's going to be hurting in a big way.

NECESSARY, NOT JUST NICE

Good relationships are not just nice; they are biblically necessary. It's not just a matter of one person saying, "Well, I can live without getting close to anyone." There is much more at stake than that. Look at what Paul tells us:

> Brothers, if someone is caught in a sin, you who are spiritual should restore him gently. . . . Carry each other's burdens, and in this way you will fulfill the law of Christ.
> —*Galatians 6:1-2*

We can't restore a brother unless we are close enough to him to know he's hurting, or unless he feels comfortable enough with us to say, "I need help."

Let me show you a biblical example of how important relationships are, even to the survival of a nation. In Exodus 17:8-13, we find the story of Israel's battle with the Amalekites. This is the famous incident where Moses told Joshua, "Choose some of our men and go out to fight the Amalekites. Tomorrow I will stand on top of the hill with the staff of God in my hands."

You may remember the story. Moses, Aaron, and Hur went up to the top of the hill, and Moses raised his staff. When he did that, Israel took charge of the battle. But Moses got tired, and his hands dropped. The Amalekites started winning, so Aaron and Hur sat Moses on a rock and supported his hands. In the end, Israel won the battle.

You need to understand that Joshua obeyed Moses because he loved him like a father. And Aaron and Hur did their part because they loved Moses too. But there was something bigger going on here.

The nation of Israel was at stake. Therefore, supporting Moses wasn't just an act of kindness to an elderly leader. Supporting Moses was saving Israel.

A GENERATION AT STAKE

My brother, the generation coming behind us is at stake. Supporting each other is not just for us. If we don't hold each other's hands up, our boys and girls will become casualties in the battle.

There are some Amalekites out there in the world who want to pervert our boys and girls, to rob them of their purity and their faith in Christ. Unless we Christian fathers and husbands and single men start holding up each other's hands, the Amalekites are going to prevail.

We all get tired. We may not talk about it, and we may not want anybody else to know we're drained. But sometimes we get tired of fighting the Amalekites and ask, "Is it worth it?" When you ask that question, you'd better have somebody near to hold your hands up.

THE VALUE OF RELATIONSHIPS

Exodus chapter 17 is one example of the value God places on relationships. The book of Proverbs is also rich with examples. Proverbs 17:17 says, "A friend loves at all times, and a brother is born for adversity."

When do you need a friend the most? Not when you're on top. Not when the times are good and the crowds are coming. Not when the money is good. Everybody wants to be your friend then. But a true friend stays with you when you're heading downhill, when times are rough.

Proverbs 18:24 warns, "A man of many companions may come to ruin, but there is a friend who sticks closer than a brother." The writer isn't saying it's bad to have lots of friends. He's saying that if everybody's your friend, something is wrong. You're not being very wise in choosing the people you hang out with.

We see illustrations of this all around us. Probably the most obvious is the politician who's a friend to everybody who will contribute to his campaign, regardless of their views.

Proverbs 27:6 is a classic: "Faithful are the wounds of a friend, but deceitful are the kisses of an enemy" (NASB). What a great word to men. Our world is full of people who "kiss up" to the boss or the coach or whoever is in charge to get ahead.

But a true friend may wound you because he loves you. An enemy kisses you because he's out to get you. Didn't Judas betray Jesus with a kiss? A true friend corrects you when you're wrong. A legitimate friend will never absolve you of the evil you do.

Look at Proverbs 27:17—"As iron sharpens iron, so one man sharpens another." We need friends to keep us sharp, to rub off the blunt edges and make us better men. We need friends who will challenge and sharpen our thinking, help us make good decisions, and help us hone our spiritual lives until they are razor-sharp.

THREE KINDS OF FRIENDS YOU CAN'T LIVE WITHOUT

Every man needs three kind of friends. The Bible says, "A cord of three strands is not quickly broken." (Ecclesiastes 4:12) It's hard to break three ropes wound together.

A PAUL

The first kind of friend we men need is an older, more mature believer, a father figure, someone who has been where we're trying to go. We need someone to be a Paul to our Timothy, a spiritual father or older brother we can hang out with and from whom we can learn what it means to be a godly man.

Finding a friend like this may require that we lay aside our pride and say, "You know, I don't really know all I need to know about being a man of God. I've a lot to learn about loving my wife and my children the way I need to. Maybe I need to hook up with an older and wiser man who is walking with the Lord."

A BARNABAS

The second kind of friend we need is a soul brother. Somebody who loves you, but is not all that impressed with you. Somebody who's not going to get nervous when you show up, but can deal with you eyeball to eyeball. This is more of a peer relationship, the kind that Paul had with Barnabas.

A brother is someone on your level, a friend who can relate to you where you are because he's going through the same stuff. He can also be an accountability partner for you. The two of you can work through things together. And you can be like Barnabas to each other by encouraging each other.

A TIMOTHY

Along with a father and a brother, you also need a son. This is the third kind of friend every man needs, a Timothy to your Paul. You and I need to provide a model that younger men and boys can look up to. They need to see Christ at work in us.

A much-used word today is *mentor*, which simply means a tutor or coach. Now this kind of Timothy or mentoring friendship might sound scary, and in one sense it is. But the fact is that it is already happening at some level in most men's lives. If you are a father, you are a mentor whether you know it or not. If you coach kids, teach kids, or even have kids in your neighborhood, you're doing some kind of mentoring. And chances are that some younger man at work is watching you for clues on how or what to do on the job.

This is really front-burner stuff for me, because I have two teen-aged sons. What I don't have is lots of extra time, so I am learning to be more creative with the time I have.

I include the boys in the things I'm doing as much as possible. For us, the problem wasn't so much finding extra time, but making good use of the time we have. The reason our church in Dallas has a mentoring program for boys without fathers is so that they don't have to grow up for eighteen years without ever knowing what a man is supposed to be like—and what a Christian man in particular looks like.

A BIBLICAL EXAMPLE OF REAL FRIENDSHIP

I know that one of the complicating factors for men in trying to form strong, healthy bonds with other men is the area of homosexuality. In a close relationship, we fear that someone might think we're something we're not.

Let me show you one of the most manly and virile, yet sensitive and intimate, relationships in all the Bible: the friendship between David and Jonathan, the son of King Saul. Let's look at their story and learn some valuable principles about relationships.

DAVID AND JONATHAN: TWO MANLY MEN

I need to introduce you to Jonathan a little bit first. In 1 Samuel 14:1-15, Jonathan decided to sneak over to the garrison of the Philistines, Israel's mortal enemies. He took with him his armor bearer, who would have been just a boy. They had worked out a signal whereby they would know whether the Lord would give them success in a fight (see verses 9-10).

So when the signal came, Jonathan said to his armor bearer, "Climb up after me; the LORD has given them into the hand of Israel." (verse 12) Johnny and his armor boy whipped twenty Philistine warriors all by themselves.

Are there any Jonathans in the house? Anybody willing to take on twenty men by himself and one young friend? Now don't get me wrong. I'm not talking about Rambo stuff, making one's own laws and blowing away anybody who gets in the way. Jonathan went out in the name and power of the Lord.

He was no wimp. He was a man's man by any definition. He was fearless and tough.

And we all know about David. He was just a kid himself when he whipped Goliath.

Notice what David said before that fight: "David said to the Philistine, 'You come against me with sword and spear and javelin, but I come against you in the name of the LORD Almighty, the God of the armies of Israel, whom you have defied.'" (1 Samuel 17:45)

David and Jonathan fought in the same name. So these were real men, but they were also God's men. They didn't just jump bad. They jumped bad for the Lord.

SOUL BROTHERS AND KINDRED SPIRITS

I'm sure you will agree that there is no problem here in grasping the manhood of David or Jonathan. We're dealing with real men. These two men were like nobody you and I have ever known or met. But look at the intimate relationship they formed:

> "Whose son are you, young man?" Saul asked him. David said, "I am the son of your servant Jesse of Bethlehem." After David had finished talking with Saul, Jonathan became one in spirit with David, and he loved him as himself.
> —*1 Samuel 17:58–18:1*

Talk about soul brothers. These guys' souls were knit together immediately. As far as we know this was the first time Jonathan and David had met. What knitted them together so quickly? I believe it was the fact that Jonathan saw right off that David was his kind of man.

Jonathan watched David go out there and kill Goliath all by himself. Now Johnny had just slain twenty men almost by himself earlier, so he said, "Man, this dude can get it on for the Lord too. He's my kind of guy. I can relate to this brother. He's one cool customer." (That's in the Hebrew!)

So Jonathan felt an instant kinship with David. And the Bible says that Jonathan loved David on the spot. He was instantly drawn in loyalty to this new friend. Wait a minute. Two men loving each other? Hmm. Are they sissies? Are they gay or something? No, we have already established that they were men's men. It's all right for real men to love each other, to be kindred spirits.

But Jonathan did more than just slap David on the back and take off. "And Jonathan made a covenant with David. . . . Jonathan took off the robe he was wearing and gave it to David, along with his tunic, and even his sword, his bow and his belt." (1 Samuel 18:3-4) This is what we used to call becoming blood brothers.

Remember when you and your best friend would cut your fingers and press them together like the Indians did in those old movies?

When I was growing up, I did that with Darrel, my best friend. Darrel lived across the alley from me. We played ball in those alleys.

Darrel and I had a good deal going. In baseball, he was the pitcher and I was the catcher. In football, Darrel was the wide receiver and I was the quarterback. In everything, Darrel was this and I was that. I remember one time we grabbed hands and I said, "I love you, Darrel."

Darrel said, "I love you, Tony."

I said, "Hey, Darrel, let's become blood brothers." He thought that was a good idea, so we got a razor blade (a bad idea because I cut my finger too deep). Darrel cut his finger, I cut my finger, and we put them together. We were blood brothers. Now we didn't understand it all, but we knew that our souls were connected.

RISKS AND REWARDS OF COVENANTAL FRIENDSHIP

This covenant Jonathan made with David was very significant because Jonathan was next in line to be king of Israel. When Jonathan gave David his armor and his sword, he was saying, "Here's my robe, because it seems to me that God wants you in this position, not me. And if that's what God wants, so be it. You don't have to take the throne. You don't even have to ask me for it. Since it's God's will, here's the robe. Here's the king's sword. You can have it because I love you." That's deep commitment.

We also see in this gesture the element of vulnerability, the willingness to take a risk, that is foundational to building good relationships. Jonathan made himself very vulnerable to David when he did that, because David could easily have abused that trust and turned on Jonathan.

Notice also the loyalty that good relationships require. Jonathan was constantly defending David against the threats of his own father, King Saul. Both 1 Samuel chapter 19 and chapter 20 record accounts of how Jonathan stood up for David against Saul. The story in chapter 20 includes an incredible scene. Saul got mad at Jonathan for protecting David and told him:

"As long as the son of Jesse lives on this earth, neither you nor
your kingdom will be established. Now send and bring him to
me, for he must die!" "Why should he be put to death? What
has he done?" Jonathan asked his father. But Saul hurled his
spear at [Jonathan] to kill him.

—verses 31-33a

Here was Saul trying to kill his own son because he was such a
good friend to David. Now when someone goes against kin for you
because of principle, that's a friend. In fact, when the whole ugly scene
was over, Jonathan was angry and grieved, not that his own daddy had
tried to kill him, but because of his father's shameful treatment of
David (20:34).

This friendship wasn't one-sided. Jonathan asked David for a
promise that when David became king, he would show kindness to
Jonathan's house as long as he had any descendants around (20:14-
17). David made the promise and always honored it.

But where you really see the extent of David's love for Jonathan
is in 2 Samuel 1, when David got the report of Jonathan's death at the
hands of the Philistines. I want to look at David's lament for Jonathan:

"I grieve for you, Jonathan my brother; you were very dear to
me. Your love for me was wonderful, more wonderful than that
of women. How the mighty have fallen! The weapons of war
have perished!"

—2 Samuel 1:26-27

What did David mean by his statement about the joy of
Jonathan's love? It's a beautiful testimony to the kind of relationships
we've been talking about all through this chapter.

What David was saying was that while he had a whole harem full
of wives to meet his sexual needs, he wasn't close enough to any of
them to count them as a friend. That shouldn't surprise us; we know
that polygamy was never God's ideal for marriage. But the idea is that
although David had no problem satisfying his physical needs, his spirit

was starved for a soul mate. He only had one that we know about, Jonathan, and now he had lost him.

So the emotional and spiritual intimacy that David might have had with a wife was not there, but he had it with Jonathan.

In that sense, Jonathan's love was better than the love David's wives could give him.

MAKING FRIENDSHIP A REALITY

Where do we go from here? First, we need to make a decision to start building relationships. The best place to start is to get on your knees and ask God to help you. The fastest way to build a better relationship with anyone, even your wife, is on your knees.

Second, we need to make time for building relationships. Notice I said make time, not find time. If you go looking for extra time, you won't find it. It's not there. You've got to make time for others. We have a men's fellowship at our church that gives men lots of chances to cultivate friendships and develop prayer partnerships with other men.

Third, realize the truth of the old saying that the best way to make a friend is to be a friend. Work hard at affirming others. This is a trait most men don't come by naturally. It somehow feels a little funny to give out the kind of affirmation and encouragement we all need at times. But it can be a powerful thing.

I think of the story of John Wesley writing to William Wilberforce when Wilberforce was fighting against slavery in England. He was about to give up because the effort was going nowhere. But then he got Wesley's letter, who wrote as a friend to say, "I love you, keep fighting, God wants slavery ended."

Wilberforce was said to be so encouraged by Wesley's letter that he took new courage and fought on. It took him thirty years, but slavery was finally abolished in the British Empire.

A friend of mine once gave me a card on which was a whole list of questions. He told me, "Tony, every month I'm going to ask you these questions, and I want you to ask them to me." Here are the questions:

- Have you set a daily time in the Scriptures and in prayer?
- Have you had any flirtatious or lustful attitudes, tempting thoughts, or exposed yourself to any illicit materials that would not glorify God?
- Have you been completely above reproach in your financial dealings?
- Have you spent quality relationship time with your family and friends?
- Have you done your 100 percent best in your job?
- Have you told any half-truths or outright lies, putting yourself in a better light to those around you?
- Have you shared the Gospel with a nonbeliever?
- Have you taken care of your body through daily physical exercise and proper eating and sleeping habits?
- Have you allowed any person or circumstance to rob you of your joy?
- Have you lied to me on any of the previous questions?

When that man gave me this card, I knew I had a real friend. My brother, let's not play at church. Let's not play at family. Let's not play at relationships. I'm not asking you to cease being a man. I'm asking you to be a *real* man.

THIRTEEN

NO MORE OWNERSHIP

"WHAT'S MINE IS MINE. I'VE WORKED HARD FOR
EVERYTHING I HAVE, AND IT BELONGS TO ME."

The story is told of a dying man who wanted to take his money with him. He had $30,000, so he called his pastor, his doctor, and his lawyer to his deathbed and said, "I want to take my $30,000 with me when I go. So I'm going to give each one of you an envelope with $10,000 in it. At my funeral, I want each of you to come and put your envelope in my coffin."

The man died, and each of the three did his job. Later they met to talk about it. The preacher said, "I'm sure that Brother Smith would have wanted to help out with the new church organ, so I took out $2,000 and put $8,000 in the coffin."

The doctor said, "Well, he complimented me on how well I treated him during his declining years, and I know he would have wanted to help out with my new clinic. So I took $5,000 out and deposited $5,000 in the coffin."

The lawyer said, "I did better than both of you. I took out the $8,000 you left, preacher, and I took out the $5,000 you left, doctor. I also kept my $10,000, but I left behind a check for $30,000."

Well, that's one way to look at life. Take the cash, and leave a check. But God has a better plan for his men. It's called stewardship, and it beats ownership every time.

Now you may already be saying, "Yeah, I know all about stewardship, Tony. You're going to tell me that God owns everything and I own nothing, right?"

In a word, yes. But hold on, because by the time we're done you'll discover that being a steward under God is the only way to fly. In fact, let me give you two very good reasons right now for my contention that stewardship beats ownership any day.

The first reason is that this is God's will and plan for His people. In fact, God has set up creation to operate as a stewardship. Now He's not going to revamp His eternal plan, so our choice is either to get on His program or wind up fighting against the way things are designed to work.

A second reason that stewardship beats ownership is best illustrated like this. From time to time Congress will start toying with ways to get more money. One that comes up occasionally is the idea to eliminate the deduction for the taxes and mortgage interest that homeowners pay on their property.

Suppose that got implemented. It might change your mind about being a homeowner. One of the big advantages of owning over renting is that big deduction off your income taxes.

But if that were gone, you might be better off to rent. Why? Because when someone else owns the house, he is responsible for it, not you. If the water heater goes out, you just call him. If the roof leaks, it's his job to get it fixed. All you have to do is live there and keep the yard mowed.

So stewardship has real advantages. It's the way to live in obedience to God. And as the Owner, God takes the responsibility.

But before we delve into that, let me define the term *stewardship*.

What Stewardship Is All About

Biblically, the word refers to an administration or an economy. A steward in Bible times was someone who administered or managed another person's property. Therefore, a steward didn't own anything, but he oversaw everything for the owner. He was accountant, foreman, field boss, and office manager, all rolled into one. It was a very responsible position.

WHAT STEWARDSHIP LOOKS LIKE

A biblical illustration of stewardship is Joseph in the house of Potiphar, the Egyptian official who bought Joseph as a slave.

According to Genesis 39:6, "[Potiphar] left in Joseph's care everything he had." When Potiphar's wife tried to seduce Joseph, his reply showed that he understood his role: "'With me in charge,' he told her, 'my master does not concern himself with anything in the house; everything he owns he has entrusted to my care. No one is greater in this house than I am. My master has withheld nothing from me except you, because you are his wife. How then could I do such a wicked thing and sin against God?'" (39:8-9)

A modern-day illustration is the house-sitting Lois and I used to do when we were in seminary. People in Dallas would often call the seminary to get the names of students who did house-sitting. So Lois and I would get to live in some fancy house for a weekend or even longer. It was a great way to make extra money for school.

Since a lot of these people lived in the elite areas of Dallas, we felt like we were king and queen for a day or a weekend. Now I'm a casual kind of guy. I make myself at home anywhere. So I would go acting like it was my home, and my wife would have to remind me regularly that it was not our house.

I remember one time when we were house-sitting, I was going to invite some friends from seminary over. Lois said, "No, you're not. This is not our house." She had the right idea. We were just the overseers, the *stewards*, of that house, caring for it in the owner's absence.

So the nature of stewardship is very easy to grasp. A steward owns nothing, but he manages everything. When a steward starts acting like he owns his master's stuff, there are problems (see Luke 16:1-2).

GOD MADE IT, SO HE OWNS IT

The Bible declares that God owns it all. "The earth is the LORD's, and everything in it, the world, and all who live in it; for he founded it upon the seas and established it upon the waters." (Psalm 24:1-2)

That's about as clear as it gets. God owns everything because He created everything. Now unless you and I helped Him do that, we don't really own a thing. This is important to understand and believe, because we men are into ownership.

That's where we get a big part of our masculine identity. It's sort of the Tarzan thing. Was there any doubt who owned the jungle? Tarzan was king of his domain, and we want to be king of our domain too.

But since we can't swing through trees and fight lions, we collect stuff. Then we compare our stuff with other guys' stuff to see who has the most stuff. Like the bumper sticker says, "He who dies with the most toys, wins."

MAN'S GOD-GIVEN ROLE

You and I were born with nothing but our skin on. And even though we will be buried in a nice suit, it's only because somebody else dressed us. And there will be no U-Haul following the hearse. On that day, everyone around us will realize that everything we had was only borrowed from God.

What God did when He created man was to make us stewards of His creation. God said to Adam, "I want you to oversee my domain, to rule over it for Me. I put it in your care. It's yours to use and enjoy, but I want you to do with it what I want done with it" (see Genesis 1:28-30; 2:16-17).

The psalmist wrote, "Not to us, O LORD, not to us but to your name be the glory, because of your love and faithfulness. Why do the nations say, 'Where is their God?' Our God is in heaven; he does whatever pleases him." (Psalm 115:1-3)

Why is the glory all God's? Why can He do whatever He wants? Because it's all His. And that includes you and me. God didn't create us for our pleasure but for Himself. He's the owner; you and I are just the managers. Since the universe is God's place, He does whatever He pleases with it.

THE FOLLY OF TRYING TO PLAY OWNER

Suppose I came to your house today and said, "Look, I don't like your furniture. It's got to go. You need to replace this antique stuff with contemporary. All of this has to be changed."

What are you going to say to me? "Excuse me, you're in my house. I paid for this furniture, and I'm paying the house note. You haven't made one dime's worth of investment in this house. I like antique furniture, so with all due respect, mind your own business."

We haven't made one dime's worth of investment in God's creation. We haven't added one iota to what has been made, so we shouldn't live like we helped Him make this deal. A steward recognizes God as the absolute owner of everything.

The sin of Satan was that he wanted to share ownership with God. Only Satan wasn't after mere things. He wanted to be like God. "I will make myself like the Most High." (Isaiah 14:14)

Having failed at that, he got Adam and Eve to try the same thing: "You will be like God." (Genesis 3:5) That didn't work either. God will not share His glory with anyone.

That's what Paul says in Romans 11:36: "For from him and through him and to him are all things. To him be the glory forever! Amen." God created this world for Himself, and He owns everything by virtue of that creation.

DOUBLE OWNERSHIP

But if you are a Christian, you not only belong to God because He created you, you belong to Him because He redeemed you.

"Do you not know that . . . you are not your own? You were bought with a price." (1 Corinthians 6:19-20) Therefore, Paul can say, "So whether you eat or drink or whatever you do, do it all for the glory of God." (1 Corinthians 10:31)

Now it appears that God is stuck on Himself, doesn't it? Does it seem as though He's being a little absolute, a little selfish about all this? Well, I don't share my wife with another man. I don't try to correct every kid in my neighborhood. Am I being selfish?

No. Sharing partners and trying to raise everyone else's kids is just not the way God created marriage and the family to work. If You're the Creator and You created something for a purpose, You have the right to demand that it fulfill Your purpose and nothing else.

Do you like everything your boss tells you to do? Probably not. So why do you do even the things you don't like? Because the man has your money.

Now when the day comes that you can start your own business or create your own world, then you get to call your own shots. But as long as you and I live in God's world, we need to recognize that God owns it, and He shares His glory with no one. There's only one throne.

I have a wife God has given me the privilege of loving. But even she belongs to Him. I have children He's given me the privilege of raising, and I have a home God allows me to live in. But all things belong to the Maker of heaven and earth.

GIVING GOD HIS DUE

If God owns everything, how does that relate to the concept of tithing, or of giving God 10 percent of what we make?

God established the tithe with Israel in the Old Testament. He told the people that He wanted the first 10 percent of everything they produced, whether the crops in the fields or the animals born to the flocks and herds (see Leviticus 27:30-33).

The tithe was not designed to allow the Israelites to say, "OK, God, here's Your 10 percent. The other 90 percent is ours, but here's Your part." No, the tithe was a way of saying, "God, this tithe is my way of acknowledging that You own it all and gave it all to me. I realize the 90 percent is Yours too."

We tend to get it all mixed up. We figure that if we give God ten dollars out of our hundred dollars, the other ninety belongs to us. But giving is designed to remind us that the whole hundred bucks belongs to God. He graciously allows us to keep ninety dollars for our needs, but it's all really His.

The tithe was also to be given *first*, to remind the Israelites that God would meet their needs if they honored Him. So returning God's portion before you pay any bills is a way of saying you know who the real owner is.

This is a view of stewardship most of us aren't used to. We're used to digging into our pockets when the collection plate comes around, finding something that jingles, and dropping it in. But God says, "I want you to let Me know that you know that I own all of it."

WHAT IT MEANS TO YOU

Now if God claims ownership of everything, it follows that He also has first lien on everything. The way you let God know you understand that you are His steward is by giving Him first priority in every aspect of your life.

NO LEFTOVERS

The test of our stewardship is whether God winds up with our left-over time, energy, and resources, or whether we give Him our first and best. To put it another way, Jesus is either Lord of all, or He is not Lord at all.

There's a great example of this principle in the book of Malachi. The Israelites of Malachi's day dishonored the Lord by giving Him the worst of their flock for sacrifice, rather than the best as the Mosaic Law prescribed (Malachi 1:7-8).

The people would look among their sheep, see a nice fat one, and say, "No, we can't give that one to the Lord. It's worth too much money." They'd see another nice one and say, "Can't use that one for sacrifice. He's got a great coat of wool."

So they would set aside the valuable sheep for themselves. Then they would find the sheep that were born with defects, that were lame, or that were diseased and going to die anyway, and offer these to the Lord, hoping He would accept their sacrifice.

222 · NO MORE EXCUSES

These people were giving God their leftovers, the junk they didn't want, and saying, "Lord, You ought to be happy I'm giving You something. I'm doing You a favor, so be happy with what You are getting from me."

But God said, "Oh really? If you think that kind of offering is acceptable, trying giving it to your governor. Go to your earthly ruler and offer him what you are offering Me, and see whether he will take it."

You get the point. If an earthly ruler would be insulted by an offering of our leftover junk, how much more would the Ruler of heaven and earth be insulted by such an offering?

Look how seriously God took this insult. "'Oh, that one of you would shut the temple doors, so that you would not light useless fires on my altar! I am not pleased with you,' says the LORD Almighty, 'and I will accept no offering from your hands.'" (Malachi 1:10)

PUTTING GOD FIRST

God says to shut the temple, close down the church, if that's all we are going to give Him. One reason many of us Christian men are not seeing God actively at work in our lives is that we are still giving Him our leftovers and expecting Him to be satisfied. What He wants is to be first in everything.

When we give God any lesser priority in our lives, we are relegating the Owner to the demeaning position *below* that of His steward or manager. That's never going to work because it doesn't work on the human level. Your employer would not be satisfied with your leftover time, energy, and skills.

Neither is God. You can give God a million dollars, but if it's out of your leftovers, He finds it unacceptable. That's the principle of priority we need to understand.

WHAT'S IN STORE FOR THE GOOD STEWARD

But let's turn this around, because I want to show you what God has in store for the man who makes stewardship a priority. In Matthew

6:25-34, Jesus gives us the greatest reason in the world to offer God our best instead of our excuses.

The first reason is stated in verse 25: "Therefore I tell you, do not worry about your life." For what reason? The reason is given in verse 24: "No one can serve two masters." Jesus says you will hate one master and love the other.

Then He comes back with this statement about not worrying. What's the connection? Jesus knows that if He can get you to love Him alone and Him supremely, you won't be worried about anything.

THE SIN OF WORRY

Did you know that the word *worry* is from a word that means to strangle? That's what worry does to us. It chokes us. It cuts off our emotional and spiritual air supply so that we get frustrated and angry.

Worry is like fog. I'm told that a fog that can cover up to seven blocks contains less than one glassful of water. Fog is a lot of smoke and almost no substance. It's the same with worry. It's like a rocking chair, taking you back and forth but never getting you anywhere.

Jesus tells us not to worry about what we are going to eat or drink or wear. He asks, "Is not life more important than food, and the body more important than clothes?" He is saying not to worry about your food or clothing. If you want to worry, worry about whether you are going to get up tomorrow. It's hard to get dressed if you're dead. It's hard to eat if you're dead.

Jesus' point is that if God gives you life, He's going to take care of what you need to sustain that life. If you wake up alive tomorrow, that means God has obligated Himself to take care of you for at least one more day.

What Jesus is doing is helping us get things in the right perspective. Most of us *don't* worry about whether we are going to get up tomorrow. We assume we will. When we go to bed at night we already have tomorrow planned. We don't worry about whether our heart is going to stop while we're sleeping.

But we worry about things like how we are going to pay the bills tomorrow, how we are going to straighten this or that out tomorrow, what we are going to wear to work tomorrow, where the money is going to come from for the kids' braces tomorrow.

Jesus says we are worrying about the wrong things. If your heart stops, you won't have to worry about any of that. We are worried about earthly details while God is saying, "I'm the One who controls life and death. Seems like I'm the One you ought to be concerned about."

GOD'S PROMISE: "I WILL PROVIDE"

Do you see how this relates to our stewardship? If we get our lives straightened out before God and learn to trust Him and rely on Him, He's going to assume responsibility for our tomorrows. If you want to see how this works, Jesus says, "Look at the birds of the air." (6:26)

When you look at the birds, you see creatures with plenty to eat. But what you don't see is a bird plowing with a tractor. You don't see birds getting together to raise a barn and then stock it with hay or corn. You don't see any of that.

But notice the end of verse 26: "Yet *your* heavenly Father feeds them. Are you not much more valuable than they?" (my emphasis). God is the Creator of birds, but He is not their Father. He's your Father. So if He takes such magnificent care of birds He's not even related to, what are you worried about?

If you saw me feeding birds in my backyard, would you wonder if I'm feeding my kids? You would probably think that any father who takes the time and trouble to feed birds is going to feed his children. That's what Jesus wants us to think about our heavenly Father.

Now it's true that birds dig for their worms. They work for their food. They don't just sit on a limb with their mouths open waiting for God to drop worms from heaven. But birds don't stockpile worms either.

Birds search and dig for food, but they do so because they expect to find worms. In other words, they don't worry about finding a worm. They figure if they found a worm today, they are going to find one tomorrow because God is going to have one out there somewhere for them.

Now remember, we're talking about the priority of stewardship; that is, the attitude of the mind and heart that says we recognize God owns it all, that we are just managers of His property, and that therefore He deserves first place in everything. Jesus is building toward this as He unfolds His teaching here in Matthew chapter 6.

When you see how God takes care of the birds and the flowers (see verses 28-29), you can see why it's a sin to worry. Did God wake you up this morning? Then you're sinning to worry because you are saying that while God may have the ability to keep you alive, He doesn't have the ability to clothe, feed, or shelter you. When you worry, you're saying, "My Daddy doesn't care."

Not only is worry sinful, it is also useless. According to verse 27, worry doesn't extend your life. "Who of you by worrying can add a single hour to his life?" It may, in fact, shorten it. There's one thing you and I need to know about our lives, and that is that our days on earth have been appointed by God.

Now that's not fatalism. That's biblical reality. God has allotted to all of us our life span, and when He's ready to take us home, no amount of jogging or oat bran or anything else will delay it one day. Those things will just help you look better on your way out. So if God has your days firmly in His hand, worrying about the next one won't do a thing for you.

You say, "But, Tony, I'm just a worrier. I can't help it." Yes, you can. Worry is a decision. You can decide to worry or not to worry. Jesus wouldn't command you not to worry if you weren't able to do just that.

GIVING GOD HIS PLACE

The real issue isn't whether you worry, but whether God is first. If He isn't, then you *should* be worried. Why? Because that means you are assuming the responsibility of providing for your own needs. You are trying to act like the owner rather than just the manager who works for the real owner.

How do you know if God is first in your life? One way is by how

you handle your money. People who think that the church and preachers are always trying to get their money may be confused. That attitude is based on the false assumption that if I give something to God,
that means I now have less.

But that's not it at all. God says, "If you will honor Me first with
your money and your time and your abilities, I will make what you have
stretch further than you ever could." The problem comes when we try
to hang on to all of it on the excuse that we earned it and it's ours.

What happens when we take that attitude is that the paycheck
never seems to go far enough. The prophet Haggai told the people of
his day, who were living well while God's temple was in ruins, "You
earn wages, only to put them in a purse with holes in it." (Haggai 1:6)

Guess who was cutting the holes? God has a way of seeing to it
that if we don't honor Him, we don't get to hold on to what we have.
Suppose God reversed things and gave us *His* leftovers. You wouldn't
want just leftover oxygen or water, would you? I wouldn't either. So
let's get to Jesus' bottom line on this:

> "So do not worry, saying, 'What shall we eat?' or 'What shall
> we drink?' or 'What shall we wear?' For the pagans run after
> all these things, and your heavenly Father knows that you need
> them. But seek first his kingdom and his righteousness, and all
> these things will be given to you as well."
>
> —*verses 31-33*

The word *kingdom* means God's rule, or God's plan, or God's
program. God says if we will seek His eternal program first, He will
work with us on the temporal stuff.

Brother, that takes the pressure off. I'm not under any pressure
because God says that if I will look after Him, He will look after me.
That doesn't mean I don't have to work and save and be responsible,
but it does mean I can turn the worry over to the Owner. It's His stuff,
so if something breaks He gets to fix it.

Now I'm not perfect at this because I worry sometimes, just like you do. But it's a sin for me to worry, because God says, "Stop worrying, Evans. It's a sin for you to call Me Father and then act like I'm not going to feed or clothe or shelter you."

Verse 34 has another good word for us. "Therefore do not worry about tomorrow, for tomorrow will worry about itself. Each day has enough trouble of its own." Jesus is saying that God is not going to give you tomorrow's grace today. He is only going to give you enough for today. So if you are worried about tomorrow and next week and next year, you are in trouble because God is not helping you with tomorrow yet. He is only helping you with today.

Back in 1989, I went into the hospital. The doctor thought a lump I had was cancer. The night before the surgery, as I lay on that hospital bed, was I worried about what I would wear the next day or what would be on the menu? Do you think I was worried about whether the roof would shelter me from rain?

I assure you I was not. In that hospital, the only thing that counted was God and my relationship to Him. Praise God, the lump was not cancerous, and I left the hospital. Now God says, "Evans, I gave you your life back. I let you walk out of that hospital. So don't insult Me by worrying about whether I'm going to feed you. I'll feed you until I'm ready to take you home."

If God is first, you can stop worrying. But only if He's first.

THE PRIVILEGES OF STEWARDSHIP

Now it's getting real good. Not only does God assume the responsibility and the worry when we turn the ownership over to Him. He even rewards and blesses us when we're faithful in doing the comparatively little that we're asked to do.

CONTENTMENT

One reward for faithful stewardship is contentment, a quality of life so elusive that the world has been chasing it for centuries and still hasn't found it. In Philippians 4:10-12 Paul writes:

I rejoice greatly in the Lord that at last you have renewed your concern for me. Indeed, you have been concerned, but you had no opportunity to show it. I am not saying this because I am in need, for I have learned to be content whatever the circumstances. I know what it is to be in need, and I know what it is to have plenty. I have learned the secret of being content in any and every situation, whether well fed or hungry, whether living in plenty or in want.

Paul calls the attainment of contentment a secret. So come on, Paul, tell us the secret. "I can do everything through him who gives me strength." (4:13) The secret to being a contented steward is to have such a dynamic relationship with Jesus Christ that it doesn't matter what your circumstances are. You're just tickled to death to belong to the Lord regardless.

That seems wrong to most people, because the world puts an "if" or a "when" where Christians are supposed to put a "regardless." Most people are content only when the money is good and the house is nice. Most people are content only if they are in good health.

But Paul says the secret to real contentment is found only when Christ is dynamically at work in your life. Now the reason that this is a secret even to a lot of Christian men is that we don't slow down long enough to learn it. God can't teach us this lesson when we're knocking ourselves out to get ahead and don't have time to listen.

You may be saying, "But Tony, it's a dog-eat-dog world out there, and I'm one of the dogs. It's tough making a living. I've got to scratch and scrape just to keep up sometimes, let alone get ahead. I really don't have time to sit around trying to be super-spiritual about this thing."

GREAT GAIN

I hear you. I know what's it like out there. Everybody wants to get ahead. So how would you like to know another secret—the secret to making a great gain? Here it is: "Godliness with contentment is great gain." (1 Timothy 6:6)

Now Paul isn't saying that if you're godly, you'll do better on Wall Street than the next guy. He isn't necessarily talking about material gain. That may be a byproduct of getting your priorities straight before God, but it's not the focus. Great gain comes when you understand that you are just a manager of all you have, and that you can't afford to put God last.

Notice that great gain comes from godliness, which itself comes from God. Paul is saying that godliness is the only thing that can produce great gain. You can get a good job or improve your profit margin, but you can't get great gain without putting God in His rightful place.

So if the "great gain" of 1 Timothy 6:6 isn't money, what is it? Well, part of it is contentment, which we have already briefly discussed. Verse 7 gives us another reason to be content with what we have: "For we brought nothing into the world, and we can take nothing out of it."

We talked about this earlier in relation to God's ownership. You and I arrived bringing nothing of this material world with us, and when we depart we will go the same way.

Why break your neck trying to gain material things that God may give you anyway if you will live as His steward, faithfully giving back to Him a portion of what He has given you and trusting Him to meet your needs? You say, "But wait a minute. We don't have a house yet. We only have one car."

Verse 8 says, "But if we have food and clothing, we will be content with that." Does this mean you should never try to get a house if you don't have one? Does this rule out ever moving to a bigger house if you have the opportunity?

No. I don't think God is saying never to desire these things. But He *is* saying to be content until He pleases to give them to you. But don't let them become your obsession, because you will leave them behind someday, and in the meantime they can divert your focus away from striving for godliness.

Take a pair of newlyweds. They are deeply in love. Yes, they want a house one day, and they hope to get into a better financial situation. But they are content because there is great gain in their relationship. They enjoy just being together.

Ten or fifteen years later, this husband and wife are looking good in their designer clothes. Both of them have a car and a career. The home is nice. But wouldn't it be tragic if, in all they've achieved, they've lost that "great gain" because now they are living like two strangers in the same house?

That could happen because money can buy a house, but it can't purchase a home. Money can buy you medicine, but it can't buy you health. Money can buy pleasure, but it can't buy peace. There's nothing wrong with houses and cars and careers, but when you leave out godliness, God says He won't give you great gain, because great gain is the things money can't buy.

BEWARE OF THE LOVE OF MONEY

Now look at verse 9: "People who want to get rich fall into temptation and a trap." Paul is talking about those whose passion is to get rich. It's their single great obsession. A Christian who succumbs to that passion has fallen into temptation and sin.

You know how a snare or a trap works. The trapper covers it with brush and uses bait to lure the animal into the trap. Just when the victim thinks he has a meal, the trap has him.

That's how money works. You think you have it, but it has you. How do you know if money has you? Go back to what we've been talking about all the way through. What's number one in your life, God or gold?

The rest of verse 9 reminds us once more that God is not trying to hold out on us or keep us from something good. An inordinate desire for money leads to "many foolish and harmful desires that plunge men into ruin and destruction." Does that sound like a route you want to take?

The problem is that the love of money doesn't make you more generous and loving. It doesn't make you a better husband or father or

Promise Keeper. Instead, "the love of money is a root of all kinds of evil." (verse 10) Don't misread that. Money itself is not evil. It is neutral. The problem is in the heart, not in the paper. What you love comes first.

You know you love money if your passion for it outweighs your passion for God. You know you love money when you have to choose between money and God, and money wins. You know you love money when your career keeps you off your knees, out of the Word, and out of fellowship with the saints.

This is why God required His people to give Him a tenth of their income as a minimum, and why He required it to be given first. He wants to help us learn not to love money, but to love Him. Stewardship is His way of making us think of Him first. So Paul told Timothy, "Flee from all this, and pursue righteousness, godliness, faith, love, endurance and gentleness. Fight the good fight of the faith." (verses 11-12a)

Satan is going to try and change your priorities. He's going to try and get you to fix your hope on the uncertainty of riches rather than on God, "who richly provides us with everything for our enjoyment." (verse 17)

SEE FOR YOURSELF!

Now I realize that for some guys, messages on money come under the category of, "That's easy for you to say." So let me just close by saying, don't take my word for it. Try it for yourself.

Go to God and say, "You're going to be number one with me. I'm going to arrange my life by Your priority scale. I'm going to stop owning stuff and start being a manager. I'm going to stop giving You what's left over. And I'm going to trust You to fulfill Your Word and take responsibility for my needs."

My brother, once you understand that you can't shortchange God and expect to come out right, once you see that you can't outgive God when you put all you have in His hands, then making God number one will be no problem for you.

FOURTEEN

NO MORE CLOCK-PUNCHING

"WORK MUST BE PART OF THE CURSE. A JOB THAT'S EIGHT HOURS OF DRUDGERY EVERY DAY OR ONE I ENJOY BUT THAT CONSUMES ME—I CAN'T WIN."

A man was walking down the street one day and passed a major construction project. He went up to one of the workers and asked, "What are you doing?"

The man answered, "I'm laying bricks."

Another laborer was working a few feet away, so the man asked him, "What are you doing?"

The second man said, "I'm building a cathedral."

Some men lay bricks, while others build cathedrals. The difference has to do with one's perspective on work. If you have the wrong perspective, you'll lay bricks. If you have the right perspective, you'll build cathedrals.

There are a lot of excuses men give about work. The lazy man says, "I don't want to work." The frustrated man says, "I don't like my job." The purposeless man says, "My job is not getting me where I want to go." And of course the broke man speaks for all of us when he says, "I'm not making enough."

Well, the Bible has a lot to say about work because God is big on work, particularly for men because of our leadership role as providers for our families. It's unfortunate that we live in a world where people are finding ways to get out of work, or to do illegitimate things to sustain themselves, because work is a gift from God.

THE GIFT OF WORK

Let me place work in its theological setting. I want to talk about the significance of work from God's vantage point.

Work existed before sin did. So if you only look at work as part of the curse that came because of Adam's sin, you've missed it. Work was always a part of God's plan. The first chapter of Genesis brings this out, because it shows us God Himself at work.

The first thing the Bible says is that "God created the heavens and the earth." So the Creator was busy from the beginning. In Genesis 1:2, God's Spirit was "hovering over the waters." In verse 5, God was busy giving names to the entities He had created, calling the light "day" and the darkness "night." Verse 7 says that "God made the expanse."

Then God said, "Let the water under the sky be gathered to one place, and let dry ground appear." (1:9) And in verse 17, God placed the sun, moon, and stars in the heavens, orchestrating more of His creation. God was very busy organizing His creation.

What we see God doing in Genesis 1, before there was ever humankind or even sin, is expressing Himself by doing productive work. God is the ultimate Worker, and because He decided to work we have a magnificent world that was brought into being.

This is powerful stuff, because God was having a good time as He worked. We know this because every time He made something, He congratulated Himself. He said, "That's good."

Then when He made man and woman, His crowning achievement, He looked over everything He had made and said, "It's all very good" (see Genesis 1:31). God felt a definite sense of accomplishment in what He had done. He felt good about His work.

You're supposed to feel good when you work too. It's the feeling an accountant gets when the numbers come out right and he says, "Yeah, that's good." It's the feeling an athlete gets when he scores, or the sense of accomplishment a businessman feels when he closes the deal. When you can say about your work, "That's good," you're imitating God. That's how it was meant to be.

We were made to be producers like God because we are created in His image. You were created in the image of a working God. That's why one of the first things God did when He created Adam was to give him a job—to work the Garden of Eden and take care of it (Genesis 2:15).

Remember, sin still had not entered the human race, so Adam's job as the overseer and manager of Eden had nothing to do with a curse.

God gave Adam a job, and then He gave him the authority to do something creative by naming the animals (Genesis 2:19-20). God had given the day and the night their names, but now He allowed Adam to share in this aspect of the creative task. Adam was free to make up the names, because God said, "Whatever you want to call these creatures is cool with Me" (see verse 19).

Adam had an awesome job—cultivating the Garden of Eden. Then God gave him a helper, Eve, to work alongside him and help him fulfill the divine mandate. What I want you to see is that when God created man, He created him to be a worker because God Himself is a worker. God always has a deal going.

As men, we were not made just to react to God's creation. We were given the authority to help *shape* His creation. You and I were not put here just to watch what someone else is doing. We were put here to help cultivate, manage, and shape God's creation. What an awesome honor! We get to do what God does. We get to work.

AFTER THE FALL CAME THORNS AND THISTLES

Now you may say, "That sounds great, but my job's not like that." It may not be, because sin entered in. When Adam and Eve rebelled against God, it affected their work. When they decided to be independent, the marketplace was affected. When they tried to go their own way, it affected their economic well-being. One of the judgments for sin was a curse on work:

"Cursed is the ground because of you; through painful toil you will eat of it all the days of your life. It will produce thorns and thistles for you, and you will eat the plants of the field. By the sweat of your brow you will eat your food until you return to the ground, since from it you were taken; for dust you are and to dust you will return."

—*Genesis 3:17b-19*

Now there is a problem. God says that from now on, creation will resist your work. In the Garden, everything was clean and pure. You didn't need a Weed Eater in Eden. But with the introduction of sin came thorns and thistles to jab and prick and resist man's efforts in work. Now man would sweat because he was going against a created order that was not going to cooperate with him.

This is why so many men feel like work is a life sentence rather than a blessing. This is when you start hearing the excuses for the haphazard and shoddy way some men approach their work. When you are in a job you don't like, when you feel like your job is meaningless, what you're feeling are the thorns and thistles of the curse. It's part of our fall into sin.

This also explains why men can be so creative in doing evil. We were born to create, but what sin has done is distort that ability so that now we use our creative ability to create evil. Isn't it amazing how ingenious evil people can be? They can come up with the most clever ways to do wrong.

Therefore, you and I not only have to work against a created order that grows thorns and thistles. We have to work against people who are themselves thorns and thistles. So when man fell, work fell with him.

REDEEMING YOUR WORK

That's the bad news. But the good news is that in Christ, God offers us the redemption of work. Even though men have fallen and the created order is now messed up and uncooperative, if you are a Christian you have the opportunity to regain a significant measure of the meaning of work.

INCLUDE GOD IN YOUR EVERYDAY

How can you do that? If you know Jesus Christ as your Savior, God can now plug you back into His will, into His plan. My brother, if you are going to find meaning in your work, you will only find it when you are in right relationship with God.

Otherwise, you can have the best job in the world and still be empty inside, because work in and of itself can't give you meaning. Look at James 4:13-17:

> Now listen, you who say, "Today or tomorrow we will go to this or that city, spend a year there, carry on business and make money." Why, you do not even know what will happen tomorrow. What is your life? You are a mist that appears for a little while and then vanishes. Instead, you ought to say, "If it is the Lord's will, we will live and do this or that." As it is, you boast and brag. All such boasting is evil. Anyone, then, who knows the good he ought to do and doesn't do it, sins.

Your work can actually become a source of sin when God's will is excluded. Conversely, it becomes blessed when God's will is included. The Bible is very practical about this. The degree to which you integrate God into your work is the degree to which you will find meaning in what you do every day.

REMEMBER WHOM YOU REPRESENT

What I'm saying is that if a couple of hours on Sunday is the only time for you and God to be together, don't be surprised if Monday through Friday is meaningless for you. The idea is to take God with you to the job in terms of your attitude. In Colossians 3:22-24 Paul writes:

> Slaves [employees], obey your earthly masters in everything; and do it, not only when their eye is on you and to win their

favor, but with sincerity of heart and reverence for the Lord. Whatever you do, work at it with all your heart, as working for the Lord, not for men, since you know that you will receive an inheritance from the Lord as a reward. It is the Lord Christ you are serving.

Put another way, if you don't go to work tomorrow thinking, "I'm going to work for the Lord," then you've missed the meaning of work. The quickest way to transform a bad job is with a new attitude. And the quickest way to get a new attitude is to change bosses.

Paul says if you work for the Lord, you get your reward from Him. If you're just working for "the man," the man can give you whatever reward he wants. But if you're working for the Lord, the man has to give you what the Lord tells him to give you.

This is a subtle yet significant reorientation to work. God wants you to find meaning in your work, but the thing that makes it meaningful is not the task itself, but your relationship with God in the task.

Tasks can change. But even if you get a project you're not excited about, if your attitude is that you are participating with God in the project, He can change the meaninglessness of work into the meaningfulness of work.

FIND JOY IN YOUR JOB

If you're struggling with your job, you need to read the book of Ecclesiastes. Solomon has a lot to say about finding meaning in our work, even in a sinful world. For example:

> A man can do nothing better than to eat and drink and find satisfaction in his work. This too, I see, is from the hand of God, for without him, who can eat or find enjoyment?
> —*Ecclesiastes 2:24-25*

Where have we heard this idea that work is good? God said it in Genesis chapter 1. But if you leave God out, you can have a great job and still not have joy. With God in the picture you can have a bad job and still possess joy in your work. In Ecclesiastes 5:18-19, Solomon advises:

> Then I realized that it is good and proper for a man to eat and drink, and to find satisfaction in his toilsome labor under the sun during the few days of life God has given him—for this is his lot. Moreover, when God gives any man wealth and possessions, and enables him to enjoy them, to accept his lot and be happy in his work—this is a gift of God.

You and I have a relatively few years to live and do productive work. Solomon is telling us to make the most of our work opportunities. In other words, don't be satisfied with a job you don't enjoy. Don't make it your goal just to punch the clock if that's all your job means to you.

God can give you the ability to enjoy your labor. Now that starts with your relationship to Him, but it should extend to the environment where you are expending your labor. God wants you to have a job you enjoy doing and can do well for His glory.

There's nothing worse than having to get up and go to a job you hate. Tell the truth and shame the devil. But do you know why a lot of men feel that way about their work? Because all they're doing is laying bricks instead of building cathedrals. It's a perspective problem.

The goal of work is not for you to put in your forty hours a week for forty years so you can quit and go to Florida to retire. Nor is the goal of work the accumulation of wealth so that you don't have to work anymore.

The goal of work is the joy and sense of achievement you get when you accomplish a God-given task. That's what God is after, so that's what you should be after. It would be better to make less money wanting to get up tomorrow morning than to make more money wanting to stay in bed.

STAY FOCUSED

I know we need money to support our families. But that's a long way from what the Bible calls the desire to get rich, which Paul warns will plunge men into great temptation, ruin, and potential destruction (1 Timothy 6:9).

There's nothing wrong with being rich. There's everything wrong with making riches your goal. If God has a Kingdom reason for making you rich, that's fine. But your joy should be in the accomplishment of your work under Him.

I like the attitude expressed in Proverbs 30:8-9, where the writer asks God not to give him too much for fear that he will forget God, or too little for fear that he will be tempted to steal. What he asks for is that God will meet his needs so that he can keep his focus where it ought to be.

GIVING YOUR WORK TO GOD

The beauty of this thing is that once you get God's perspective on your work, you can deliver your work into His hands. That way you don't have to stay up all night or work all day Sunday trying to get ahead or make ends meet.

THE SABBATH: A CHANCE TO RELAX, REST, AND FOCUS ON RELATIONSHIPS

The Bible teaches that there should be a day in every week when you cease from your labor. God didn't create us to be workaholics. We do that to ourselves. I'm guilty of this because I love what I do. So I tend to neglect Scripture in the area of the limitation of work, just as I know many other men do.

But even God rested from His work of creation on the seventh day (see Genesis 2:1-3). To enjoy His accomplishments, He stepped back and looked at them. He was finished, so He rested. Now God didn't rest because He was tired. His rest was the rest of accomplishment, of a job well done. It was the rest of reflection on and enjoyment of His work.

God thought it was such a good idea to rest one day in seven that He commanded His people to do the same. The seventh day on which God rested became known as the Sabbath. Now this was a big deal with God. In the Old Testament, breaking the Sabbath actually carried the death penalty.

We're not under law, but as Christians we are to cease from our work and take a day to worship the God who provided for us all week long. This concept worked its way into our culture in the form of the "blue laws" that prohibited the selling of certain items on Sunday. Those laws were a way of respecting the concept of the Sabbath, a time of worship and rest.

The Sabbath was serious because it was the day when you were supposed to focus not on your work, but on giving thanks to God for the work He allowed you to do. It was a time to enjoy the God of work rather than the work itself.

The Sabbath also meant you were trusting God for next week's work. This is powerful, because it means that when you are working in the will of God, you can trust Him for next week's opportunity, next week's promotion, next week's challenges. So instead of knocking yourself out, you say, "God, this is it. I'm done. I'm going to stop working and trust You."

One problem with workaholism for the Christian man is that it often reflects a lack of trust in God. What's behind workaholism is the sense that we've got to do it all ourselves or it won't get done. This is too important to leave to anyone else, even God.

Another problem with workaholism is that it kills relationships. The Sabbath was designed to re-emphasize the importance of our relationships with God and with each other. The reason so many of us men are workaholics is that we're scared of relationships. If I'm not working on Sunday, I may have to sit down and talk with my wife. And I may discover we have a problem or two. If I'm working, I have an excuse for not talking to her. So for many men, work becomes a good excuse not to relate to others.

That reflects our insecurity. In chapter 12 we talked about building relationships and how hard that is for many men. We don't want to get too close to anybody, so to avoid that we focus on work. That's why a lot of conversations between men never get beyond, "How's it going at work?"

All of this is to say that one way to avoid letting work dominate us is to put limitations on it. We are not to be driven by greed. And we are not to work seven days a week so that our spiritual life dries up and dies.

My brother, if you're working so hard that you never get time with God or time with your loved ones, you're working too hard. Your work was never meant to replace God in your life. Work had its limits even with the One who created it. He rested on the seventh day. In imitation, His people are to rest on the Lord's Day.

GOD'S PROVISION

Let me show you one more thing about Sabbath rest and what it means for you and your work.

In Hebrews 4:3, the writer says, "We who have believed enter that rest, just as God has said." In verse 10, he says, "For anyone who enters God's rest also rests from his own work, just as God did from his."

In the Old Testament, the Israelites entered into God's rest, which was the land of Canaan. It was a land flowing with milk and honey. It was a land where God had already provided everything they needed. All they had to do was trust the God of Abraham and enter into His rest.

When you know Christ, you likewise enter into His rest. He's already making provision for you. Look at Psalm 127:1-2:

> Unless the LORD builds the house, its builders labor in vain.
> Unless the LORD watches over the city, the watchmen stand
> guard in vain. In vain you rise early and stay up late, toiling for
> food to eat—for he grants sleep to those he loves.

Do you know what that means? While you're sleeping, God is cutting a deal. While you're sleeping, He's arranging things. While you're sleeping, He's fixing the system.

In other words, when you place limitations on your work by entering into God's day of rest, you begin to tap into His supernatural provision. He cuts the deals, He works the promotions, He gives the raises, He adjusts the scenarios, and He gives meaning to your work.

Jesus' friend Martha missed the point (Luke 10:38-42). She was so busy working in the kitchen that she didn't have time to sit at Jesus' feet. She was working too hard, trying to do too much—and she was irritated and aggravated.

So she lit into Jesus. "Why don't You tell Mary to get up off that floor, get her lazy self out here, and help me in this kitchen? I've got twelve preachers plus You to feed. The grease is popping from the chicken, and Mary won't budge."

Jesus told Martha, "I won't tell Mary any such thing. If I send her in there with you, I'll have *two* frustrated women on My hands. Mary has chosen the better part. So instead of fixing us a seven-course meal, do a casserole and then get in here" (another Evans paraphrase).

Now don't get me wrong when I talk about limitations on your work. When you work, you should work hard. But when you rest, you rest well. God has given us a Sabbath rest, and if we'll observe it as a step of faith in obedience to Him, He will cover us even in our sleep.

THE REWARDS OF WORK

God has arranged the universe so that productive work is designed to bring a reward. It's not always a monetary reward, although that is sometimes included too, but a reward that builds character and helps to make us the kind of people God wants us to be.

DIGNITY

The first reward I want to talk about is the dignity that productive work brings. When a man works, he gains a sense of dignity that nothing else can bring.

We know there is inherent dignity to work because God worked at creation, and He continues to work in our world. Just as Jesus' presence at a wedding in Cana dignified and sanctified marriage, so God's decision to work dignifies work.

If you take from a man his ability to work, you have removed from that man his sense of dignity and worth. Work gives a sense of worth. Now obviously it doesn't determine our ultimate worth, but it affirms our worth in a genuine way nevertheless. It fulfills our built-in need for a sense of dignity.

We know that God worked at creation. But Jesus had work to do also. On the cross He said, "It is finished." (John 19:30) In other words, "I have achieved the work I came to do. I have accomplished what I came to accomplish."

The word Jesus used in John 19:30 means "paid in full." His work of redemption was utterly finished—He paid off the sin note that hung over all of us. There's nothing like the feeling of being able to make the last payment on a bill because you worked hard and earned the money to retire the note.

In a much greater sense, Jesus had that feeling of accomplishment. In fact, Jesus spent His whole earthly life working. We can assume He worked hard in Joseph's carpenter shop. And He spent His entire ministry working out the will of His Father. He said on one occasion, "My Father is always at his work to this very day, and I, too, am working." (John 5:17)

RESPONSIBILITY

Another benefit of work is that it teaches you responsibility.

If you have a job, you have to get up. If you don't work, you don't have to get up, and chances are you won't get up. That's why you have to keep fighting the good fight with your kids to teach them responsibility.

What father hasn't wondered if his teenagers—boys in particular—will ever learn responsibility? Not long ago I told Jonathan, my youngest son, "It's time for you to go to work at the church. On Saturdays you're going to give the church a few hours of work."

He said, "You mean like a janitor's job, Dad?"

I said, "Yes, like a janitor's job."

"I don't want to be a janitor."

"Well, you're going to be a janitor. You're going to set up chairs and break down chairs. You're going to work."

Then he hit me with the big one. "But I'm the pastor's son."

But I had him there, so I said, "That's right. All the more reason to obey your father and learn the biblical responsibility of work!"

My point with Jonathan was that if he didn't learn to work now, he might get the idea, "I don't have to work." And when a person gets the idea that he doesn't have to work, he begins to rip off other people who *do* contribute. I don't mean necessarily hitting them over the head, although that's one way to steal.

But there are other ways to rip people off, like sitting home collecting a check without working, which involves ripping off the tax dollars that you and I have to pay. Worse yet is a man who lets a woman support him because he doesn't want to work.

These guys must think they're something. "I don't have to do anything. My lady takes care of me." Well, she's a fool to do that, and he's a fool to let her.

So if you're concerned about how the younger generation is going to learn responsibility, that's a legitimate concern—because we have a generation of people who are irresponsible. I don't know if you have noticed, but everybody is blaming somebody else for everything. Nobody is saying, "I messed up. It's my fault. It was me."

No, everybody blames the society. "If society didn't have these unfair conditions, then I wouldn't be here. If I were not in a poor neighborhood, then I wouldn't have this problem."

My father worked like a dog on the waterfront in Baltimore. He'd take me out there sometimes when he had to pick up his check on his day off, and he'd show me these guys working. They didn't have all the fancy equipment they have today for loading and unloading ships.

I remember thinking of my father that this man really works. What that did was create a work ethic in me. I saw my father work, as you probably saw your father work, and it helped to teach me responsibility.

A SENSE OF ACCOMPLISHMENT

As we have already discussed, work provides a challenge and a sense of accomplishment, so that when you're finished, you can say, "That's good."

By the time Sunday morning is over, I'm spent. After two sermons, I am physically and mentally wrung dry. But no matter how tired I am, by the time I finish the second service and pronounce the benediction, if I feel like the message accomplished the goal the Holy Spirit had for it, I feel that sense of accomplishment that comes from work well done.

The key to satisfying work is having the right job for the right reasons, which gives you the right reward. That's why you always want to move toward what I call your motivated gifts or talent. Let me explain what I mean by that term.

We have two kinds of talents. The first is just raw ability to do a job, whether you're motivated to do it or not. It's just something you know how to do. You may hate doing it, but you can do it.

The problem with unmotivated talent is that you only do it because you have to. There's no real feeling of accomplishment or satisfaction with it. At night you say, "Oh shucks, I've got to get up and go do that again tomorrow."

But motivated talent says, "You mean I get to do this again tomorrow?" That's what preaching is for me in terms of a job. It's a motivated talent. It's the idea, "I get to do this again next week," or "You mean people will actually give me a plane ticket to fly there and do this?"

Preaching is a motivated gift for me. Nobody has to coax or beg me to preach. They have to beg me *not* to preach. It turns me on. That's what God wants to move you to. You may not be there now, but that's why you want to link up with Him. You want Him to begin to steer you.

Using your motivated talent in your work gives you confidence. When David was a shepherd boy, he didn't know God wanted him to be king. All he knew was that he wanted to be God's top shepherd boy. So when the lion and the bear came to take his sheep, he killed them. When Goliath defied God, David was ready. He had already killed ferocious animals. This guy would be no problem. David's work as a shepherd gave him confidence to face deeper challenges.

DOLLARS AND CENTS

The most obvious reward of work is the paycheck we receive, but I saved it until last because it's not first on God's list.

But God isn't a miserly boss. He knows the laborer is worthy of his hire, and He always makes sure that His people are paid a fair wage. You deserve to be paid a fair wage for your work, or for the ability of your enterprise to produce.

WHATEVER YOUR WORK, GIVE IT YOUR ALL

My brother, we have to establish the right attitude about work. We've already covered Colossians 3:22-24, which says that we work for the Lord. In 2 Thessalonians 3:10, Paul says any man who won't work doesn't get to eat.

Now if a man *can't* work, you help him. But if he *won't* work, you don't help him. When he gets hungry enough, he'll change his mind. That's why the church is not like the welfare system, paying someone not to work.

I'm a terribly anti-welfare person. Welfare started out as a temporary, stop-gap measure to help the farmers and then to help people through the Great Depression. That was good, but then welfare became a permanent institution that now rewards people for being irresponsible and lazy.

The Proverbs are full of the lazy man's excuses for not working. Some of them are really pretty humorous. "The sluggard says, 'There is a lion in the road, a fierce lion roaming the streets!'" (Proverbs 26:13) In other words, the lazy man makes up excuses not to go to work. "Hey, there's a lion out there. I might get eaten." Anything to get out of honest work.

Let me lay this one on you. A sluggard says, "There are no jobs out there." Why is that a sluggard's mentality? Because if you're a man, and especially if you know Christ, you were made to be a producer, not just a job finder.

Now there may not be any openings in your field, but a man who understands his responsibility before God does whatever it takes to provide for his family, even if it means flipping hamburgers for a time.

Granted, it's not the best job. And it certainly isn't the best income. But it can be done with integrity—even with joy. Why? Because you can flip hamburgers to God's glory.

Read verses 14-16 of Proverbs 26 and you'll get the rest of the picture of a sluggard. It's not pretty. So my closing challenge to you is, be zealous in your work. Don't give excuses for giving less than your best in your work.

Begin to think in terms of being a producer rather than just a consumer. Remember that you are working for the Lord, not just for "the man." If the only time you work hard is when you know your boss is looking, you've got an attitude problem about your work.

Working for the Lord means working with integrity and being honest. When Zacchaeus came to Christ, he paid back the people he stole from fourfold (Luke 19:8). He became a man of integrity and honesty in his work.

And of course, make sure you are a witness for Christ at work. People ought to know you are a Christian. I don't mean necessarily that you stop working so you can witness. I mean that both by your words and by your outstanding work habits, you give witness that you belong to Christ and that you're working for the Kingdom. It should be evident to your coworkers that the hand of God is on you by what you say and what you do.

The great thing is that, as Paul said in Colossians 3:24, when you work for the Lord, you get your reward from the Lord. And no one knows how to reward like He does!

FIFTEEN

NO MORE
BUSINESS AS USUAL

"WHO HAS TIME TO WORRY ABOUT A VISION?
THAT'S PIE IN THE SKY. I'VE GOT MY HANDS FULL
TRYING TO MAKE A LIVING."

In case you haven't figured it out by now, someone has done a number on us men. The world, the flesh, and the devil have joined forces to so radically redefine and distort manhood that this generation of men has been left damaged.

The results are all around us. Some men have reacted passively. They haven't seen too many examples of godly manhood and leadership, so they are satisfied just to sit back and let others do the leading for them—sometimes transferring the burden of leadership to the women in their lives.

Other men are misguided leaders. This is the guy who wants to be a leader and thinks he is a leader, but doesn't really know what it means to be a leader in any biblical sense of the term. So he often leads from insecurity. He makes sure folks know he is in charge. But if you have to tell people you're a a leader, nobody knows it but you.

Another false brand of male leadership is the guy who uses violence to push others around, trying to establish his place by beating his wife, for example. This is false leadership gone completely bad, right up there with the man who defines leadership as sexual prowess.

THE NEED FOR A VISION

Now this chapter isn't on leadership in general, so here's my point. One of the key aspects of leadership is vision, the ability to see a goal others don't see, help them see it, and then help them reach it. A man with vision sees where he needs to go and motivates others to go along too.

I want to talk about the need for a vision, what it consists of, and how to develop a vision for yourself, your family, your business, or whatever. To show you how it works, I've also included a sample vision, which you'll find at the end of this chapter.

Many of the principles we are going to talk about apply whether you're married or single, although our primary attention will be on the family. Since the man is the head of the home, he is responsible for guiding the family in the way it should go. It comes with the territory.

If we are going to put away the excuses that stand between us as we are and the men God wants us to be, we must be men of vision. We must see beyond the ordinary, the everyday, the expected. We must not settle for what's routine or safe.

A FATHER'S INFLUENCE KEEPS GOING . . . AND GOING . . .

Why? Because Exodus 20:5-6 says that the actions of a father have repercussions for generations. What a father does not only relates to *his* life. It spills over to his children and his children's children.

That is a sobering thought. It would not be so bad if my mess was left with me. But my mess gets passed on and on to many succeeding generations. Of course, the principle works the other way too. My faithfulness can bless my family for generations.

It's no wonder that Satan targets men. He understands this generational relationship. He knows the damage he can do if he can produce generations of children who grow up never knowing the touch of a father, never experiencing a father's blessing.

There is only one thing to do: raise up a new generation of godly men who will change the trend. You and I have the challenge of being that kind of men and raising that kind of children. The stakes are terribly high. To our forefathers, faith was an experience. To our fathers, faith was an inheritance. To us, faith is a convenience. To our children, faith is a nuisance.

Turning that around involves getting a new vision from God. The Bible shows us how much we need a vision. According to Proverbs 29:18, "Where there is no vision, the people cast off restraint." That is, they just bounce off the walls and go in every direction. That is true for nations, for families, and also for us as individuals.

ASSUME THE RESPONSIBILITY

My brother, our families need leaders with a vision. Otherwise, the members will make decisions that are in their own interest rather than in the interest of the larger family agenda. That's just human nature.

If you don't provide a vision for your family, your family will create one on its own. A lot of husbands and wives have totally different ideas of what their family should be, so they live in conflict. Many wives create their own vision either because their husbands don't provide one, or because they never share it. So the wife has to guess what her husband expects.

People will not operate without leadership, even if they have to become their own leaders. But obviously, when everyone is going his or her own way, you're not going to make much forward progress in any one direction.

SETTING YOUR SIGHTS

You and your family also need a vision to provide you with a challenge to meet and a target to aim your lives at, resulting in a sense of significance and fulfillment.

It's true that if you aim at nothing, you'll hit it every time. If you want meaning and purpose, you have to have a goal, something to reach for. To give you that sense of significance, your vision needs to be connected to something that reaches out and grabs you, a passion that stirs your heart and gives you a reason to get up in the morning. For the Apostle Paul, that passion was knowing Christ: "I want to know Christ and the power of his resurrection and the fellowship of sharing in his sufferings, becoming like him in his death." (Philippians 3:10)

There has to be more to our existence than putting in our time at work and trying to keep up with the bills. Those things are important, but they are not strong enough or big enough in themselves to fulfill the need all men have for significance, the feeling that they are somehow making a difference.

But I suspect that if you ask the average man where he is going, his basic answer will be limited to his job and his income. But if that is all you have going for you, you aren't going very far.

If there is no call of God on your life, you will have no real sense of destiny. Destiny produces a sense of vision and a willingness to dream dreams to get there. A visionless man is a man with little or no sense of calling.

All of us as Christian men ought to get on our knees and say, "Lord, give me Your view for my life." People give up when they don't see anything out there worth living for. If you want a new spark for yourself and your family, give your family a new vision of what they can do.

THE INGREDIENTS OF A VISION

If you and I are meant to be leaders as the heads of homes, and part of that leadership is providing a vision, then we need to find out the ingredients of a meaningful vision.

A CLEAR SENSE OF GOD'S WILL

This is one thing that should make the vision of Christian men distinctive. We are not simply looking for what *we* want to do or what turns *us* on. We are to seek *God's* purposes for our lives and our families, and fall in line with them. This will keep our vision on track spiritually.

Making sure your vision is in line with God's vision is crucial because if you are trying to act independently of God's vision or God's will for you, you won't get the Master's help to accomplish your goal. So the will of God is very critical, because we need to know what He wants and expects of us.

A CLEAR STATEMENT TO YOUR FAMILY

A second ingredient of a biblical vision is the need to communicate it clearly to your family.

Your family members should be able to restate to you the key aspects of the family vision and the role they are expected to play. The only way I know that my family knows where we are going is that I have shared the vision with them—and they can give it back to me.

Now this may sound easy, but I realize that many men have a problem in this area. They just don't tell anyone what they're thinking. If you want to know whether you're really coming across clearly to your wife and kids, see if they can tell you what your goals and desires are for the family.

Let me show you a man who failed to communicate his heart to his family. His name was Lot, and he lived in Sodom (Genesis 18–19). Lot's relative Abraham had pled with God to spare Sodom if he could find just ten righteous people in the city.

Now Lot had a wife, at least a couple of sons, two daughters, and two men who were engaged to his daughters. So that could have been almost ten people right there. But Lot had failed to pass on his values, so his sons-in-law didn't take his warning that the Lord was about to destroy Sodom seriously (Genesis 19:14), and the city was in fact destroyed.

Go back to Genesis 17:26-27 and notice the contrast in Abraham's household. "Abraham and his son Ishmael were both circumcised on that same day. And every male in Abraham's household . . . was circumcised with him." If you lived in Abraham's house, you were going to be circumcised, as God had told Abraham to do.

Because my father sometimes had to work on Sunday, I sometimes had to walk to church. Now the church was about five miles away, but I could not say, "Dad, because you are not here to drive me today, I'm not going to church." It was understood that if you lived in Arthur Evans's household, you went to church. The man had a vision for his family.

A CLEAR STRATEGY FOR REACHING THE GOAL

Third in the mix of vision ingredients is a plan to get you where you want to go. A vision is not just a nebulous, hazy concept out there in the future. That's a pipe dream, not a vision.

If your vision is of the Lord, that means He has something He wants you to accomplish. If a person says he wants to be a doctor, for example, but has no plans to go to college, we have a definite problem. This person's goal and the track he plans to run on to accomplish his goal don't match. You need to have measurable steps you can take to get you to the goal.

A NEED FOR GOD

Pursuing a vision always involves taking some risks. You must be willing to step out in faith and dependence on God.

According to Hebrews 11:1, faith involves acting on what we can't see and hoping for something that is not always a visible reality. That's why you must depend on Somebody bigger than yourself to fulfill your vision. Any vision that you can accomplish on your own without God's help isn't big enough!

It's only when you get hold of something that is much bigger than you that you sense your need for God and begin to call on Him. That doesn't mean that all aspects of your vision will come true, but it does guarantee that you will have something worth going for. If only God can make it happen, we're talking about a powerful vision.

A GROWING VIEW OF GOD

This fifth ingredient of a vision follows naturally from the one above. The formula is simple: small God, small vision; big God, big vision.

What we have is too many maintenance men, guys who like to keep things as they are rather than dreaming of things as they ought to be. The size of your view of God will have a lot to say about the size and significance of your vision.

My wife Lois doesn't like to fly, especially in small planes. One time we were scheduled to fly to Iowa in a four-seat private plane. Lois said she wasn't going with me. I said, "Honey, you have a little faith."

She replied, "No, the problem is you have a little plane." But the plan changed and we wound up flying a commercial airline. She was now ready to go. I said, "Oh, your faith grew."

"No, the plane grew."

My wife's willingness to take a risk was tied to the size of the airplane. If you have a growing view of God, you'll be willing to take on the big challenges of life.

I want an ever-expanding view of God. I want my view of God next year to make what He did this year seem minor in comparison. Don't expect your vision to grow if your view of God doesn't grow with it.

AN ACCOUNTABILITY GROUP

You also need some sort of accountability structure to keep your vision on track.

This will help make sure you don't go off the deep end. At our church in Dallas, we are working hard on small-group ministry among our men, so we can hold each other accountable to our vision.

Our wives are also a great source of accountability, because if we're doing things right they will be the ones who share the vision and are committed to helping reach it. A family gives us built-in accountability.

A DISCIPLINED COMMITMENT

Another ingredient of a worthy vision is a disciplined commitment to stick to it and avoid things that will distract you from reaching your goal.

I always think of the story of George Allen, when he was coaching the Washington Redskins in the early seventies. He was invited to the White House for a dinner, but the problem was that the dinner was the last week of January. So Allen turned down the president's invitation.

Why did Coach Allen do that? Because he was preparing his team for the Super Bowl, and he didn't want anything to distract him from his task, even if it was the president. Allen had no objection to dining at the White House. The dinner just wasn't in line with his priorities.

A SHARED ENTHUSIASM

A vision must also include a clear demonstration of its ideals, one that pulls rather than pushes people toward the goal.

You don't want to force people toward your vision; you want to pull them toward it. If you are forcing people, then it is not a shared vision. If your vision is from the Lord and in line with His purposes, He can put the same desires in the hearts of your wife and kids, or any others you are leading.

Your challenge is to demonstrate your own excitement about and commitment to the vision. When it's clear to everyone that you're on board for the long haul, you won't have nearly as much trouble getting others to ride with you.

A WILLINGNESS TO DELEGATE

A final ingredient of a biblical vision is the importance of delegating parts of it to others, so that those who share in and benefit from the vision participate in its implementation. You want others to feel the ownership of the vision as well.

There is no better way to do this than to involve the family in reaching the goal. If you want your children to feel like this is their dream as well as Dad's, give them some responsibility at home or at church or wherever you can.

Howard Hendricks always said, "When you do for others what they can do for themselves, you make them emotional cripples."

DEVELOPING A VISION

How do you develop a vision? First of all, clearly identify the various areas of family life that need to be addressed, such as spiritual issues, education, career, finances, and entertainment. Then develop a strategy for each area that you believe incorporates God's will for you.

Remember to discuss this with your wife and come to a shared vision that incorporates her ideas and goals as well. You don't want to go to your wife and say, "This is the vision, no discussion."

Far too many men leave their wives behind as they pursue their life's goals. I told Lois that in order to do what I felt God was calling me to do, I needed her to help me through college and seminary.

But then I asked her what she wanted to do, because my commitment to her was that after I had completed my education and was on solid footing, I would double back to support and empower her in what she felt God wanted her to do.

So Lois gave up her education and stayed home with the kids while I progressed in my education and ministry. But later I supported her while she got her degree. Today much of what has been achieved in my ministry is traceable to the contributions Lois has made.

Next, communicate your vision to your children as appropriate and ask them for their ideas and input. Let your kids see that you have a dream and that your dream includes them. Then help them think about how they can contribute to the achievement of the vision, especially in the areas that affect them.

One thing that will help you in developing your vision is to try and express it in a clear, simple, and easy-to-remember summary statement. Make it easy to grab hold of; then ask God regularly to guide and even adjust the vision as necessary.

KEEPING THE VISION ALIVE

Once you get a vision, how do you keep it alive and growing? The most obvious way is to make sure your vision stays linked into God's will. To do that, we'll want to regularly submit our dreams to God's plan, His program, and His goals. Our prayer should be, "Lord, not my will, but Your will be done. I will adjust to You."

Another way to keep your vision going is to plan an annual weekend getaway with your wife to review and update the family vision. Most men need a special time like this because they have trouble talking in a meaningful way with their wives in the midst of the daily routine. When the guy comes home from work, his wife says, "Let's talk."

Most men simply want to say, "OK. I went to work. Work was fine. I'm hungry. What's for dinner?"

A lot of wives complain that their husbands won't talk to them. Now when you were dating your wife, talking to her was no problem. The reason was that you had a goal of winning her. Then there was the marriage and plans for a life together. You were shooting for something.

If you aren't shooting for anything now, you don't have anything to talk about. But if you have a vision and your wife is part of it, you have plenty of stuff to talk about.

I would also plan regular updates with the whole family to keep the vision before them so they can continue to pray over it. And don't forget to review your vision with an accountability partner who can help you in the pursuit of it.

Let me give you one word of caution here. Make sure the people you share your vision with are visionaries too. If not, they will tell you why you can't do it.

I don't hang around people who tell me I can't do something, unless they have a biblical reason for saying so. But to simply tell me it can't be done or give me a list of reasons why it will never be done doesn't help me. My reaction is, "It's never been done before? Well, let's try to be the first."

THE PLACE TO START

We've covered a lot of ground, and you may be saying, "Tony, I just don't know where to start putting a vision together." Well, let me finish up by giving you a biblical pattern that I think will also convince you that the effort is worth it. I'm talking about Psalm 128, which gives us God's vision for a family.

YOURSELF

The first aspect of God's vision for your family is His vision for you as the leader. The psalmist writes: "Blessed are all who fear the LORD, who walk in his ways. You will eat the fruit of your labor; blessings and prosperity will be yours." (Psalm 128:1-2)

The man who "fear[s] the LORD" is the man who learns to obey and submit to Him. Don't demand that your wife or kids follow your leadership if you are not willing to let God demand that you follow His leadership.

The word *fear* has the dual idea of awe and judgment. It means looking up to somebody, holding that person in high esteem. To fear God is to have the highest regard for His glory, His greatness, His holiness.

The result will be peace within yourself. You will be able to enjoy where you are until you get to where you want to go. When you are right with God, you can have confidence that He has your future in His hands. You can relax, because it will be well with you. So we must start with ourselves.

We don't have enough men who take God seriously. They'll go to church and say a prayer at dinner, but that's not what I'm talking about. We need men who will say, with Joshua, "As for me and my household, we will serve the LORD." (Joshua 24:15)

YOUR WIFE

Then the psalmist turns to a man's leadership in the life of his wife. "Your wife will be like a fruitful vine within your house." (Psalm 128:3a)

A lot of brothers don't like to hear this, but the fact is that when we come home from work, we are coming home to our second job. I know, you come home to watch TV, read the paper, and eat dinner, but that's not all you come home to.

Now I can hear some guy saying, "Wait a minute. I'm tired. I have been working all day, relating to people. I don't want to come home and relate. Besides, my wife doesn't just want to relate. She wants to emote. She wants me to feel it. I can't pull that off after a long day."

Really? Then let me ask you this. What would you do if you were getting ready to leave work at the end of a long day and your most important client called, saying he needed to see you right away? What you're going to do is make a way out of no way—and you'll be nice about it too.

Why? Because your client has your money in his pocket. You adjust based upon the significance of the person who interrupts you. The more significant the person, the more the interruption is allowed. Our wives often don't feel all that significant because when we come home, all they get are the leftovers.

The man with a vision has a wife who becomes like a "fruitful vine" in his house. The psalmist is picturing a grapevine loaded down with luscious grapes. When a man starts getting it right, his wife begins to flourish.

Let me tell you something about grapevines. The ripeness of the grapes is determined by one thing, the weather. If the weather is good, the grapes will grow nice and juicy. If the weather is bad, they'll be small and stale.

One reason many of our wives are so unfulfilled, so emotionally dry and withered instead of flourishing, is because the "thermostat" is set so low in the home. When it comes to your home, my brother, you are the thermostat. You determine the emotional and spiritual temperature in the house.

Don't expect to have nice grapes if the thermostat is turned down low. Don't expect the juice to flow if it's cold inside. Don't expect exuberant sexual response from your wife if the temperature isn't set right. Don't expect a warm, summer woman if you're providing winter temperature.

What we do determines what our wives become. You don't find the right wife, you develop the right wife. One way you do that is by serving her. Jesus said, "The greatest among you will be your servant." (Matthew 23:11) So as the leader, you should be doing more for your wife than your wife is doing for you.

Our wives married us because they got excited about what we offered them, which was somebody who would live for their well-being. When you were trying to win your wife, you showed her a man whose passion was to live for her alone. So you took her places she wanted to go and did things she wanted to do.

What she saw was a man who so valued her that he would inconvenience himself for her pleasure. So she began to say, "This is a man I can love."

Now you didn't like shopping then, and you probably still don't like shopping. But the difference is that before you were married, you faked it. "Oh, you want to go to the mall? Sure, baby, I just want to be with you." Now you say, "You want to go the mall? Well, go right ahead, but I'm tired. I'm not going to any mall."

When you ask your wife to share with you in developing a vision that includes helping her to become all she can be, you communicate to her that she is of the highest value to you. When you commit yourself to helping your wife flourish, you want to talk about her, not you or the kids. You want to focus on her.

When that happens, your vine will grow and you will get to enjoy the fruit of that vine. A grapevine doesn't drink its own juice. It's grown for the enjoyment of others. If your wife is like a fruitful vine in your house, both of you will enjoy the result.

You may say, "I don't see any fruit on my vine." That may have something to do with the thermostat's setting. Some husbands are not interested in talking to or loving their wives apart from sex. These guys are good when they are in the right mood. Then they can make stuff up about how beautiful and wonderful their wives are. But the wife knows she is not going to hear anything like that until the next time her husband wants his desires fulfilled. It is simply true that the husband sets the emotional temperature in the home.

YOUR CHILDREN

Psalm 128:3 goes on to say, "Your sons [children] will be like olive shoots around your table."

This is God's vision for your children. Olive plants were very important in biblical days because they had a lot of uses. Olive oil was used for cooking, for medicine, and for massages, among other things.

Notice that the psalmist talks about olive shoots because these are not yet full-grown trees. What a great picture of the way we should be tending and nurturing our children. They are little shoots off the big plant that need to be cultivated and cared for.

You know how it is with young plants. You have to make sure they are watered and packed in good soil. The idea is that our children are filled with potential that needs to be developed and brought to full growth.

One reason children were so valued in biblical days was that a man knew if he dealt right with his kids, his own future would be secured when he was old. In helping his children grow into productive adults, he found his joy and some of his own success.

Now you won't know how well your children are growing up around your table unless you are at the table too. That means your vision must include a major commitment of time to your kids.

I'm convinced there are a lot of boys and young men who would go the right way if they only had the right man at home challenging them in the right way. The problem is, there aren't enough good men in the homes challenging them. So these boys and young men are influenced by the drug pushers and the gangs.

Sixty-three percent of black boys are growing up without a father. By the year 2000, it will be 70 percent. Only 38 percent of American men attend church, and only 25 percent are members of any church. This is a crisis. The man is not only the thermostat of the home. He's the filter, catching and filtering out stuff that shouldn't get inside.

YOUR CHURCH

God's vision for you includes your church. "May the LORD bless you from Zion." (Psalm 128:5a) Zion was Israel's place of worship. Hebrews 12:22 uses Zion to refer to our place of worship too. "But you have come to Mount Zion, to the heavenly Jerusalem, the city of the living God."

What we need is men who are not ashamed to be true church-men, men whose wives (or whose pastors) don't have to prod them into taking the lead spiritually. But what we have are too many church "hitchhikers."

The problem with a hitchhiker is that he doesn't invest in the car or buy the gas. He just wants a free ride. And you'd better not have an accident or he may sue you.

Other men are "McChristians." They want drive-through Christianity. No getting out, no going inside, no commitment, no sacrifice, no inconvenience. But God calls us as men to develop a vision for the church, because the church is His representative on earth. It is our extended family, the family of God.

YOUR COMMUNITY

Finally, God wants you and me to be men with a vision for our communities. "May you see the prosperity of Jerusalem." (Psalm 128:5b) If we get our homes and our churches right, our neighborhoods will have peace and our cities will be better places in which to live.

We cannot let our communities go to seed while good men do nothing. We must be involved. Taking an interest and a place of leadership in the community, no matter how small-scale that involvement may be, gives us the chance to help others and witness to our faith.

So God's vision for a man starts with his personal life, moves to his wife and children, and encompasses his church and his community. Everybody is better off when a man becomes a man of God, a leader with God's vision operating through his life.

What's the result? "Indeed, may you see your children's children. Peace be upon Israel!" You get to see your godly influence passed on from your children to your grandchildren. You build a legacy. A new climate has evolved; a new environment has taken over. There is peace in Israel. The community has been tamed.

"BLUE-COLLAR" CHRISTIANITY

What we need is some "blue-collar" Christianity, some "roll up your sleeves" kind of faith among the men of God. I'm talking about men who decide it's time for a new vision. It's time to dream a new dream.

Now some of us fathers have not been all that we should be. But the good news is that God can take lemons and make lemonade. He can hit a bull's-eye with a crooked arrow. Maybe you can't fix what went wrong yesterday, but you can do a lot about what happens today!

Getting a vision may mean you start turning off the television thirty minutes earlier and spend time on your knees with your wife and family. It may mean sitting down with the family one Sunday afternoon, opening Psalm 128, and asking, "How are we going to implement this in our home?"

As the father, you need to be in control of your family's future. Satan is going to try to thwart and discourage you. Maybe the kids won't cooperate at first. Your wife may wonder what's happened to you for a while. You may feel like there's no use trying.

But once you decide that you and your family are going to be guided by a God-given vision, the Lord will honor your leadership because you are His representative. May God bless and help you as you develop a vision for your home.

A SAMPLE VISION

VISION STATEMENT:

To develop my family in a spiritually responsible, technically excellent way so that each member maximizes his or her full potential in Christ.

I. *Spiritual Life*: To make sure each member of my family is maturing in Christian faith.
   A. Church Worship
      1. To regularly attend church as a family and review what has been learned.
      2. To be actively involved in a ministry of the church.
      3. To develop a relationship with another family in the church whose children are the same ages as ours.
   B. Family Worship
      1. To pray as a family on a daily basis.

2. To have a family worship time on a weekly basis.

3. To have a special spiritual retreat on an annual basis.

C. Personal Worship

   1. To set aside at least fifteen minutes for personal devotions each day.

   2. To teach my children how to develop a personal devotional life by the time they are teenagers.

   3. To meet with an accountability partner on a monthly basis.

II. *Recreational Life*: To promote meaningful fellowship and relationships that build up the members of the family.

A. To romantically date my wife at least twice a month.

B. To have a family outing at least once a month.

C. To take a family vacation annually.

D. To have at least two weekend getaways with my wife annually.

E. To spend personal time with each child monthly.

F. To make at least one affirming statement to each member of my family daily.

G. To set aside thirty minutes, at least three times a week, for a focused time to talk with my wife.

H. To work out at least three times weekly for my physical well-being.

I. To spend time each month with another Christian couple or family.

III. *Financial Life*: To be financially secure and stable.

A. To be debt-free within five years, except for the house and car.

B. To pay off my outstanding bills, beginning with the smallest bill first.

C. To pay off our house in fifteen years or less.

D. To develop my own business in five years.

E. To develop a family budget that is reviewed annually.

F. To teach my children how to give, save, and spend.

IV. *Education and Career:* To maximize the opportunities and abilities of each member of the family.

A. To complete my next degree or sharpen my skills so that I can move to the next level in my occupation over the next three years.

B. To read at least one book a month in my area of work.

C. To make sure my children are keeping up with their schoolwork.

D. To read at least one a book a year on some aspect of family life and responsibility.

E. To identify, help to develop, and use the skills of my wife.

F. To expose my family to culturally diverse and enriching experiences.

V. *Community Life:* To tangibly contribute to the stability, progress, safety, and development of the community in which I live.

A. To miss no more than two PTA meetings annually in my children's school(s).

B. To be involved in one quality community organization that helps others as well as provides the opportunity for Christian witnessing.

C. To be a registered voter who participates in every election that affects my community.

D. To get to know some of my neighbors personally.

SIXTEEN

NO MORE
HALF-STEPPING

"LOOK, I'M A CHRISTIAN. I TRY TO DO MY BEST.
BUT I DON'T WANT TO BECOME A FANATIC
LIKE THOSE GUYS ON TV."

Y ou may have heard the story of the chicken and the pig. They were walking down the street one day and came to a grocery store. There was a sign in the window that said, "Bacon and eggs needed." The chicken looked at the pig and said, "Let's help the grocer out."

The pig responded, "You must be crazy. For you that's just a contribution, but for me that's a total commitment!"

That's how a lot of men feel about the Christian life. "Hey, I don't mind contributing a little here and there. But let's not go overboard. Let's not get into this total commitment thing." That sounds a little too scary for a lot of guys, as if the Christian life is going to cost them too much. So they give a part of themselves to Christ, but hold back the rest in case the Christian life gets too demanding.

Where I grew up, they call that "half-stepping." That's when you try to walk with Christ and walk with the world at the same time. You might call it "two-timing."

Whatever you call it, it's what happens when you try to love Christ and love the world at the same time. But love doesn't work that way. It always calls for commitment. That's why I appreciate movements like Promise Keepers that are calling men to total commitment to Christ and to their families. The seven promises of a Promise Keeper call a man to commitment.

What I want to do in this chapter is to call you past the excuses men make and show you the excitement, the spiritual power, and the overflowing joy that await the man who is committed, sold out, to Jesus Christ.

THE ANATOMY OF COMMITMENT

In Romans 12:1-2, Paul gives what I call the anatomy of commitment:

> Therefore, I urge you, brothers, in view of God's mercy, to offer your bodies as living sacrifices, holy and pleasing to God—this is your spiritual act of worship. Do not conform any longer to the pattern of this world, but be transformed by the renewing of your mind. Then you will be able to test and approve what God's will is—his good, pleasing and perfect will.

Since everything we do is expressed through our bodies, Paul calls us to present our bodies as living sacrifices to God. The concept of a living sacrifice is interesting because it sounds like a contradiction.

In the Mosaic system, a sacrifice was killed. Yet Paul wants us to remain alive. We are literally to be walking dead people. How is this possible? Paul's understanding of his own life helps us here when he says, "I have been crucified with Christ and I no longer live, but Christ lives in me." (Galatians 2:20)

If you were to ask Paul what his goals in life were, he would probably have said, "I don't have any. Dead people don't set goals." If you were to ask him what his dreams were, he would have responded, "Dead people don't dream." But if you were to ask him what God's goals and dreams for him were, no doubt he could have talked all day long, because even though Paul was dead to himself, he was alive to God.

God's goals had become Paul's goals. God's desires had become

Paul's desires. The only life he had was the life of Christ. This is why no one could intimidate this brother.

If his enemies threatened to kill him, he could say, "To die is gain." (Philippians 1:21b) If they said, "No, we're going to let you live," he could answer, "That's fine. 'To live is Christ.'" (1:21a) If they said, "We're going to whip you," he could say, "I consider that our present sufferings are not worth comparing with the glory that will be revealed in us." (Romans 8:18)

If Paul died, he would go to be with Christ. If he lived, he would serve Christ. And if he suffered, he would get more reward from Christ. Therefore, since his whole life belonged to Christ, Paul's attitude was that it really did not matter what happened to him.

This kind of commitment is so important that Paul calls it our "spiritual act of worship." Notice that Paul doesn't say, "If you want to be committed, go to church." Worship starts with the commitment of our lives, not with our church attendance. We should go to church to do corporately on a weekly basis what we are already doing individually on a daily basis.

It's tragic that we have so many people worshiping God on Sunday who ignore Him—or even worse, worship themselves—the rest of the week. When you're a living sacrifice, every activity of your life becomes an act of worship.

THE MOTIVATION FOR COMMITMENT

Look at the reason Paul gives as to why we should present our bodies as living sacrifices to God. It's because of "God's mercy."

Now there's so much packed into that word that it would take the rest of the chapter to develop it fully. Basically, "God's mercy" refers to all that has gone before in the first eleven chapters of Romans. Let me summarize what this means for you and me as Christians today.

The first three chapters of Romans explain that the whole world, you and me included, is guilty before God. "There is no one righteous, not even one." (Romans 3:10) This is the bad news.

But then in the second half of Romans chapter 3, Paul gives us the good news of Jesus' sacrifice on the cross that brought humankind into right relationship with God. We were justified or declared righteous before God because Christ's blood satisfied the demands of a holy God against sinful men (3:21-26).

Then in the fourth chapter of Romans, Paul explains that salvation is granted to us in response to faith, not works (we're going to talk about the importance of faith later on). This means that our salvation is free and cannot be gained through any human merit. Rather, God gives it away to undeserving sinners. That's mercy!

But salvation is just the beginning of new life in Christ. Romans chapter 5 tells us that in Christ, we gain back the quality of life that the sin of Adam took away from us. We are introduced to a whole new dimension of life that provides a brand-new existence, joy in tribulation, and hope in time and eternity.

Now that doesn't mean all our problems are solved, because according to Romans chapters 6 and 7, we still struggle with the principle of indwelling sin. In fact, this is why we need to present our bodies to God.

When we do present our bodies to God, we can be assured of victory, as the eighth chapter of Romans shows. God has given us the indwelling Holy Spirit, who empowers us to experience all the rights and privileges God has for His children. This power is awesome, assuring us that "we know that in all things God works for the good of those who love him, who have been called according to his purpose." (Romans 8:28)

In a nutshell, those are the mercies of God to you and me. They deserve only one kind of response, the response of total commitment.

REJECTING WORLDLINESS

In Romans 12:2, Paul expands on what it means to commit ourselves to God. "Do not conform any longer to the pattern of this world, but be transformed by the renewing of your mind. Then you will be able to test and approve what God's will is—his good, pleasing and perfect will." (Romans 12:2) He tells us that as Christians, we are not to let this world order define who we are. Total commitment includes rejecting the attempts of this satanically controlled world system to get us to exclude God from our lives.

The essence of worldliness is independence from God. Being independent is especially tempting to men, and we've already talked about the spiritual damage men have suffered from an overdose of male independence. On a constant and unrelenting basis, this world order seeks to get you and me to leave God out of our lives.

Being worldly doesn't only mean committing gross sins. Nor does it mean going to so-called worldly places. The heart of worldliness is simply leaving God out, excluding His rulership from our daily lives.

Nor do you have to kill anybody or commit immorality to be worldly. All you have to do is let the world conform you to its shape, the way a potter takes a lump of clay and conforms it into a bowl or pitcher. Rejecting that pressure is impossible unless you are committed without reservation to Jesus Christ. A mushy, "half-stepping" kind of Christian life won't get the job done.

A TRANSFORMED MIND

Why does God want our minds? Because that is where the decisions of life are made.

If we are going to be committed to Christ, He must have control of our minds. This word *transformed* in Romans 12:2 is passive. In other words, the transforming work is done by someone other than us. If we commit ourselves to God and reject the world, the Holy Spirit takes over and begins the renewal and growth process. The implications of this are staggering, as we will now see.

YOU WON'T PRODUCE UNLESS YOU GROW

If you are a committed Christian, you will be a growing Christian. Growth follows commitment like day follows night.

Spiritual growth is possible because the Christian life is a dynamic, living thing. That's why Jesus used the analogy of a vineyard to deliver one of His most important messages on the process of spiritual growth:

> "I am the true vine, and my Father is the gardener. He cuts off every branch in me that bears no fruit, while every branch that does bear fruit he prunes so that it will be even more fruitful. You are already clean because of the word I have spoken to you. Remain in me, and I will remain in you. No branch can bear fruit by itself; it must remain in the vine. Neither can you bear fruit unless you remain in me. I am the vine; you are the branches. If a man remains in me and I in him, he will bear much fruit; apart from me you can do nothing. If anyone does not remain in me, he is like a branch that is thrown away and withers; such branches are picked up, thrown into the fire and burned. If you remain in me and my words remain in you, ask whatever you wish, and it will be given you. This is to my Father's glory, that you bear much fruit, showing yourselves to be my disciples. As the Father has loved me, so have I loved you. Now remain in my love. If you obey my commands, you will remain in my love, just as I have obeyed my Father's commands and remain in his love. I have told you this so that my joy may be in you and that your joy may be complete."
>
> *—John 15:1-11*

When Jesus refers to a branch "in me," He is not talking about those who are merely acquainted with Him. He is referring to people who are in a vital, personal relationship with Himself. But some of these branches do not bear fruit, so the Father has to throw them away.

Such branches are "picked up"—a common practice in grape growing. Sometimes branches that droop too close to the ground get covered in dust. They fail to get the sunlight they need and begin to wither. The vinedresser will lift these branches up off the ground and brush off the accumulated dust, making sure they get the life-giving light they need.

If possible, these branches are tied to poles or posts to keep them from drooping to the ground. In other words, the nonproductive branch is given every opportunity to produce fruit.

How does God "pick up" His people? Through encouragement, for one thing. I've seen it again and again, especially with new Christians who haven't had time to grow their branches very far from the ground.

I've seen God answer prayers that seemed impossible. I've seen Him make a way out of an inescapable situation. I've seen Him solve problems that appeared insurmountable. All the person on the receiving end could say was, "Thank You, Jesus!" Their praise was the beginning of fruit-bearing, the continuous offer to God of "a sacrifice of praise." (Hebrews 13:15)

THE PRUNING PROCESS: SHORT-TERM PAIN
FOR LONG-TERM GAIN

Going from producing no fruit to producing some fruit is an important step. But it's still just the beginning. Once you become committed to Christ and start reflecting a Christian character, God prunes your branches in hopes of producing more fruit.

Pruning is the process of trimming off unwanted shoots that can rob the branches of the nourishment they would otherwise receive from the vine. In grape growing, these are called "sucker shoots," little branches that grow where the vine and branch intersect. As they grow larger, they begin to do exactly what their name suggests; they suck away the life-giving sap on its way from the vine to the branch.

Even committed Christians need pruning, and it hurts. When God starts trimming off the stuff that should not be in our lives, it's painful. Now God knows that, but like a good father, He weighs the long-term benefit against the short-term discomfort and does what needs to be done.

THE CLEANSING POWER OF GOD'S WORD

In John 15:3, Jesus reminds us that we have been made clean, or saved, by the word He has spoken to us. Just as we are saved by hearing and trusting the word of Christ, we are also kept clean by hearing and heeding that same word. That's why it is critical for us to maintain regular exposure to the Bible, which is God's fixed revelation to us.

As David said, "I have hidden your word in my heart that I might not sin against you." (Psalm 119:11) The Word of God is our spiritual cleansing agent, purging out the undesirable junk—the sucker shoots—that collects in our lives so that we can become fruitful for Christ.

THE SECRET TO YOUR SPIRITUAL SUCCESS

The real secret to growth and fruitfulness in your spiritual life is remaining in Christ (15:4).

The word *remain* means to stay or abide. It's what happens when you put a tea bag in a cup of hot water. As the tea bag remains or "abides" in the water, it influences the water so that the water begins to reflect the color and taste of the tea.

Of course, the longer the bag abides in the water, the stronger the tea. This is exactly what happens when you abide in Christ and He abides in you. The influence of Christ so pervades your life that you begin to reflect the character and nature of your Lord.

Now the beauty of abiding is that all we have to do is maintain our contact with Christ to have the desired result. A tea bag really doesn't have any excuse not to produce results once it is dipped into the cup. In fact, it doesn't need any excuse as long as it stays put. The trouble with many of us men is that we are not good "abiders." We think we can survive apart from the vine. We provide for our families, so why ask God for our daily bread? We work, so why depend on someone else, even God, for our needs? You and I may work and do a lot of other things, but according to Jesus we can do "nothing" without Him.

Now you may say, "Wait a minute, Tony. Is that really true? Didn't you just mention some of the things we can do?" Sure, there's a lot we can do without Christ. But taken as a whole, it amounts to nothing. Jesus is saying that without His indwelling presence, we can do nothing that's pleasing or acceptable to God. We can do nothing to further our spiritual growth without Christ.

FOR THE STUBBORN, GOD LIGHTS A FIRE

This matter of abiding is pretty serious stuff, because Jesus goes on to say in John 15:6 that if we fail to abide, we're gathered up like a bunch of dried-up grape branches and burned.

Since we've already established that Jesus is talking to true believers, we need to be clear that the fire here is not hell. It's the fire of God's discipline. In other words, if we try to survive without abiding in Christ, we can look forward to fiery trials. If God can't get our attention any other way, He will do it by lighting a fire.

Now since men tend to be a little stubborn and often have to learn the hard way, there's a good chance you know what it's like to be burned by a fiery trial from the Lord. I've got burn marks all over me from learning the lessons God has wanted me to learn!

Whatever the circumstances of your fiery trials may be, God's purpose is not just punishment. His aim is to get you reconnected to the vine so that you can bear fruit.

AN OPEN-ENDED OFFER

In verses 7 and 8 of John chapter 15, Jesus gives us the flip side of the coin. Going it alone results in fiery trials. But abiding has incredible benefits: "If you remain in me and my words remain in you, ask whatever you wish, and it will be given you. This is to my Father's glory, that you bear much fruit."

I know this promise is often quoted by unscrupulous and unscriptural preachers on religious television. But they don't give you the whole picture. Jesus did not simply say, "Ask for anything." He said to *abide*, then ask. Our world is full of people who ask but don't abide.

But I don't want to rob this promise of its power. Jesus can make such a promise to His abiders because He knows they will ask only for what pleases Him, helps them bear "much fruit," and thus glorifies the Father.

How does one know one is abiding in Christ? The measuring rod is obedience (verse 10). If you lack obedience to Christ's commands, forget about praying. If you are not obeying Christ, you might as well get up off your knees, unfold your hands, open your eyes, and go for a walk.

Jesus said that only those who abide *in Him* can expect to receive what they ask for, and obedience is the key to abiding. But if you are vitally connected to Jesus Christ and completely committed to obeying His commands despite your flaws and failures, then don't hesitate to tell Him what's on your heart. Why? Because what you want from Him is identical to what He wants for you.

And while you're waiting for the answer, God gives you something to make the wait worthwhile: joy. "I have told you this so that my joy may be in you and that your joy may be complete." (verse 11) Joy is different from happiness. Joy has nothing to do with how things are going. Instead, it has to do with a God-given, internal quality of life. It can produce peace in the midst of panic, calm in the midst of chaos, and tranquility in the midst of turmoil.

Therefore, for the committed Christian, spiritual growth is a process, just like growing grapes is a process. The fruit God wants to see in our lives is likeness to Christ, from which will flow the good works that please God and demonstrate our faith to others.

THE IMPORTANCE OF FAITH

If we as men are going to stop "half-stepping" with Christ and move out in commitment, we need to understand what that commitment involves. We need to understand the process by which we grow as Christians. And we need to grasp the importance of faith to the life of commitment. After all, Hebrews 11:6 says, "Without faith it is impossible to please God."

It's safe to say that we cannot live powerfully on earth as Christian men without a significant measure of faith. So I want to help you see how important it is that we learn to live by faith. To do this I want to back up to verse 1 of Hebrews 11, which says, "Now faith is being sure of what we hope for and certain of what we do not see."

GENUINE FAITH FOLLOWS THROUGH

To believe in what you can see requires no faith; it's right there in front of you. But to be convinced that what you cannot see is real, and to have as much confidence in its reality as you do in what you can see, hear, taste, touch, and smell, is genuine faith.

But there's more to this word *certain* than just a firm belief. It refers to a certainty or a conviction that we are willing to act upon. In other words, we have to do more than talk about faith actually to have faith.

I'm reminded of the story of a high-wire walker around the turn of the century who had been wowing audiences from coast to coast. In what was billed as the biggest stunt in history, this daring young man stretched a wire from one side of Niagara Falls to the other.

Then, as an enormous audience looked on, he walked casually back and forth across the wire. He followed this with another round trip, this time riding a unicycle. For his next feat, he pushed a wheelbarrow loaded with bricks across and back. After executing each of these tasks flawlessly and without even working up a sweat, he stood on the platform and addressed the crowd.

"Do you believe I can cross the falls on this wire with a loaded wheelbarrow?" Of course, the crowd applauded. They had just seen him do exactly that.

"Do you believe I can push this wheelbarrow across the falls with a man riding in it?" Again, the crowd roared, eager to see him try.

"Very well," he said, motioning to a gentleman in the front row who was clapping his hands furiously. "Get in." Before he even had a chance to stop clapping, that man discovered the difference between genuine faith and mere "mental assent"! Faith requires follow-through.

ACTING ON YOUR FAITH

When I talk about faith in the context of Christian commitment, I'm talking about that quality of trust in and reliance on Christ through the power of the Holy Spirit that enables us to do what He has asked us to do. The book of James has several good examples of what I'm talking about.

In James 2:14, we learn that our faith must be demonstrated by our works. "What good is it, my brothers, if a man claims to have faith but has no deeds?" Now you know right away that James is not talking about faith as it relates to our salvation. We know that salvation is by faith alone, apart from any works on our part. But we don't stop exercising faith once we come to Christ. In fact, the Christian life is a faith-life from start to finish.

But James is saying that the faith we are to exercise as Christians has to be more than just talk. The illustration he uses in James 2:15-17 brings this out. If someone comes to you hungry and ill-clothed, he doesn't need just a pat on the back and the assurance that if he will just trust God everything will be fine. He needs food and clothes.

The point is that the benefits of faith do not happen to Christians just because they believe the right things, but rather because they execute the right actions based on that belief. If you are a defeated Christian today, it could be that you suffer from the problem many of James's readers suffered from: theology without practice, which James argues is useless to God.

The issue James wants us to wrestle with is not whether we have faith. That's already been established. He is concerned about the usefulness of our faith. You can see this in his illustration of Abraham (2:21-23).

Abraham offered up Isaac, validating his faith in God. Now that occurred in Genesis chapter 22, but Abraham was justified by faith back in Genesis chapter 15. However, it was only after Abraham obeyed God in the sacrifice of his son that "his faith was made complete by what he did." (James 2:22)

This is crucial to grasp if you want your commitment to Christ to result in spiritual victory. You grow in your faith only as you grow in your works. Only when you trust God enough to obey Him will you make progress on the road to victory.

Many Christians seek more faith. But Jesus made it clear that "mustard seed"-sized faith is really all that's needed to do great things (see Matthew 17:20). Most of us don't need more faith. What we need is a more obedient application of the faith we have.

James reinforces his point with an illustration of the harlot Rahab (2:25; see Joshua 2:1-16). According to Hebrews 11:31, Rahab demonstrated faith when she received the spies from Israel. But James adds the interesting note that she "sent them off in a different direction" to prevent them from being caught, thus proving that she believed in the God of Israel.

Now notice James's conclusion: "As the body without the spirit is dead, so faith without deeds is dead." (2:26) Many Christians could be pronounced dead spiritually for all the value that their faith is to them and to the cause of Christ. Day after day they move around like spiritual corpses because they refuse to take what they believe in their heads and make it part of what they do in their lives. You and I must rise above this spiritual "zombie-ism" if we are to become men of commitment. A committed Christian puts his faith to work.

THE BIG EIGHT: BLESSINGS OF COMMITMENT

Sometimes we preachers are guilty of talking about commitment like it was some terribly hard step that most Christians, and men in particular, must be almost dragged toward kicking and screaming.

Well, my brother, this preacher is here now to tell you different. I want you to know that there is no sweeter or more blessed way to live than being a man of rock-solid, sold-out commitment to Jesus Christ.

How do I know that? Because Jesus pronounced an eightfold blessedness on His followers who lived authentic, committed lives of faithfulness and obedience to Him (see Matthew 5:3-12). We call these blessings "the Beatitudes," derived from a word that means blessed or happy. As we look at these verses, I want to you note especially that Jesus directed them to His men, the disciples.

This blessedness is not a happiness derived from our circumstances. The word was used of the happiness the Greek gods experienced when their worshipers kept them pleased and satisfied.

Therefore, what Jesus is saying is that in order for us to be truly blessed or happy, we must find that happiness in our relationship to the true God. Commitment to God allows us to share in His happiness. Let's study the profile of a committed disciple and learn about the happiness such commitment produces.

A PROPER ATTITUDE TOWARD SELF

First, men of Christian commitment who are blessed of God and share His happiness maintain a proper attitude toward themselves. They are "poor in spirit." (5:3) They recognize their complete dependence upon God.

To be "poor in spirit" is the opposite of being rich in pride. It means you realize that you cannot possibly live the Christian life in your own strength. We learned earlier that Jesus said, "Apart from me you can do nothing." (John 15:5)

This word *poor* was used of beggars. The only way beggars can make it from day to day is to rely totally on the gracious gifts of those who pass their way. We must unashamedly depend on God, knowing that unless He dispenses His grace into the emptiness of our lives, we will remain spiritually bankrupt.

The happiness that comes to those who see their spiritual poverty is that "theirs is the kingdom of heaven." Heaven will be at the disposal of those who are dependent on God. They are the ones who get their prayers answered, who see God intervene in life's circumstances, and who enjoy their Christian walk.

A committed Christian man not only sees himself as poor in spirit, but he also mourns (verse 4). Jesus is referring to sorrow over sin. It means to hurt so much over our sin that we cry out to God in repentance (see 1 John 1:9).

Far too many Christians join the world in laughing at sin, tolerating sin, or simply being passive to it. But when our Lord saw sin, He wept (Luke 13:34-35). When Peter was confronted with his sin, he broke down and wept bitterly (Mark 14:72). And when Paul saw his sin, he cried out in spiritual pain (Romans 7:14-24).

Sin is like carbon monoxide in an enclosed car. You can get so used to it that it will put you to sleep and then kill you. But those who mourn over their sin will be comforted. When we feel the pain of God over our sin, then we experience the comfort of God.

A PROPER ATTITUDE TOWARD GOD

Second, committed Christian men maintain a proper attitude toward God. They are "meek" or "gentle" (NASB) and they "hunger and thirst for righteousness." (Matthew 5:5-6)

I prefer to use the *King James* and *New International Version* translation here—"meek," because I think it strikes a chord in us as men. Say the word *meek* to most men, and they think of a Casper Milquetoast, Barney Fife kind of guy who's afraid of his own shadow.

But meekness is not synonymous with weakness. The term was used in reference to bringing wild horses under control. A trainer would take an uncontrollable, undisciplined, and rebellious horse and break it to the bit and bridle. When the process was finished, the horse was said to be meek.

The horse did not lose its strength. Its strength was just under the control of the trainer. Meekness, then, can be defined as "strength under control." For us as Christian men, meekness means the strength to submit ourselves to the will of God. It means obeying God even when we don't want to. It means doing whatever God says because we have been domesticated by heaven.

The blessing on those who are meek or gentle is that "they will inherit the earth." Only meek Christians will see God take the earth and make it work for their benefit. Only meek Christians will see God work all things together for good by intervening in life's circumstances and bringing them to a well-defined conclusion for His glory and their good.

Committed Christian men also have a deep appetite for the things of God. Great men of God throughout history have all had this characteristic. David said, " As the deer pants for streams of water, so my soul pants for you, O God." (Psalm 42:1) He was spiritually parched.

The blessing God has for hungry and thirsty Christians is that "they will be filled." Far too many Christian men are following the world's path to satisfaction: money, power, entertainment, sex, etc. It's a dead-end street. Jesus is the only real thirst-quencher. He alone can feed you with satisfying bread from heaven.

A PROPER ATTITUDE TOWARD OTHERS

Third, committed Christian men who are blessed by God possess a proper attitude toward others.

The person who is "merciful" (verse 7) puts grace into action. Just as God looked down and pitied us in our hopeless, sinful condition, we must also show pity to others. A picture of mercy is the Good Samaritan, who got his hands dirty helping someone.

The blessing for givers of mercy is that they will also be *receivers* of mercy. If we are too busy to help others, God will be, so to speak, too busy to help us. If we are only known for giving people what they deserve rather than what they need, then do not be surprised if heaven is not available to us in our own time of need. Just as we want mercy and not justice from God, we also must extend mercy to others.

Committed Christian men are also "pure in heart." (verse 8) They are not hypocritical. They do not have to edit their lives, always cutting and pasting so you do not get to see them as-they really are. And when they do blow it, pure people confess their sins rather than cover them (Psalm 32:1-5). With pure people, what you see is what you get.

The blessing for the pure in heart is that "they will see God." That is, they will see God operating in their lives. He will not be a distant stranger to them, but rather an intimate friend.

Committed Christians are also "peacemakers." (verse 9) They pursue unity, not divisiveness. They seek to pull people together, not tear them apart. They seek to bring unbelievers into relationship with God and lead believers into intimate fellowship with God and others.

The blessing for these believers is that "they will be called sons of God." There will be public recognition of the godliness of those who promote harmony in the body of Christ. God will ensure a strong and vital testimony for those who keep the unity of the Spirit in the bond of peace (Ephesians 4:3).

Finally, committed Christians are "persecuted because of righteousness." (verse 10) A friend once told me, when he was ticketed for speeding, that he was suffering for righteousness's sake. I told him, "No, you are suffering for speeding's sake."

The idea here is to look so much like Christ in our actions and attitudes that what happens to Christ happens to us, and for the same reason that it happened to Him. The blessing for those who are persecuted and insulted for identification with Christ is a great reward in heaven.

In other words, the heavenly register rings each time we suffer because of our Christian commitment. If no one ever insults or rejects us, if no one ever talks against us, it may be because we are not committed. I say that because Paul says, "Everyone who wants to live a godly life in Christ Jesus will be persecuted." (2 Timothy 3:12) Persecution now means promotion later.

Are you tired of half-stepping with Jesus Christ? Then take that full step of committing yourself without reservation, and start enjoying all the good things He has for you.

· SEVENTEEN ·

NO MORE
STANDING ON THE
SIDELINES

"HEY, THERE'S ONLY ONE OF ME.
WHAT CAN ONE MAN DO?"

It doesn't take a genius to recognize that no matter where you live or where your children go to school, our communities are in a desperate situation today. There is a crying need in our world for men of impact.

I think it's an excuse to ask, "What can one man do?" because history is full of examples of individual men who did incredible things. These were men who rose above the crowd and made a lasting difference.

In fact, whenever you see change taking place in a home, a community, or even a nation, you can ultimately attribute it to the influence of some person. In other words, one man can do a lot. When we fail to see that, we miss the power of being a man—particularly when that man is a man of God.

Now when I talk about the impact one man can have, I don't mean we're all going to wind up on the cover of *Time* magazine as their "Man of the Year." What I am saying is that each man can make a difference in his sphere of influence. Every man matters. And if we get enough men making the right kind of difference, we will see real transformation taking place around us.

We forget that a lot of the wrong kind of impact is being made by one person. Not long ago, I conducted the funeral of the twenty-year-old son of one of our church's deacons. This young man was gunned down for making a turn in traffic and interfering with another driver. That driver made a tremendous impact on our church—a horrible impact, but an impact nonetheless.

One gang leader can impact a lot of other young people. It's the wrong kind of impact, but it can change young lives and even ruin our lives when we have to lock our doors and keep our children in at night for fear of the gangs.

It's been said that one of the worst things that can happen is for good people to do nothing. I'd like to amend that to say that one of the worst things that can happen is for Christian men either to do nothing or to do the wrong thing. So in this chapter I want to show you how you can be a man of impact.

As I began thinking about a man in the Bible, aside from Jesus of Nazareth, who embodies what it means to be such a man, my attention was drawn to Nehemiah. If you want to know what a single godly man can do, look at Nehemiah. That's what I want to do, drawing principles that you can put to work in your life as you seek to make a difference for Christ.

A MAN OF SPIRITUAL PERCEPTION

The first thing we need to understand is that a man of impact is a man of deep spiritual perception.

Nehemiah was a Jew living in Persia as a servant of Artaxerxes, the king of Persia. Now Nehemiah was a descendant of the Israelites who had been carried into captivity by the Babylonians, who were then conquered by Medo-Persia. So Nehemiah had no personal history in Israel, but his heart was there because that's where God's people and God's heart were.

So when Nehemiah heard the report from his brother that the

Jews back in Jerusalem were "in great trouble and disgrace. The wall of Jerusalem is broken down, and its gates have been burned with fire" (Nehemiah 1:3), he was crushed. He was crushed for the sake of his people, but also for the sake of his God, because he knew that these conditions were a reproach to God's name.

You and I know neighborhoods like that, where the walls are broken down and the gates are burned, so to speak. There is no question that the people in these communities need help, but the issue is the kind of help they need.

Nehemiah could have started pushing for a political solution. Get the right person in office, get the right laws passed, get the right programs in place, and things will get better. But Nehemiah knew better.

So the very first thing he did was go on his face before God with tears and prayer and fasting (1:4). He also turned to God's Word for the right perspective on his problem. Read his prayer in Nehemiah 1:5-11 and you'll see that Nehemiah knew Israel's spiritual history, and he also knew God's warning that He would send His people into exile if they did not repent (see 1:8).

This man understood that the root of the problem was his people's sin. But Nehemiah also used the Word to remind God of His covenant promises to restore Israel if they would turn back to Him and obey His commands.

If you want to be a man of impact, you don't start with political or social or economic solutions, although all three of these eventually came into play in Nehemiah's case. Rather, you fall before God in fasting and prayer, and you go to the Word.

Some of us men need to impact our wives because our wives don't respect us anymore. Some of us need to regain the respect of our children or perhaps of our employer, employees, or coworkers.

But whatever the case, whatever walls are broken down in your life, the first place to go is to God. What He will do through prayer, fasting, and searching the Word is bring to your heart and mind the things you must do to correct the problem.

You can go to your pastor or someone else for advice, but nobody can do what God can do in your life. When you seek God, what you do is send up an antenna that tracks a spiritual satellite and gets you in tune.

A man may say, "I don't see any way out of my dilemma. My predicament has no solution." It may seem that way now, but if we will get serious with God and get our spiritual "receptors" functioning, we'll witness some marvelous things done in our lives.

Nehemiah was facing a whole city in disarray, not just one person or family. But he had the right perspective; he knew a city wasn't too much for God to handle.

Now let me show you something interesting that happened when Nehemiah prayed. The last line of Nehemiah 1:11 says, "I was cupbearer to the king." Do you know what I think happened? I think God put this thought in Nehemiah's mind: "Wait a minute. I work for the king. I'm already in a position of influence."

As Nehemiah prayed, it dawned on him that God had already given him the answer he needed. Now I don't know how long Nehemiah had been praying, but it wasn't until he prayed that God brought the answer to his mind.

When you get on track with God, He brings ideas to mind. He shows you answers you wouldn't see if you thought and fretted about the problem all day.

I can't tell you how many times I have gone to God in prayer, and He has brought ideas and solutions to my mind that I wasn't even thinking about. They only came when I prostrated myself in prayer before Him. If you want to be a man of impact, become a man of spiritual perception, a man of prayer, of fasting, and of the Word.

A MAN OF INFLUENCE

Because Nehemiah was spiritually perceptive, he became a man of influence where the plight of God's people was concerned.

A cupbearer tested the king's drink to make sure it wasn't poisoned. That meant a cupbearer was very close to the king, and as a trusted servant he often became a trusted advisor to the king. So Nehemiah was certainly in an influential position.

Therefore, when he appeared sad before King Artaxerxes one day, Artie took note of it and asked Nehemiah what was wrong (2:1-2). Notice how Nehemiah responded:

> I said to the king, "May the king live forever! Why should my face not look sad when the city where my fathers are buried lies in ruins, and its gates have been destroyed by fire?" The king said to me, "What is it you want?" Then I prayed to the God of heaven, and I answered the king, "If it pleases the king and if your servant has found favor in his sight, let him send me to the city in Judah where my fathers are buried so that I can rebuild it."
>
> —*Nehemiah 2:3-5*

Did you catch that? Nehemiah said, "I want to rebuild the city." Have you ever thought about rebuilding a city, or your community? When people tell me that the vision I believe God has given me for rebuilding our communities and our cities can't be done, I tell them it *has* been done. Nehemiah did it.

Lots of guys have dreams, but they don't have plans. Now we talked about developing and having a vision back in Chapter 15, so I won't repeat that here. Let me just point out that Nehemiah had a plan already worked out when the king asked him what he wanted (2:6-11).

Where did Nehemiah get the plan? God put it into his mind as he fasted and prayed and reflected on the Word. God gave Nehemiah an idea, and then He gave him the influence he needed to pull it off, first with the king and then with "the priests or nobles or officials or any others who would be doing the work." (2:16)

Nehemiah was also wise in the way he used his influence to execute his plan, because he brought people into the plan who had a vested interest in getting it done. These people were living in Jerusalem in its broken-down condition, so they were motivated to get to work. "Let us start rebuilding," they said (2:18).

If you are going to develop and carry out a plan, a vision for your family, you want to get your family in on the action. You want them to own the vision as their own, not just Dad's.

Simply announcing, "I'm the head of this house. We're going to do this" may not get the job done. Your wife and kids may tell you, "Go ahead." A wise man uses his influence to get others on board.

Now let me tell you a secret. The moment you try to carry out a plan that is designed to promote a righteous vision, Satan is going show up. And he will show up "jump street"—up front, real close. Satan is going to get in your face because his job is to stop God's plans in the lives of God's men.

In Nehemiah's case, Satan showed up right away in the persons of some characters named Sanballat, Tobiah, and Geshem. "When [they] heard about it, they mocked and ridiculed us. 'What is this you are doing?' they asked. 'Are you rebelling against the king?'" (2:19)

In other words, they tried to turn this thing into a political issue. Satan isn't fussy about the method he uses, as long as it works. But Nehemiah appealed to a higher source, the God of heaven, for his vindication.

Nehemiah got everybody involved in the rebuilding project at the point of their ability and their interest. For example, in 3:1 we are told that the priests were put to work rebuilding the Sheep Gate. Now why would Nehemiah assign the priests to this gate? Because it was the gate through which the sheep would be brought for sacrifice by the priests.

So Nehemiah put people where they would be most interested in doing the job and where they had the most at stake in getting the work done. He also had people working close to where their homes were built into the wall.

Now obviously, if a man was building close to his home, he would have a definite reason to do the best job he could. He would have to live with the results.

In other words, Nehemiah didn't try to force square pegs into round holes, to use an old expression. A man who is going to make an impact on his world must know where people belong. He needs to know what their gifts and abilities are, and how those can best be used in executing God's plan.

This principle is especially important for us to understand in relation to our wives. Our wives are unique people with a unique blend of skills, interests, and gifts. The challenge for us is to help them identify and develop those abilities and gifts as they partner with us to accomplish our family's vision.

Too many men try to force their wives into uncomfortable roles according to what they, the husbands, think is best. That's why we saw earlier that men are to live with their wives in an understanding way (1 Peter 3:7), to study them until we know them well.

If you and your wife can forge a common vision using your different skills and strengths, you are on your way to accomplishing great things for the cause of Christ.

A MAN OF FAITH

Another quality we need to develop if we want to become men of impact is faith.

Why does it take faith to make a lasting impact for God? Well, according to Nehemiah 4:7-8, Sanballat and his gang got very upset when they saw that those "nuthin'" Jews were actually rebuilding the walls of Jerusalem. So they issued a military threat to try and stop them.

Read on in Nehemiah chapter 6 and you'll see that Nehemiah's enemies also used compromise, slander, and trickery to try and get him. They even plotted to assassinate him.

What's the point? Well, we already know that Sanballat and his cronies were Satan's boys. The point is that if you start to make spiritual progress in your own life and in your family's life, Satan is not going to let that go unchallenged. If he can't stop you by ridicule, he's going to turn up the heat.

Sanballat could only be strong as long as Israel was weak. As long as the walls of Jerusalem lay in ruins, Sanballat, who was the governor of Samaria, could control things without much effort because the Jews were defenseless.

As long as we aren't doing anything significant for God, Satan can control us without much effort. As long as he knows we present no challenge to his kingdom, he doesn't even have to get on us much to keep us in line.

But the moment the devil realizes that you and I are serious about praying and fasting for ourselves, our families, our communities, and our cities; the moment he knows that we are going to ask God to give us a vision and a plan to carry it out; the moment Satan knows we are committed to winning back our wives and children, he's going to throw the heavy stuff at us.

That's why when a man reaches out to his wife or his children in an effort to repair a bad relationship, he may encounter resistance from them at first. It takes a man of faith not to give up in the face of that resistance. It takes a man of faith to be obedient, knowing God can break down the barriers. Resistance comes because Satan doesn't want this to happen.

Sanballat was also jealous of Nehemiah. To Sanballat, Nehemiah was this nobody from nowhere who came to Jerusalem and started turning that whole mess around. When Sanballat's threats didn't stop Nehemiah, the jealousy turned to envy. Let me explain the difference.

Jealousy says, "I'm upset because I don't have what you have." But envy goes one step further. Envy says, "I'm not only upset because I don't have what you have. I'm going to make sure you don't have it either." Envy is jealousy gone crazy.

That's why Nehemiah had to be a man of faith to make the impact he made. He had to depend on God to take care of these guys, because he didn't have time to stop his work and try to defend himself against their taunts and accusations. He prayed, "Hear us, O our God, for we are despised. Turn their insults back on their own heads." (Nehemiah 4:4)

I love this. Nehemiah said, "God, I have a problem down here.

Would You take care of it for me?" Then he kept on working. He did not let people keep him from getting where God wanted him to be.

Don't let folk who don't want to make an impact stop you from making an impact by making you feel bad about your impact. You don't have to apologize for your impact. If you don't have any vision, apologize for that. But don't apologize to people who want to hold you back and put you down.

A man who isn't interested in doing the required work shouldn't expect to have any impact. Now we have to put work in perspective. God doesn't want us to be workaholics, but it does take hard work to do anything of real significance.

Nehemiah didn't ignore the threats made against him or pretend they weren't real. He prayed for God's protection, but he also put his faith into action:

> From that day on, half of my men did the work, while the other half were equipped with spears, shields, bows and armor. The officers posted themselves behind all the people of Judah who were building the wall. Those who carried materials did their work with one hand and held a weapon in the other.
>
> —*4:16-17*

In other words, Nehemiah and the men of Jerusalem said, "We are not going to let the criminals run us out of our community." Now a lot of men are involved in things like a neighborhood watch program, but in cities like Dallas and Ft. Worth, where I live, it sometimes has come down to men taking turns watching their streets so their families can go to sleep safe at night.

Now don't get me wrong. I'm not talking about playing vigilante or exercising "street justice" like the tough guys in the movies. I'm talking about men of faith taking a stand to keep evil from taking over.

While Nehemiah had the men prepared for battle, when it came down to it, he was still a man of faith. "Wherever you hear the sound of the trumpet, join us there. Our God will fight for us!" (verse 20)

294 · No More Excuses

Let me say one more thing about faith. In order to be a man of faith, your view of God must be bigger than your view of your enemies. If you have a bigger view of your enemies, then they will control you.

Wind can't move an iceberg because most of an iceberg is beneath the surface of the water. But the current can move an iceberg, even in the face of a fierce wind, because the pull of the current is stronger than the push of the wind.

If the pull of God is stronger in our lives than the push of our enemies, then God's influence will win out. I've been intimidated at various times, especially when my life was being threatened. That's not a good feeling. So I'm far from perfect here, but if I ever allowed the threats of the enemy to control me, I would have quit what I'm doing a long time ago.

What I'm saying is that if we are going to do anything lasting for God, we must be men of faith. And there will come those times when we need to take our stand together, "man to man, shoulder to shoulder," as men who believe God.

A Man of Justice

In Nehemiah 5, the situation in Jerusalem took a different turn:

> Now the men and their wives raised a great outcry against their Jewish brothers. Some were saying, "We and our sons and daughters are numerous; in order for us to eat and stay alive, we must get grain." Others were saying, "We are mortgaging our fields, our vineyards and our homes to get grain during the famine." Still others were saying, "We have had to borrow money to pay the king's tax on our fields and vineyards. Although we are of the same flesh and blood as our countrymen and though our sons are as good as theirs, yet we have to subject our sons and daughters to slavery. Some of our daughters have already been enslaved, but we are powerless, because our fields and our vineyards belong to others."
>
> —verses 1-5

What did Nehemiah do? According to verse 6, "When I heard their outcry and these charges, I was very angry." He got angry at the injustice. Oppression made him hot. Part of the explanation for Nehemiah's impact was that he was a man of justice.

The people of Jerusalem were mortgaging away their children and putting each other under slavery. Nehemiah fought for righteousness. He called a large meeting to deal with the people.

Look at his rebuke in verse 9: "Shouldn't you walk in the fear of our God to avoid the reproach of our Gentile enemies?" Excellent question. Nehemiah held the leaders of Jerusalem accountable for being men of honesty and justice. Then he reinforced the seriousness of the situation and the need to make things right. Nehemiah didn't let God's people get away with their unjust business practices, with holding their brothers in slavery. In this case, the problem was classism, the wealthy oppressing the poor.

In America today, racism is often the problem. Racism is having an errant view of another person simply because of the shade of that person's complexion—and that's wrong.

People have the right to be different, even people of the same race. Our brothers in Christ don't have to like the music we like. They don't have to talk like us or do everything the way we do it. As long as they are not disobeying God, they have the right to be different.

And we men must give each other that freedom in Christ. We must be men of justice. As a black man, I must have the freedom to say to another black man who may be acting wrongly toward a white or a Hispanic man, "Brother, I love you in the Lord. But what you are doing is wrong."

White and Hispanic men must also have the freedom to say the same thing to white or Hispanic brothers who may be acting wrongly toward a black brother. All of us need the freedom in Christ to say, when necessary, "Brother, what you are doing is wrong. That joke may be funny, but it's wrong."

Let's be honest with each other. Some of the stuff we as Christian men tolerate isn't even on the borderline. It's just wrong. So if we are going to be men of godly impact, we must be men of justice like Nehemiah. We must practice it, insist on it, fight for it when necessary. The question we need to ask ourselves is, "What does God think?," not "What will men think?"

A MAN OF PERSEVERANCE

Nehemiah was also a man of perseverance. He didn't quit too soon.

In the sixth chapter of Nehemiah, Sanballat showed up again. I alluded to this briefly above, but let's look at it in more detail. Sanballat and Geshem tried to get Nehemiah to come to a meeting on the plain of Ono, nineteen miles north of Jerusalem (verse 2).

But Nehemiah answered, "I am carrying on a great project and cannot go down." (verse 3) He said, "Oh, no" to the meeting in Ono. Now he knew they were out to get him, but the point is that Nehemiah wasn't about to quit his work to go to a useless meeting. He stayed with the job.

If you want to make an impact, don't stop doing what God wants you to do. Don't give up the dream God gave you just because trouble shows up. Keep rebuilding. Don't let other people knock you off the wall.

Too many of us are hearing the world say, "You can't make any difference. Don't even try. It's not worth the effort." Who says? I'll tell you who says. Sanballat says. The problem is, we're listening to Sanballat rather than continuing with the work. Keep on going. Don't let those who have no spiritual perspective stop you.

The great thing is, when you persevere in what God called you to do, you make an impact that carries on for generations. Nehemiah 7 is a long chapter, and when you look at all those lists of the tribes who returned to Jerusalem and Judah you may be tempted to skip it. But wait a minute.

Nehemiah was doing something more than just rebuilding the wall of Jerusalem. That's what he's known for, and that's what we talk about. But he was also interested in reestablishing the people who were going to live within the rebuilt walls.

After he had settled the problem in chapter 5 (helping the poor) and finished the wall, Nehemiah wanted to make sure that God's people were ready to carry on. So he appointed leaders for the city (7:1-2). Then he organized the people by their families in order to register them. Notice that from verses 8-65, it's sons and men all the way through.

Why doesn't Nehemiah talk about wives and daughters? It's not that the women weren't important, but rather that the women would come alongside their men when the men got their act together spiritually. And it was understood that the sons would carry on that spiritual leadership and keep the impact going.

Do you know that we have a virtual army of committed Christian women out there who have no one to marry? They can't find enough men who are serious about their commitment to Christ, who are through making excuses, and who are willing to make their personal interests secondary to God's call on their lives.

That's what Nehemiah is all about, men rising and keeping the family institution strong so the impact will keep on going. That takes perseverance by godly men in each generation. Nehemiah was a man of perseverance in his generation. My brother, it's our turn!

A Man of Spiritual Leadership

Nehemiah chapter 8 gives us our final ingredient in what it takes to be men of impact:

> All the people assembled as one man in the square before the Water Gate. They told Ezra the scribe to bring out the Book of the Law of Moses, which the LORD had commanded for Israel. So on the first day of the seventh month Ezra the priest brought the Law before the assembly, which was made up of men and women and all who were able to understand. He read it aloud from daybreak till noon as he faced the square before the Water Gate in the presence of the men, women and others who could understand. And all the people listened attentively to the Book of the Law.
>
> —verses 1-3

Now Ezra the priest was the preacher. Nehemiah was the layman, the governor. But did Nehemiah leave all the spiritual stuff up to the preacher? No, he was among those who led in this incredible experience of confession, repentance, and worship (8:9).

Now we've already considered the issue of a man's spiritual leadership, but I want you to notice it again because it comes up here. The principle is obvious: a man of impact is a man who takes spiritual leadership.

I regularly challenge the men of our church by asking them, "When was the last time you led a Bible study with your family? When was the last time you got on your knees with your kids? When was the last time you reviewed the Sunday sermon with your family and talked about what they learned or what they didn't understand?"

You don't have to be a preacher to take spiritual leadership. You don't need a seminary degree to pray with your wife. But look at the impact you can make. Most of Nehemiah chapter 9 is a prayer the Levites made as they led the people in repentance.

In verse 38, the leaders agreed to make a covenant of obedience to God, putting it in writing and signing their names to it. They were making a commitment to God and to each other to do what was right, binding themselves to their promises with their signatures.

That's what we must do as men of God today—bind ourselves together as brothers and make a commitment to God to be the spiritual leaders He calls us to be. If we will do that, we'll see God build walls that no man can ever tear down.

I think of the runaway slave Frederick Nolen, fleeing for his life. He hid from his pursuers in a cave, and then a spider came and built a large web over the mouth of the cave. By the time Nolen's pursuers got to the cave, they concluded he couldn't possibly be inside, because the spider's web wasn't broken. Nolen wrote after the event, "Where God is, a spider's web is like a wall. Where God is not, a wall is like a spider's web."

Finally, notice Nehemiah 10:39. One part of the commitment the people of God made was this: "We will not neglect the house of our God."

After your family and the work you must do to provide for them, I think your involvement in your church should be next. Every man should have some significant involvement in a church where God's Word is honored and taught faithfully.

No, it doesn't necessarily mean you are there every time the doors are open, but it means you are taking your place of leadership at some level. A man who wants to impact his world needs to be a vital part of the body of Christ. If not, he is hurting the program of God.

NEHEMIAH: A MAN WORTH REMEMBERING

Let's wrap up by looking at Nehemiah's prayers in chapter 13:

> Remember me for this, O my God, and do not blot out what I have so faithfully done for the house of my God and its services.
>
> —*verse 14*

> Remember me for this also, O my God, and show mercy to me according to your great love.
>
> —*verse 22*

> Remember me with favor, O my God.
>
> —*verse 31*

Isn't that what you want to be able to say? "O my Lord, remember me for the good I have done in Your name and for Your glory." Nehemiah wasn't a perfect man, but he could pray that way because he was a man of great impact. He was a man worth being remembered, as we are remembering him now.

You can pray this way even when you have to add, ". . . and forgive me for the times I have messed up." We all have to pray that, don't we? "Lord, have mercy, I'm just a mess."

But when we confess and come clean with God, He develops a bad memory concerning our mess-ups. He doesn't remember the bad stuff. "I will forgive their wickedness and will remember their sins no more." (Hebrews 8:12) As men of God, let's give God and our generation something good to remember us by.

And if we are going to do that, we need to remember that we can't please God and please everybody else at the same time. It will never happen, because people change their opinions all the time.

There was once an old man walking along leading his donkey while a young boy was riding on it. As they passed by, someone said, "Look at that boy riding on that donkey while that poor old man is walking." When they heard that, the boy got off the donkey and the old man got on, and they continued on.

But then they passed by some other people who said, "Look at that old man making that young boy walk." So this time the boy got on the donkey with the old man, and they both started riding.

But sure enough, they passed by another group of people who said, "Look at that old man and that boy overburdening that poor donkey." So they both got off and walked.

But then someone else said, "Look at that foolish old man and boy, not taking advantage of the availability of that donkey." So the next time they were seen, the boy and the old man were walking and carrying the donkey!

Brother, if we listen to too many people, we may wind up being remembered as those crazy guys who lugged a donkey around instead of riding it. If we're people like that, we won't make a lasting impact for God. Let's follow Him—and start making some godly memories!

EIGHTEEN

NO MORE "LOSER'S LIMP"

"MAN, I DON'T KNOW. YOU'RE ASKING ME TO
DO A LOT. I'M NOT SURE ALL THAT
EFFORT IS WORTH IT."

I hear you, brother. I get where you're coming from. So let's talk bottom line. Let's talk about what is waiting for the guy who "runs the race" God's way and wins the prize in eternity.

I don't think I've ever met a man, Christian or otherwise, who said he didn't want to be a winner. I'm convinced most men don't want to go through life with a "loser's limp" like the one we talked about in the introduction to this book. We males are taught to be winners from the crib. Winning is held up to us as everything.

Well, God has nothing against winners. There is nothing wrong with wanting to be the best. There is nothing wrong with wanting to be a winner. We just need to make sure we're competing in the right game to win the right prize. So let's talk about what it takes to put away the excuses and be a winner from the viewpoint of heaven.

THE CHALLENGE: WIN ONE FOR GOD

As we wrap up our study, I want to challenge you to make the greatest commitment you could ever make. I want to challenge you to develop a passion to be a winner for God.

A PASSION TO WIN

That's my passion. I want to close my eyes every night knowing that I did my best for God. I want to be able to say at the end of the day, the week, or even the year, "I lived it for God. I competed to win for the Kingdom."

When your passion upon getting up each morning is to say, "How can I make God look good today?"; when the passion of your life is to someday open your eyes in eternity and hear Jesus say, "Well done, My good and faithful servant"; when that becomes the consuming passion of your existence, it absolutely transforms your everyday experience.

The apostle Paul had that kind of passion. He knew what it was to compete for a prize. In likening the Christian life to a race, Paul urged us, "Run in such a way as to get the prize." (1 Corinthians 9:24)

GO FOR THE GOLD—AND NOTHING LESS

You can go to the store and get a nice jogging suit, but that doesn't make you a runner. You can go get a great-looking tennis outfit, but that doesn't keep your ball inside the baseline. You can wear a football jersey with the name and number of a star player on it, but that doesn't make you a football star.

Paul is saying, don't be satisfied simply to be part of the pack. Don't compete just for show. A winner breaks from the pack, and it's clear that Paul was intent on winning his race.

The problem is, a lot of us want to walk the Christian race or jog the Christian race. But if it's a race, the idea is to run as fast as you can to get to the finish line as soon as you can.

There are two good reasons why we men who know Jesus Christ as Savior ought to have as the overwhelming, dominating goal of our lives to know Christ better and to serve Him more.

One reason is simply because Jesus loves us and saved us. We are on our way to heaven. We have received a transfer slip out of hell. That ought to be reason enough to serve Christ without reservation and without excuses.

The second reason we ought to serve Christ is because there is going to be a payday someday. One day God is going to reward us for how we served and loved Him. In verse 23 of 1 Corinthians chapter 9, Paul said, "I do all this for the sake of the gospel, that I may share in its blessings."

Paul was saying, "I love Jesus, but I also see a prize at the end of this deal, and I want to go for it. I want to be a partaker in the victory celebration." Because of that desire, he says in verse 24 that he was going to run to win. We also need to run to win.

I don't think there is enough teaching about the rewards promised for faithful service to Christ, and I'll talk about these rewards in more detail later. God never asked to us to run aimlessly (1 Corinthians 9:26).

DO EVERYTHING WITH YOUR EYE ON THE PRIZE

But if we're going to run to win, we need to make some decisions. "Everyone who competes in the games goes into strict training. They do it to get a crown that will not last; but we do it to get a crown that will last forever," Paul says in 1 Corinthians 9:25.

Paul was referring to the Isthmian Games, an event held every two years that was similar to the Olympics. The games were held in the city of Corinth, so naturally the Corinthian believers knew exactly what Paul was talking about. Thousands of people would come to watch the athletes compete, so this was a big deal.

The athletes would begin their training ten months before the actual games. Certain activities and foods were laid aside—not always because they were bad, but because they didn't contribute to the goal the athlete had in mind.

In other words, every decision these Isthmian Games athletes made was measured against the goal of winning the race or wrestling match or whatever event the athlete planned to compete in. The prize governed the decision, not the athlete's momentary pleasure or desire to take it easy, or pain, or fatigue, or anything else.

Now if you wanted to win a wreath at the Isthmian Games, you had to be ready to exercise a lot of self-control. Why? Because you can't live any way you want and still be a winner.

Talk won't get the job done here. We're so used to "trash talking" athletes today that we forget games aren't won in front of microphones. Saying you are going to win has never made anybody a winner. "I should have," "I'm going to," or "I need to" will not get you across God's finish line.

One reason so many men don't keep the New Year's resolutions they make every year is that they get hung up on those one or two areas and lose sight of the prize. The athlete who is in training to win a contest understands that his training is just a means to a much larger end. He is after the winner's wreath, the gold medal.

He wants this prize so badly that it controls his life. His sleeping habits change. His eating habits change. His relationships change. Everything changes because the serious athlete has his eye on the prize.

If you make glorifying God and living for him your consuming passion, you won't have to struggle very long trying to decide whether you should pick up your Bible or the TV remote control. You won't have to grunt and groan trying to bring yourself to a point where you actually spend time in prayer, in worship, and in serving others.

Now there's nothing wrong with resolving that you are going to pray more or serve Christ more faithfully. My point is that once you get the larger goal in sight, it will help you make the daily decisions you need to make to get there.

LAY OFF THE DISTRACTIONS

The writer of Hebrews put it this way: "Therefore . . . let us throw off everything that hinders." (Hebrews 12:1) Those are the things holding you back from being a winner for God, from receiving heaven's approval. It's the small stuff that consumes so much of our time and energy.

Maybe it's too much television. You say, "Aw, Tony, I knew you were going to get around to that." Don't worry, I'm not going to rag on television. It's not that television in and of itself is wrong.

The problem with television for most men is that they can't seem to get past it to get to their Bibles. I have a friend who puts his Bible on his television so that in order to turn on his TV, he has to see the Word. That reminds him to raise the question, "Have I been with God in the Word today?"

Even if you don't own a television with a 180-station satellite dish, your problem may still be too little time with God. Or your problem may be people. You may have to back away from some people because they keep distracting you from the goal you have set for yourself.

Whatever the encumbrance is, it's worth getting rid of because of the prize we're running toward: "God has called me heavenward in Christ Jesus." (Philippians 3:14)

The amazing thing to me about the competitors in the Isthmian Games is that they broke their necks for a little garland wreath on their heads. All they got a was a little twig. Ten months of exercise with no fried chicken and no ice cream, just for a piece of greenery that the athlete would put on his mantel and one month later it would be dried up.

Paul says, "That's not our plan. What we are dealing with is something that does not rust or rot because it has to do with the award system of God."

A young concert pianist was asked one day, "How did you learn to play the piano so well?" She answered, "By planning to neglect anything that did not contribute to my goal of becoming a concert pianist." She was saying that even if some things were fine to do, she was going to lay them aside because her goal was far more than to be a merely competent piano player. That's the idea here.

ALL RUNNERS MUST REPORT TO THE JUDGES' STAND

Now the imagery of a race implies a finish line with judges there to determine who won and who lost so that prizes can be awarded.

For us as Christians, the judging stand at the end of the race is the judgment seat of Christ (2 Corinthians 5:10). We must all appear at this judgment, Paul says, "that each one may receive what is due him for the things done while in the body, whether good or bad."

GOD'S "EDITING STUDIO"

The Greek term for this judgment seat is *bema*, which was the judgment stand where the competitors in the Isthmian Games were judged.

At the *bema*, the athletes were judged according to whether they competed by the rules. Those who did and won their events were awarded their wreaths.

When I think about how the judgment seat of Christ may actually operate, I think of the process that is used to prepare my messages at Oak Cliff Bible Fellowship for broadcast over radio and television and for use in other areas of our ministry at The Urban Alternative.

A message is recorded on a tape and then transcribed. Lois will then take the typed manuscript and go through it, crossing out things that would be inappropriate for a national radio audience, such as remarks that were meant for our Oak Cliff people and would not make sense to the broader Christian public.

So by the time the message is turned over to the radio or television people, what I preached has already shrunk because not all of it is pertinent to the listening or viewing audience.

But that's not the end of the editing process. The producers have to work with the message even more to make it fit into the time constraints of the program. So they cut out even more of my stuff, which means that by the time the message is broadcast over radio or television, it is a much shorter version of what I actually preached.

In fact, we sometimes get letters from listeners who are upset because I did not explain a point more fully and left them hanging. Well, the fact is that I probably did explain that point more thoroughly in my original message. But because of the necessary editing process, those few minutes did not make the cut.

Now picture the judgment seat of Christ as one big editing studio where God is going to take the reel of your life since conversion and then edit it. Every act, every thought, every word, and every intent of your heart is on that recording, made with God's cosmic recording equipment and the Holy Ghost as the engineer. At the judgment seat, that tape will be edited so that the only things left on it will be those of eternal value.

TESTED BY FIRE

I'm not sure if that's the way this thing will work. But one thing is clear: our Christian lives will be revealed with fire (1 Corinthians 3:13). The judgment consists of three things: our words, our deeds, and our faithfulness.

Since the fire will burn up all the junk we did and said, the judgment seat of Christ will be a day of loss for some believers. These are the people who stood up on Sunday morning and said, "Lord, You have been good to me," but somehow never let God's goodness motivate them to love and serve Him Monday through Saturday.

But the opposite is also true. The judgment seat of Christ will be a day of triumph for those believers who, although they were not perfect, lived for the glory of God and made pleasing and serving the Lord their passion.

Now the loss I'm talking about is not the loss of salvation, so let's be clear on that. This is a judgment to dispense rewards, not to determine whether we make heaven.

But don't miss Paul's point. This is still a judgment, and we need to be ready to account for what we did with what God gave us. On that day, "shuckin' and jivin'" won't work. When I would try to pull something over on my mother, she used to tell me, "You can jive the baker because he will give a bun, but you can't jive me because I have none."

On that day we won't be able to "jive" Jesus Christ either because He is not only going to examine what we did, He is going to examine why we did it.

In fact, Hebrews 4:12 says that the Word of God is going to penetrate to the intents of our hearts. His fire will burn away those things that have no eternal value: areas where we were self-centered and not Christ-centered, the opportunities we had to glorify Him that we failed to capitalize on.

But on that day Christ is also going to hand out glorious rewards for those who were faithful. On that day, my brother, you and I will be glad that we made living for God the consuming passion of our lives.

As I said, I really believe that not enough has been preached about rewards. Yes, we ought to serve God simply because we love Him. But God knows that men in particular are creatures of challenge, and so He sets before us rewards we cannot even dream of.

One missionary told me that whenever someone asks him why he would waste his life going to the boondocks to serve Christ, his answer is, "This is not a waste. There is a reckoning day. God sees me and knows why I am serving Him. One day I am going to get my crown."

THE CROWNS TO BE WON

Paul's point is pretty simple. If those ancient athletes were willing to discipline their bodies for months to win a garland of greenery that would soon fade to brown and die, how much more should we as Christians be willing to discipline ourselves to win God's imperishable prize in eternity?

Answer: we should be willing to do whatever it takes to win. But before we talk any more about that, let me show you the imperishable crowns waiting at the "winner's stand" in heaven for the man who is determined to win.

THE CROWN OF MASTERY

The first crown is the crown of mastery, the reward for faithful obedience, which we have already alluded to in 1 Corinthians 9:24-25.

What distinguishes the man who wins this crown or wreath is his commitment to discipline himself that he might compete successfully. No one ever becomes good at anything without disciplining himself.

My youngest son, Jonathan, wants to be a star basketball player in the NBA. Sometimes when I walk by his room, even late at night, I can hear him pretending he is dribbling the ball. He'll be talking to a coach who isn't there or telling a teammate to pass him the ball.

At other times I will hear him in the garage bouncing the basketball, dribbling all over the place. When he messes up, he fusses at himself. I don't know if Jonathan will make the NBA, but he's got the right idea on how to get there.

Winning this crown at the *bema* of Christ will be determined by your faithful commitment to discipline yourself in following the Lord. If you can say yes to the things that make you a better Christian and no to the things that make you a poorer Christian, you're moving in the right direction.

Paul told Timothy to discipline or "train" himself for the purpose of godliness (1 Timothy 4:7). We need to measure and weigh our choices by the standard of whether or not they are going to help us reach the winner's stand at the judgment seat of Christ.

Now in case you don't already know it, you aren't going to get much, if any, help from the culture on this one. We live in an undisciplined world where most men do what they do because they feel like doing it, not because they have weighed their actions against any long-term goals.

THE CROWN OF REJOICING

Paul wrote to the Thessalonians, "For what is our hope, our joy, or the crown in which we will glory in the presence of our Lord Jesus when he comes? Is it not you? Indeed, you are our glory and joy!" (1 Thessalonians 2:19)

This is the crown of rejoicing, which I believe is the crown awarded for faithfulness in the work of evangelism. God is going to give a higher level of honor to those who made winning others to Christ the passion of their lives.

It's good for us as Christian men to stop regularly and take inventory. When was the last time we led someone to Christ or even shared the Gospel? Who will be there to welcome us into heaven because we were responsible for them coming to know Christ?

I have a friend who joined a community service club so he could be around non-Christians and make a concerted effort to win them to Christ. He tries to witness to at least one person a week, and a number of the people have come to faith in Christ.

Let me ask you, my brother, what intentional choices have you made to put yourself among people who do not know Christ? We can get so comfortable in our Christianity that we forget we got here because someone shared the Gospel with *us*.

Now this crown is not a piece of gold on your head. Paul says it's the people you won to Christ, your welcoming committee in heaven. That's what the Thessalonians were for Paul. The honor is the applause that greets the faithful person who has brought others to heaven.

Someone may say, "Yeah, but I don't have the gift of evangelism." That may be, but you still have the responsibility to witness for the faith. If evangelism is not a major part of our spiritual agenda, we are missing out on a crown, as well as being disobedient to the Great Commission.

THE CROWN OF GLORY

The third crown I want to show you is the crown of glory, the crown given for faithfulness in discipleship and building people up in the faith.

The Apostle Peter speaks of this crown when he tells his fellow elders: "Be shepherds of God's flock . . . not lording it over those entrusted to you, but being examples to the flock. And when the Chief Shepherd appears, you will receive the crown of glory that will not fade away." (1 Peter 5:2-4)

The idea of being a shepherd is to lead someone in such a way that that person desires to follow you in a given direction. Now Peter was writing specifically to the leaders of the church, but the principle of leading other believers in the right way is valid for all of us.

According to Peter, those who lead others on to maturity in Christ will be rewarded. They will be put in God's Hall of Fame. The word *glory* means to put something on display, to make it manifest.

God is going to grant "celebrity status" in the kingdom to those who disciple others and help them grow. Now I like that "not fade away" part, because glory sure does fade fast down here. Just ask any athlete. The guy who's the hero one day is a bum the next day. Not so in God's ballpark.

THE CROWN OF LIFE

This crown has to do with faithfulness in suffering and enduring trials.

The risen Christ told the church at Smyrna, "Be faithful, even to the point of death, and I will give you the crown of life." (Revelation 2:10) Some men seem to go from one trial or hard circumstance to another. God says that does not go unnoticed in heaven.

When you endure, when you refuse to throw in the towel and make excuses, God has a crown waiting for you. If you hang in there in suffering, knowing that God is working His purposes in your life even if you don't know exactly all that He's doing, you will receive a crown.

Now it's hard to suffer by faith. Men like to feel like they're in control, that they have the situation pretty well sized up and in hand. But when you are suffering, when you are being persecuted for your faith in Christ, you lose that sense of control. You are extremely vulnerable.

It's obvious that this crown is not one every believer will gain, although Jesus doesn't limit it to a select few. It's just that our natural tendency is to run from trials, to duck suffering, to ask God to let us sit this one out.

But if you decide this is a crown that you want to win, you've got all kinds of help in making it. You have the indwelling power of the Holy Spirit to help you endure. You have God's promise not to bring on you more than you can bear (1 Corinthians 10:13), and you have the promise of God's wisdom in your suffering if you will ask for it (James 1:2-5).

THE CROWN OF RIGHTEOUSNESS

The fifth and final crown I want to encourage you to seek is the crown of righteousness, which is the crown given for faithfulness in ministry. Paul wrote to Timothy near the end of his life:

I have fought the good fight, I have finished the race, I have kept the faith. Now there is in store for me the crown of righteousness, which the Lord, the righteous Judge, will award to me on that day—and not only to me, but also to all who have longed for his appearing.

—2 Timothy 4:7-8

Paul said there was an unrighteous judge, the Roman emperor, who was about to cut off his head. But it was all right, because the righteous Judge was going to be there to present His award.

By the way, there is plenty of room on this winner's stand, because any believer who longs for Christ's coming is eligible for this crown.

Now some Christians don't love Christ's appearing. They would be saying, "Don't come yet." Why? Because they are not ready. Not in the sense of their salvation, because that is assured. But ready in the sense of things they haven't done yet, things that Christ has asked them to do a long time ago. But when you're being faithful, you can say "Any time, Lord."

The good news about these crowns is that there is no special secret you have to know to qualify for them. They are not just for "super saints." Winning them is a matter of everyday faithfulness, of getting up every morning and saying, "Lord, I give You my life today. I want to obey You, to love my wife and children, to honor You in everything I say and do."

If the hope of winning five crowns from Jesus Christ doesn't convince a Christian man that running a faithful race is worth the effort, I don't know what else to say. Being awarded any one of these crowns will be an honor beyond anything we can imagine. Let's go for them all!

DON'T BE DISQUALIFIED

One of the things that can make athletic competition hard is the distractions athletes have to deal with. We've already talked about the importance of shutting out those things that don't contribute to winning the prize. Let's see what Paul said about these distractions.

Back in 1 Corinthians 9:26, Paul says, in effect, "I don't know about you, but I'm going to run, and I'm out to win the prize. If you don't want to run, that's up to you. But I am not going to let those who refuse to run hold me back or discourage me."

Some of us are not running very well because we are looking at all the aimless non-runners around us. But Paul says, "Don't let the aimless wanderers around you distract you. Don't use their lack of discipline as an excuse to quit yourself. I'm running with an aim in mind. I have a clear goal out there, and I know where I am going."

Then Paul changes the metaphor to boxing and says, "Because I know where I am going, I don't waste my time punching the air." To win the prize, Paul said, "I buffet my body" (verse 27, *New American Standard Version*). He literally beat his body—he gave his body a black eye to bring it under control.

Now please note. Paul did not say, "I buffet (buff-ay) my body," as in the buffet line down at the local cafeteria! He disciplined himself. But I'd better leave that one right there!

Why was Paul so consumed by his passion to serve Christ? ". . . so that after I have preached to others, I myself will not be disqualified for the prize." (verse 27b) Paul knew he was running a race in which his performance would be judged, and he didn't want to mess up and get himself disqualified.

As I said above, one of the tasks of the *bema* was to determine who qualified for the winner's wreath and who had to be disqualified because he didn't make the grade.

Remember Ben Johnson, the Canadian runner who won an Olympic gold medal in 1988 in a record-setting 100-meter dash? Johnson ran around the arena waving a Canadian flag as the crowd showered praise on him.

But we know what happened to Johnson when the judges got through testing his qualifications. He was found to have used performance-enhancing steroids and was forced to give back his gold medal.

Johnson then went home to Canada showered with shame and cloaked in disgrace because he had been disqualified.

Using drugs is one obvious way to be disqualified from a race. Another way is by not finishing, by quitting too soon. You should never get too excited about how somebody starts off, because God measures your Christian life not by how you start but by how you finish. Some people start slow but finish well. Others burst out of the starting blocks, but then fade fast and never finish.

Paul had some friends like that. Hymenaeus and Alexander were two of them (1 Timothy 1:20). Another was Demas, who had left Paul for this present world (2 Timothy 4:10). These men started out well but faded. On the other hand, Mark, whom Paul mentions in 2 Timothy 4:11, started out a little shaky, but ended quite well.

If You're Not Dead, God's Not Done with You!

Let me tell you something, my brother in Christ. If you are not dead yet, you are not finished yet. You still have time to get in the race! You may be coming to the starting blocks with regrets over personal, family, or spiritual failure.

You may look back and say, "I've got a lot of stuff following me into the race. I've got a lot of junk from the past weighing me down as I try to run."

You may have stumbled coming out of the blocks. You may have tripped up during the race. You may even be starting the race a little late, but God can help you make up for lost time. He can help you pick up speed in the last half of the race and cover more ground in less time than the average runner.

I like Paul's attitude. He forgot the things that were behind him. His eyes were straight ahead, focused on the prize (Philippians 3:13-14). You have never seen a runner win a race looking backwards. He has to keep his eye on the goal.

As I often tell my Christian brothers, you can't change yesterday, but you can do a lot about what happens tomorrow. Don't let other folk stop you from running for God. Don't let other people distract you from seeking His approval.

Let me tell you something about God. He loves to dispense His grace. If you will come to God with your regrets and your failures, and start loving and serving Him as the driving force in your life, He has an unmistakable, amazing way of using even failure to bring about success.

There is only one passion in life worth your total pursuit. And that is to love and serve Christ in such a way that you win the race and receive His approval. Everything must be brought under that umbrella. If you make that your commitment as a man of God, everything else will take care of itself.

Right now you may be wondering how you're going to make the changes you need to make. Maybe you're still debating whether it's worth all the effort.

In either case I want to leave you with this word. Jesus Christ said, "I am the Alpha and the Omega, the First and the Last, the Beginning and the End." (Revelation 22:13)

Brother, that just about covers it all! That means Jesus Christ rules from A to Z, and everything in between. Whatever your need may be, whatever excuse may be dragging you down, if it fits between those two extremes, Jesus Christ can do something about it. So you have nothing to lose by going for the prize!

EPILOGUE

I 'm a big fan of the old *Rocky* movies with Sylvester Stallone. Here is this guy from inner-city Philadelphia going nowhere, except that he has the skill and the heart of a fighter. He's aggressive, so he fights his way to the top and becomes the heavyweight boxing champion of the world.

But by the time of the movie *Rocky V*, Rocky Balboa is getting older. He's still the champ, but his quickness is gone. He's been hurt, and he would risk his life to go back into the ring. His wife tells him, "Rocky, you can't fight anymore."

Rocky wrestles with it and finally decides to throw in the towel. But then a young man named Tommy Gunn shows up. He has admired Rocky Balboa and wants to be just like him. He says, "Rocky, will you teach me what you know?"

Here is an opportunity for Rocky to be in the ring again in the person of Tommy. So he teaches Tommy, and Tommy demolishes everyone he comes up against. But then, when he's successful, Tommy decides he doesn't need Rocky anymore. He decides to go out on his own. Rocky tries to talk him out of it, but he decides to go anyway.

In the climactic scene of the movie, Tommy has become a big shot and starts standing outside Rocky's house, calling him names and daring him to fight. Rocky takes off his shirt and goes outside, and they get it on.

Tommy beats Rocky to a pulp. As everyone watches, Tommy sends Rocky flying with a right hand. Rocky lies there in the street, beaten down and bloodied by his circumstances. Then he begins flashing back to his earlier days.

He sees his old opponents. But nothing happens until he sees the image of Mickey, his former trainer who is now dead, standing over him, saying, "Get up, get up, you bum. Mickey loves you."

When Rocky hears these words again from his friend who had made him everything he was, he shakes off the daze as the movie's theme music comes up. All of a sudden, having heard that voice on the inside, Rocky gets up on the outside.

Tommy is on his way back to his car when Rocky calls out, "Yo, Tommy. One more round." Rocky draws new strength from within, and soon he's standing over Tommy. The trial that was knocking Rocky down was now on the ground, and Rocky is standing over it.

What men need to hear today is a voice saying to them, "Get up, get up, you bum." They need to get up from their trials, get up from their defeats, get up from their circumstances.

Most of all, men need to get up from the excuses that have allowed them to trade their families for their careers and produce a generation of directionless kids.

Men need to get up from the excuses that allow them to devalue, mistreat, and exploit women for selfish purposes, failing to demonstrate servant leadership, leaving us with a generation of women who seek to be liberated from bad male leadership.

Men need to get up from the excuses that cover them when they sire children but refuse to raise them, overflowing our prisons with a generation of undisciplined and violent boys who no longer have a conscience.

Men need to get up from the excuses that drive them to love the power and money of the marketplace more than their wives, sending the divorce rate skyrocketing even among Christians.

Men need to get up from the excuses that put them on the golf course on Sunday rather than taking their families to church, contributing to spiritually anemic homes and churches dominated by women.

Men need to get up from the excuses that cause them to leave charity to the government rather than expressing it through the church, producing the welfare nightmare that is now engulfing us.

Men need to get up from the excuses that blind them to the fact that they love TV more than they love their Bibles, leading to a dangerously low spiritual temperature in our society.

And finally, men need to get up from the excuses that keep them more committed to their culture than to Christ, crippling efforts to deal with racism and other wrongs in this country.

Gentlemen, we need to hear the voice: "Get up, get up, you bum." Why? "Because Jesus loves you!"